THE
50
GREATEST
Red Sox
GAMES

THE
50
GREATEST
Red Sox
GAMES

CECILIA TAN
BILL NOWLIN

WILEY

John Wiley & Sons, Inc.

Copyright © 2006 by Cecilia Tan and Bill Nowlin. All rights reserved

Published by John Wiley & Sons, Inc., Hoboken, New Jersey
Published simultaneously in Canada

All photos reprinted by permission of the National Baseball Hall of Fame and Library, Cooperstown, NY.

Design and composition by Navta Associates, Inc.

For general information about our other products and services, please contact our Customer Care Department within the United States at (800) 762-2974, outside the United States at (317) 572-3993 or fax (317) 572-4002.

Wiley also publishes its books in a variety of electronic formats. Some content that appears in print may not be available in electronic books. For more information about Wiley products, visit our web site at www.wiley.com.

Library of Congress Cataloging-in-Publication Data:

Tan, Cecilia, 1967–
   The 50 greatest Red Sox games / Cecilia Tan, Bill Nowlin.
      p. cm.
   Includes index.
   ISBN-13 978-0-471-69751-0 (cloth)
   ISBN-10 0-471-69751-6 (cloth)
  1. Boston Red Sox (Baseball team) I. Title: Fifty greatest Red Sox games. II. Nowlin, Bill, 1945-
III. Title.
   GV875.B62T36 2006
   796.357'64'0974461—dc22

                                  2005020002

Printed in the United States of America

10 9 8 7 6 5 4 3 2 1

To generations of Red Sox fans past, present, and future
—BN

For corwin, who understands divided loyalties
—CT

Contents

Cecilia's Preface

I moved to New England in the autumn of 1985. I arrived just in time to get mildly interested in the pro football team the New England Patriots as they went on an incredible playoff run, only to be crushed in the Super Bowl. "Get used to it," my friends and neighbors told me, "because here comes baseball season." Having grown up in and around New York City, all I knew of the Red Sox was their rivalry with the Yankees. New Yorkers talked about the Curse of the Bambino as if it were a birthright, yet I never knew the full scope of the history of Red Sox bad luck, misfortune, and collapses until Red Sox fans started telling me about it. My friends, believe it or not, discouraged me from following the Sox. "It's a life of heartbreak," they said. "You don't want that." What happened that year, 1986, seemed to prove their point. So I tuned out the Sox, and all of baseball, for several years.

But even when the Sox are bad, they are pervasive in New England. And when they are good, they are inescapable. I joined a theater troupe in Rhode Island. All through the 1990 season the radio was on while we built sets, ran rehearsals, tore down, and toward the end of the summer, pennant fever swept through. I found it so easy to get caught up in the excitement of the game, the sounds of the ballpark coming through the little boom box sitting on the stage, the drone of the announcers, the roar of the crowd. It didn't matter to me that it was the Red Sox (my childhood enemy) or that my friends had been warning me off for years, the way they would if I were interested in a bad boyfriend. I was mesmerized by the seductive power of baseball and the home team.

I moved to Boston proper, but managed to keep my distance emotionally. I even lived only two blocks from Fenway Park, yet never went to a game. But I could see the lights, I could hear the crowd roaring from my apartment on Queensberry Street. Some nights coming home from work, if there was a game I would get out of the T at Kenmore and walk down Jersey Street (now called Yawkey Way) and buy peanuts from the roasted-nut vendor there. In those days, sometimes after the seventh inning you could walk into the park for nothing and see the last few innings from standing room. But I held back.

The first game I saw at Fenway Park was a high school game, the national high school championships that some friends of mine had tickets to. I don't remember the teams or the players, but I remember one kid hitting a home run. As the ball soared toward the Fisk Pole and then over the big green wall, I got goose bumps, and my eyes teared up. You should have heard the crowd and seen that kid's face. I knew it, right then, that Fenway Park was not just some rundown ballyard, but a baseball cathedral. I grew up going to Yankee Stadium, so I knew that feeling. This is where history was made, and is still being made, every night, I told myself. Don't you wonder what you've been missing?

It wasn't long after that I gave in, and gave my life over to baseball. I joined SABR (Society for American Baseball Research). I started a Web site about baseball. I even started to play it, for the first time in my life, with a women's hardball league here in New England. Yes, when I say baseball took over my life, I don't exaggerate.

That was in 1999. The year Pedro was so dominating and Nomar Garcia-parra the media darling. Characters such as Rod Beck and Rich "El Guapo" Garces in the bullpen. Good guys such as Bret Saberhagen. The Yankees were my childhood sweethearts, but these Red Sox were hard not to like. I rooted for them to beat Cleveland in the ALDS, tore my hair out when Pedro had to leave game one, and danced around the living room when he came out of the bullpen to be the hero in game five. I told my friends I would root for them in the World Series if they made it. (They didn't.)

Then I started to read about Ted Williams. After his awe-inspiring appearance in a golf cart during the All-Star Game at Fenway Park, I realized I had to know more about him. All I knew was that they were naming a tunnel in Boston after him and that he was the "greatest hitter who ever lived." By studying Ted's life and career I came to understand and appreciate both the history of the Red Sox and their relationship with the media and New England as a whole. What a story, I thought, every time I would read about another unbelievable feat of Ted's, or another strange twist of Fate, or a wild and woolly postseason. What a story!

No baseball fan, regardless of his or her rooting interest, can say that the Red Sox do not have one of the most compelling and interesting histories of any team, both triumphs and tragedies. And the way history has unfolded, how the triumphs were always followed by tragedies, only makes it more compelling. And each generation of fans needs to learn the history of what happened. The *50 Greatest* books concentrate on what happened on the field, because that is where baseball history is made. Ted Williams's feud with the media would not have made a ripple in history if he had not been the greatest hitter who ever lived. This book gives me a chance to tell the story of the Red Sox from their earliest days through to their 2004 world championship. Through it young fans can catch up on everything they missed, and older fans can relive the ups and downs of so many historic moments.

To provide a longer-term perspective, I teamed up with Bill Nowlin, a life-long Sox fan, a friend and neighbor, and also a writer himself (*Mr. Red Sox, Tales from the Red Sox Dugout, Ted Williams: The Pursuit of Perfection*, and more). In 2003, when we began work on the project, Bill had the first run of picking the list of games. There were a lot to choose from. Did you know that the Red Sox have 15 no-hitters, 16 if you count Ernie Shore's nine innings of perfect relief? (MLB doesn't; we do.) Nineteen players have hit for the cycle. They have won the pennant eleven times, the East three other times, and the wild card four times. Fifteen Hall of Famers played their significant years with the Sox. Heck, 11 different Sox pitchers have pitched extra-innings complete-game shutouts. There was no shortage of games to consider. Our definition of a "great game" is broad—it includes games where a single player performed a rare feat or where a record was set or broken. There are games where the team as a whole had to fight hard for victory, and others where they breezed. Some are wins, some losses.

We knew we wanted to get at least one game in each decade, and we knew, by necessity, that many of the games would be losses. But even I was surprised at some of the losses that Bill picked and some that Red Sox fans nominated in our polls on the Internet. Bill's first draft even contained the first major league game I saw at Fenway Park, a 22–1 spanking of the Sox administered by the Yankees. He tried to explain to me that the "fellowship of the miserable" in Red Sox Nation would expect a due amount of pain and suffering to be in the book, or it wouldn't be an authentic Red Sox book.

Very well. So we have Bucky, Buckner, and Boone, and some other less momentous but meaningful losses in the book. But I have always been a believer in the power of positive thinking and in the fact that the torch Red Sox Nation carried for so many years for this team burned with hope and could flare at any time. To do our part to stoke the positive vibe, I felt that we ought to leave out the 22–1 loss and put in something a smidgen happier, such as Smoky Joe Wood's no-hitter.

And lo and behold, while we were writing the book, the most unbelievable thing happened. I got to fulfill my promise to my friends. The Red Sox made it to the World Series in the most historic, fateful, unbelievable way, beating the Yankees from an 0–3 deficit. I wore my "Reverse the Curse" T-shirt—in fact, I slept in it before Game Four of the World Series. And they did it. They did the impossible. They won it all.

So guess what? We had to revise the list again. I wrote many of the chapters in this book over the winter after the World Series win, floating along on the euphoria of it. I may only be a resident alien in Red Sox Nation, but even I saw the change taking place. A fan Web site, known as the Miserable Red Sox Fan Forum, changed their name to the Triumphant Red Sox Fan Forum. Our perspective on all that pain and suffering changed. Even Bill looked at a few of the losses and decided they were no longer worthy of inclusion. Something had to go to make room for the 2004 postseason games, and it seemed only right that now that the book had a happy ending, we didn't need to pile on the ignominy too thick.

So here it is, more than 100 years of Red Sox history, told through 50 different snapshots of game action. We have done our best to re-create each game as if we were there watching them. Pretend you're sitting there at Fenway Park with us while we tell you all about the hitters who come to bat, the pitchers who enter and leave, and the players who run across the field of green. What a story!

Cecilia Tan
Cambridge, Massachusetts

Bill's Preface

When I heard that Cecilia Tan had started work on her book *The 50 Greatest Yankee Games*, I immediately wondered why in all these years no one had ever come up with such a seemingly obvious concept for a book. I also asked Cecilia about working on a companion book, featuring my favorite team: the Boston Red Sox.

I grew up in Boston, old enough to have seen Ted Williams play his last few years. I've seen a lot and suffered a lot over the seasons since then. I always thought when I grew up, I'd write some books. Finally, in the late 1990s, I started working on a book about Ted Williams, which I wrote with Jim Prime. Jim and I have collaborated on several other books since then. Our two volumes of *Tales from the Red Sox Dugout* went over very well, and the publisher asked us about writing a follow-up book consisting of tales from the Toronto Blue Jays' dugout. There might or might not have been interesting tales from the Jays' dugout, but it didn't appeal to me to try to find out. Writing is a labor of love for me, and I prefer to pursue the many Red Sox stories that intrigue me rather than pursue professional opportunities that might be more financially rewarding. I guess one could call me a quirky writer, someone who only wants to write about one team—but there's enough fodder there to keep me going for the rest of my years.

How did we compile a list of the 50 greatest Red Sox games? When we started our list, we knew the Sox had fallen short yet again, losing game seven of the 2003 American League Championship Series to the New York Yankees. That loss gave Cecilia number 50 on her list of the greatest Yankees games, but it clearly was also one of the greatest Red Sox games, too—and should have gone down as a win for the Red Sox. But that's another story, one that draws on Jason Giambi's two home runs (steroids-enhanced?) and on Grady Little's stubborn sticking with his starter when all the statistical evidence—readily available not only to him but also to tens of millions of television viewers—clearly dictated a different course. We'll assume Fate played no part in the outcome, but a generation of Sox fans who grew up on the Curse might still wonder.

Some of the games, even before the 2004 season, were pretty obvious ones, but the criterion I tried to keep in mind was a personal one: Was this a game I really would like to have seen in person? Some of them I indeed was at—Roger Clemens' first 20-K game and Game Six of the 1975 World Series, to name just two. There were some other ones I should have been at, such as Ted Williams's final game in 1960. I was doing my paper route, and while standing on the bridge at Pierce's Station in Lexington, listening to my transistor radio, I heard him hit that last home run. The bridge is still there; the station is not. I could have gone to the game. Several times that year or the year before, I'd gone to the ball game, then come home and done my paper route later. I'm still kicking myself, some 45 years later.

There was no way I could have been at Smoky Joe Wood's no-hitter back in 1911. My parents hadn't even been born yet. I did see Smoky Joe throw out the first pitch from the seats by the Red Sox dugout one day, but that's hardly the same thing. Still, I wish I had been there, just as I wish I'd been in Philadelphia in 1941 to see Ted go 6-for-8 in the doubleheader on the final day of the season, boosting his average over .400, the last batter to reach that mark in more than six decades. I wish I'd been there when the Red Sox won the World Series in 1903, or 1912, or 1915, 1916, or 1918. I wasn't sure it was something I'd ever see.

There are also games I wish I hadn't attended—probably first and foremost, the single-game playoff in 1978. But there is no question it was a defining moment in Red Sox history. There are games I saw on TV that I also wish I hadn't seen, first and foremost the crushing Game Six loss at Shea Stadium in the 1986 World Series. Game Seven wasn't nearly as crushing.

Red Sox history is marked by losses as well as wins. To borrow from the title of an old Ed Walton book, the Olde Towne Team's history is one of triumphs and tragedies. Red Sox fans are marked by those deflating defeats, but somehow we've always held on to a wary optimism. The Sox were often very competitive; in that hope rests to some extent the haunting sense of gloom that so often attended even a Red Sox winning streak in August. There was always the sense that they'd fold come September. Sox fans have been snakebit so many times that when the Bosox finally won it all in October 2004, it was days and weeks and months before some fans truly believed that the Great Day had finally arrived. And then we worried what to do with it, how to wear this unaccustomed mantle of a world championship.

Looking at Red Sox history, the first two decades of the franchise were heady ones, as the team finished first six times and won every single one of the five World Series in which they played (the New York Giants refused to play Boston in 1904). Clearly, winning the World Series is a very big deal. One would have to represent each of those triumphant years as offering some of the greatest games in team history. The 1920s? Well, that was another matter. It was a black hole. The Red Sox pretty much finished dead last every year. At first, I argued that we should simply say there were no great games at all in the 1920s, but then I found one that would really have been fun to be at, if only for a moment's light in the decade of darkness.

Game Seven of the 1946 World Series really was a great game, even if it didn't turn out the way Red Sox fans would have liked it. There are, indeed, many great games throughout Red Sox history and right up to the present day. There are so many games we could have included, but they didn't make the final cut. One of my personal favorites took place on September 21, 2000. It was an afternoon game against the Indians at Fenway, and the regular guys who worked the scoreboard couldn't make it, and I was granted the opportunity to fulfill the dream of a lifetime and work the game inside the scoreboard. It started off as a total disaster, though. The Indians scored seven runs in the first inning. Even though I got a workout changing the numbers, I wasn't happy about recording all those hits and runs for Cleveland. The Sox found themselves down 7–0 before they even got up to bat, but they rallied to win it, 9–8. Now, that was an exciting game, but it really wasn't one of the 50 greatest games in franchise history.

I was a little apprehensive about working on this book with, of all people, a Yankees fan! But when it's not head-to-head competition with the Yankees, Cecilia roots for the Red Sox. I truly doubt I'll ever be able to root for the Yankees. It's too deeply ingrained. But I can respect them as a team, and I can respect Yankees fans as truly passionate fans. Well, some of them. It was a pleasure working on this book, though admittedly it was even more fun to write the final few chapters while basking in the reflected golden glow of the 2004 World Series trophy. Others would have made other choices of the "50 greatest," but that's part of the beauty of baseball. As a Red Sox fan for life, of course, I would love nothing more than to have another dozen greatest games to add over the next several years. We'll see how it all plays out.

Bill Nowlin
Cambridge, Massachusetts

First Act

In which Big Bill Dinneen tallies the first of his three victories in the first modern World Series

In 1903 the Wright Brothers flew for the first time at Kitty Hawk, the first Model A Ford rolled off the assembly line, and the first Tour de France sent bicyclists racing up and down the Alps. It would also be the first year that base-ball offered a postseason World Series. At this point the National League had been around for 28 years, the American League only three, and the two leagues were finally coexisting more or less peacefully. Pittsburgh Pirates owner Barney Dreyfuss looked at the standings in August and, seeing that his team had a comfortable lead, challenged the similarly placed Boston team to meet his for a postseason championship.

Game One saw Boston's ace on the hill, the 36-year-old veteran Cy Young. Young had posted a 28–9 mark that season, but was bombed for four runs in the very first inning. The Americans (not dubbed the "Red Sox" until December 1907) scraped together three runs late in the game, but by then Pittsburgh had already posted seven, eventually winning the game 7–3. Deacon Phillippe, Pittsburgh's leading right-hander, pitched a better ball game.

Both teams had excellent pitching staffs during the regular season, but, as events transpired, the Pittsburgh moundsmen were hurting. Ed Doheny had won 16 games for the second year in a row; in 1903 he was 16–8 with a 3.19 ERA. This talented pitcher, though, suffered such extreme paranoia that he finally left the team on September 21. While undergoing rest and treatment, during the Series, Doheny attacked and nearly killed his

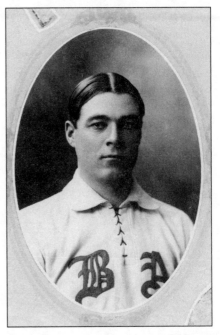

Bill Dinneen

caretaker with an iron poker before being subdued by police and committed to an insane asylum in Massachusetts.

Boston, by contrast, boasted three healthy 20-game winners (all right-handers) in Young, Long Tom Hughes (20–7, 2.57 ERA), and Big Bill Dinneen. It was up to Dinneen (21–13, 2.26 ERA) to try to beat back the Pirates before the Beantown crowd in Game Two. Dinneen had pitched for Boston's National League franchise in 1900 and 1901 and then jumped to the Americans in 1902. He had a good fastball and sported a sharp curve he called his "in-shoot."

Dinneen retired the Pirates in the first. He struck out Ginger Beaumont and Tommy Leach, sandwiched around a base on balls to Pittsburgh's left fielder (and player-manager) Fred Clarke, whom Dinneen picked off when he strayed off the bag.

Sam Leever started for the Pirates. "Schoolmaster" Sam was a righty, with the best winning percentage in the NL (25–7), and seven shut outs to his credit. He led the league with a 2.06 ERA that season. But Leever was nursing a bum shoulder, hurt by the recoil of his rifle while trapshooting in September.

Boston struck quickly—in fact, left fielder Patsy Dougherty swung at Leever's very first pitch and drove it deep to right-center. One of the fastest of the Americans, Dougherty sped around the bases and dove headfirst into home plate—an inside-the-park home run on the first ball thrown. The weather played a part here. When large crowds came to the parks in those days, the overflow crowd was often placed in the outfield, roped off but reducing the amount of fair territory. Ground rules for Boston's Huntington Avenue Grounds called for a triple to be awarded on a ball hit into the crowd. Game

OCTOBER 2, 1903: PITTSBURGH AT BOSTON

Pittsburgh Pirates	AB	R	H	RBI	BB	SO	PO	A	Boston Americans	AB	R	H	RBI	BB	SO	PO	A
Beaumont cf	3	0	0	0	1	1	3	0	Dougherty lf	4	2	3	2	0	0	0	1
Clarke lf	3	0	1	0	1	1	3	0	Collins 3b	4	0	1	0	1	0	1	1
Leach 3b	3	0	0	0	0	1	0	2	Stahl cf	4	1	1	0	0	1	1	0
Wagner ss	3	0	0	0	0	0	3	6	Freeman rf	4	0	2	1	0	0	0	0
Bransfield 1b	3	0	0	0	0	1	9	1	Parent ss	3	0	1	0	1	0	2	3
Ritchey 2b	3	0	1	0	0	2	3	3	LaChance 1b	2	0	0	0	1	0	8	0
Sebring rf	3	0	1	0	0	2	1	0	Ferris 2b	4	0	0	0	0	0	4	0
Smith c	3	0	0	0	0	0	2	1	Criger c	3	0	0	0	1	0	11	0
Leever p	0	0	0	0	0	0	0	0	Dinneen p	1	0	0	0	2	0	0	3
Veil p	2	0	0	0	0	2	0	0	Totals	29	3	8	3	6	1	27	8
Phelps p	1	0	0	0	0	1	0	0									
Totals	27	0	3	0	2	11	24	13									

Pittsburgh Pirates	IP	H	R	ER	BB	SO	HR	Boston Americans	IP	H	R	ER	BB	SO	HR
Leever (L)	1	3	2	2	1	0	1	Dinneen (W)	9	3	0	0	2	11	0
Veil	7	5	1	1	5	1	1								
Totals	8	8	3	3	6	1	2								

	1	2	3	4	5	6	7	8	9		R	H	E
PIT N	0	0	0	0	0	0	0	0	0		0	3	2
BOS A	2	0	0	0	0	1	0	0	x		3	8	0

day rains cut attendance to 9,415. In Game One, Dougherty's ball would have been declared a triple. With the smaller crowd, it had room to roll on the damp, dead grounds and remained in play, fielded just shy of the rope.

After player-manager Jimmy Collins flied out, Chick Stahl doubled and came home when Buck Freeman drove a ball up the middle, a "pretty single over second" *(Boston Journal)*. Some said Stahl's double might have gone for another inside-the-parker had Clarke not blocked it with his feet. The score stood 2–0, Boston, after one inning of play.

Leever had nothing, "neither speed, curves, nor control" *(Pittsburgh Post)*. Clarke lifted Leever after just one inning, replacing him with rookie Bucky Veil, who'd just turned 22. Veil had appeared in just 12 games (5–3, 3.82 ERA), but here acquitted himself very well. Boston touched Leever for three hits in the first, but secured just five scattered hits off Veil over the next seven frames. The *Post* commented, "The people sort of pitied the youthful pitcher. Pity soon, however, turned to wonder, and then to admiration."

Veil got himself out of trouble more than once. In the fifth inning, Boston loaded the bases with nobody out, and Hobe Ferris hit the ball hard to third baseman Leach. Leach threw home for the force at the plate. Lou Criger, Dinneen's catcher, then grounded into a 4-6-3 double play.

Despite the fact that he walked five, hit a batter, and committed an error, the only run Veil allowed was when Patsy Dougherty connected for another home run, in the sixth inning. Home runs were rare in that era; in 567 at-bats, Boston's Buck Freeman led the major leagues with 13 that season. Patsy's drive bounced off the top of the left-field fence and out of the park. Boston observers could only recall one other ball hit out of the park (Piano Legs Hickman's in 1901), and Collins later called it "the greatest hit I ever saw by a left-handed batter." Dougherty had led the league in hits, with 195 during the regular season, but only four of them were home runs.

Pittsburgh threatened just once, in the fourth inning. Ginger Beaumont walked, and Clarke singled over second. Beaumont had to hold at second base. Leach tried to bunt, but fouled off his first two attempts. With two strikes, he was swinging, but hit a weak roller toward first base that proved as good as the bunt he'd tried in vain to execute. Both runners moved up, and Leach almost beat it out, as Boston first baseman Candy LaChance grabbed the throw from Dinneen, then ran to the base. Candy collided with Leach and collapsed in a heap; Leach was ruled out on the extremely close play.

With one out—the score still 2–0 in Boston's favor—the Pirates had the game-tying runners in scoring position and Honus Wagner standing at the plate. Wagner led both leagues with a .355 average and had knocked in 101 runs. This time, nothing took the bat out of Honus's hands. Even with first base open, Dinneen challenged him, getting two quick strikes. Whiff, whiff, then whack! Honus hit the next pitch—hard. "With a sharp crack the ball left the bat, headed for right field, while two flying Pittsburgh runners were tearing round the circuit for home," wrote the *Boston Post*. Beaumont was already crossing the plate as second baseman "Hobe Ferris leaped into the air and stopped the red-hot liner in its course," speared the ball, and stepped on second base to double up Clarke for an unassisted rally-killing, inning-ending double play.

It was the Pirates' only real threat. In the eighth, Claude Ritchey led off with a hit into the left-field corner, but tried to stretch it to a double. Dougherty rifled the ball to Ferris and caught him at second. They went meekly in the ninth, and Boston recorded its first World Series victory.

Dinneen doled out just three hits and walked two, but with the pickoff, the double play in the fourth, and Dougherty's assist in the eighth, by game's end Big Bill had faced only 29 batters. He struck out eleven. The *Pittsburgh Post*'s John H. Gruber wrote that Dinneen "had everything a pitcher should have. He did grand work on the rubber, and besides was given errorless support. He was the whole shooting match, for shooting he did, with a vengeance."

Boston had a man on base in every inning but one, forcing Veil to pitch out of jam after jam, including the bases-loaded, none-out fifth. Veil, despite his fine work, didn't appear in any of the six remaining Series games—mainly because, with one exception, every pitcher threw a complete game (Deacon Phillippe throwing four of the six). Veil made but one appearance in the following season and never again reappeared in the majors despite his strong performance on the championship stage.

The win was a whitewash—a shutout to even the Series at one game apiece—but the first World Series victory for any ball club has to be counted as one of the greatest games in that team's history. Boston fans saw some outstanding pitching, some outstanding defense (and not a single Boston misplay in an era when errors were far more frequent than today), and were treated to not one, but two home runs—and very different homers at that. Though the final score was 3–0, the game was hard fought, and the outcome never certain. No Bostonian went home unhappy this early October afternoon. Boston had drawn even in the Series, and there was another game to look forward to the following day.

◀ Extra Innings

- Of Game One, which Boston had lost, there is speculation that the very first World Series game ever played was, "in all likelihood, thrown by Boston" (Glenn Stout and Richard Johnson, *Red Sox Century*, p. 38). Could this be?

The Boston team played like bumblers at key times in the game. They were officially charged with four errors, but there were "at least eight questionable plays." The next day's *Boston Post* noted that "many around town last evening asked if Boston lost on purpose" and later noted that "wholesale charges of throwing the games have been making the rounds." As with the rampant betting that took place during the Temple Cup series in the 1890s, some players may have felt the new "world's series" to be merely glorified exhibition games and have harbored little guilt over their play in games that did not "count." In 1923, Lou Criger signed an affidavit stating that he had been offered $12,000 (three times his annual Red Sox salary) by gamblers trying to arrange a fix—and had told them to shove off. American League president Ban Johnson was so impressed by Criger's statement that when the former catcher had a tubercular leg amputated, Johnson set up a pension for Criger to help pay for his retirement home in Arizona.

- Pittsburgh's Jimmy Sebring had hit a homer in Game One of the 1903 World Series. After Dougherty's two homers in Game Two, not another home run would be hit in World Series play until 1906. The next time a player hit two in a game was in 1915, when another Boston batter—Harry Hooper—hit two in the fifth and final game of that year's fall classic.

- A *Boston Herald* correspondent complained about scorecards being sold for 15 cents. This was "squeezing the dear public hard."

2

October 13, 1903: Pittsburgh at Boston

Fever Pitch

In which a bloody baseball buzzes by the Flying Dutchman

After the first four games of the 1903 Series, Pittsburgh led three games to Boston's one. The summary could also be read as Deacon Phillippe 3, Boston 1. Phillippe started and won complete games on October 1, 3, and 6: three complete games in a six-day stretch. Small wonder that Fred Clarke gave Brick-yard Kennedy the ball on the seventh (he lost to Cy Young, 11–2, in a game that included five ground-rule triples for Boston) and tried Sam Leever again on the eighth (Leever lost to Dinneen again, 6–3). In the seventh game, played on a Saturday, Young outpitched Phillippe, reversing the Game One score and outcome as Boston won, 7–3. But in 1903, Game Seven was not the deciding game. This World Series was a best-of-nine contest. Five wins, not just four, were needed to cop the title.

With the mandatory day off on Sunday, the two teams traveled back to Boston—on the same train. Rain on Monday prevented play, so the only pitcher whom Clarke truly trusted—Phillippe—was asked to come back on two days' rest for his fifth start in 13 days. He was tired. Boston had won three games in a row, pulling into a 4–3 lead in the Series. Pittsburgh faced elimination. And if they won, then what? They couldn't start Phillippe yet again. Maybe Veil? They had no four- or five-man rotation, not with the maladies that had plagued them. But you play the games, and you play them one at a time. Boston was out for blood.

And Boston had Big Bill Dinneen once more, going on a full four days' rest. The Royal Rooters, Boston's most loyal fans, marched into the Huntington Avenue Grounds and took seats in four rows of chairs placed on the field directly behind the catcher while the Letter Carriers Band played "Tessie," which had become the team's theme song. The Royal Rooters had become hoarse in Pittsburgh, though, and were not in good voice.

While Phillippe kept Boston scoreless through the first three innings, Dinneen was equally stingy. Not a runner reached first. Big Bill had a bit of a scare, though, when Jimmy Sebring led off the third with a "red hot" ball right back to the box. It split a finger on Dinneen's pitching hand, but he flipped to first for the out. Dinneen was seen to wince, and the finger "bled freely throughout the contest, each pitch causing him intense pain" *(Boston Post)*. Collins had Cy Young start warming up behind the grandstand, throwing to Charley "Duke" Farrell. Sebring's smash had literally drawn first blood.

Pittsburgh mounted another threat in the top of the fourth. With two out, Tommy Leach drew a base on balls. Honus Wagner, up next, hit a ball through the shortstop hole vacated by Freddy Parent as he covered second. With runners on first and third, and two strikes on Kitty Bransfield, Wagner took off for second as the back half of an apparent double steal. When catcher Lou Criger feigned a throw to second, Leach broke for the plate. The only trouble was, Criger held the ball, and Collins and Criger erased Leach in a rundown. End of inning, end of threat.

When the Americans came up in the bottom of the fourth, they got to Deacon. Buck Freeman led off with a ground-rule triple, a drive into the roped area of spectators in left field. Parent, hitting away, dropped an unintended bunt in front of the plate, and Pirates catcher Ed Phelps fumbled the ball. Freeman had to hold up, but Parent found himself on first base. Candy LaChance grounded out to first; Parent took second; Freeman again held at third. Hobe

OCTOBER 13, 1903: PITTSBURGH AT BOSTON

Pittsburgh Pirates	AB	R	H	RBI	BB	SO	PO	A	Boston Americans	AB	R	H	RBI	BB	SO	PO	A
Beaumont cf	4	0	0	0	0	2	4	0	Dougherty lf	4	0	0	0	0	1	3	0
Clarke lf	4	0	1	0	0	1	4	0	Collins 3b	4	0	1	0	0	0	0	2
Leach 3b	3	0	0	0	1	0	0	3	Stahl cf	4	0	0	0	0	0	2	0
Wagner ss	4	0	1	0	0	1	2	1	Freeman rf	4	1	1	0	0	0	2	0
Bransfield 1b	3	0	0	0	0	1	7	1	Parent ss	4	1	0	0	0	0	1	1
Ritchey 2b	2	0	0	0	1	1	3	1	LaChance 1b	3	1	1	0	0	0	11	0
Sebring rf	3	0	1	0	0	0	1	1	Ferris 2b	4	0	2	3	0	0	0	3
Phelps c	3	0	0	0	0	1	3	0	Criger c	3	0	2	0	0	0	7	2
Phillippe p	3	0	1	0	0	0	0	2	Dinneen p	3	0	1	0	0	1	0	3
Totals	29	0	4	0	2	7	24	9	Totals	33	3	8	3	0	2	27	11

Pittsburgh Pirates	IP	H	R	ER	BB	SO	Boston Americans	IP	H	R	ER	BB	SO
Phillippe (L)	8	8	3	2	0	2	Dinneen (W)	9	4	0	0	2	7

	1	2	3	4	5	6	7	8	9		R	H	E
PIT N	0	0	0	0	0	0	0	0	0		0	4	3
BOS A	0	0	0	2	0	1	0	0	x		3	8	0

Ferris then singled to right field, and drove in both men. When Criger bounced back to the pitcher, Ferris took second base. Dinneen followed with a single to right. Ferris tried to score but was an easy out at the plate. On the scoreboard, it was Boston that drew first blood, taking a 2–0 lead.

With two outs in the fifth, Sebring hit another hard shot, a ground-rule three-bagger, but was stranded at third. Phillippe tried to help his own cause by singling in the top of the sixth, but when Ginger Beaumont fanned, Criger fired the ball to LaChance at first and Phillippe was caught napping, picked off.

LaChance then tripled in the bottom of the inning (another one into the roped area), and scored on another Ferris single. Ferris had two hits, reached on an error, and drove in all three Boston runs. That was the end of the scoring. Dinneen set down nine more men without permitting another hit. The last man up was, appropriately, the dangerous Honus Wagner. The crowd wanted the batting champion to strike out. Dinneen threw one pitch by him, then another. He had two strikes, but Honus worked the count to 3–2. The *Boston Herald* described the final pitch: "No more artistic conclusion to the great series was possible. Slowly the big pitcher gathered himself up for the effort, slowly he swung his arms about his head. Then the ball shot away like a flash toward the plate where the great Wagner stood, muscles drawn tense, waiting for it. The big batsman's mighty shoulders heaved, the stands will swear that his very frame creaked, as he swung his bat with every ounce of power in his body, but the dull thud of the ball, as it nestled in Criger's waiting mitt, told the story."

The mighty Wagner had struck out, swinging, at another ball bloodied by Dinneen's split finger—igniting a rousing celebration from the Beantown faithful. The *Boston Journal* headlined, "Crowd Frantic in Its Expression of Joy." The Boston Americans had won the first World Series, taking the final game 3–0—the very same score by which Dinneen had blanked the Pirates back in Game One. Dinneen had given up four hits, and struck out seven. In the Series, Dinneen and Phillippe won three games each, making the 1903 World Series the only one with two three-game winners.

Boston's rooters "did not run for the exits as they usually did after a game. They began dropping into the field from the grandstand and bleachers, shouting and yelling like mad. In a jiffy, the Boston players were swallowed up in the monster rush" *(Pittsburgh Post)*. Dinneen was carried in triumph from the field, and Collins, Stahl, and Ferris were borne aloft as well. The band suddenly struck up "The Star-Spangled Banner"—the song was not yet the national anthem—and all joined in. The *Pittsburgh Post* reported "a stirring scene—a whole baseball populace worked up to a high pitch of enthusiasm." The fever would carry over into 1904 as Boston remained a powerhouse of the American League.

◢Extra Innings

- Though the Pirates pitchers were hampered by injury, and the team lost Doheny to mental illness, Boston used fewer pitchers. Only three men pitched for Boston and, of those, Tom Hughes threw two innings in his lone appearance. (He'd started Game Three but was relieved by Young after the first two frames.) Bill Dinneen threw 35 innings (3–1, 2.06 ERA) and Cy Young threw 34 (2–1, 1.85 ERA).

- With weather threatening again and thousands fearing the crowded conditions of the earlier contests, attendance at the finale was the smallest of all eight games (just 7,455). Scalpers were asking $3 or even $5 per ticket, but patrons didn't bite. As many as a thousand spectators saved themselves the official $1 ticket price by watching from rooftops overlooking the field.

- Bill Dinneen set a modern-era major league record in 1904. He appeared in 37 games, starting all 37 and completing all 37 (23–14, 2.20 ERA). (That same year, Jack Taylor set a record by starting 39 games and completing all 39, but since he also made two relief appearances for the St. Louis Cardinals he cannot claim to have pitched a complete game in all his appearances. Back in 1883, Tim Keefe made 68 appearances, all complete games, pitching for the New York Gothams.) In 1905, Dinneen threw a 2–0 no-hitter for Boston against the White Sox in the first game of a doubleheader. (Cy Young lost 15–1 in game two.) After ending his career with the St. Louis Browns, Dinneen umpired in the American League from 1909 through 1937. He was behind the plate for five no-hitters.

Farmer Young Feeling His Oats

In which "No Quaker Gets Far as First Base"

Denton True Young made his mark in the National League prior to the turn of the century. The nickname "Cy" was short for "cyclone," inspired, some said, by the speed of his "jump ball" (fastball), others by the twisting of his body in his windup, in which he turned his back to the batter. He joined Boston in 1901, and his mound magic made him one of the American League's first stars.

The reigning world champions got off to a terrific start in 1904, winning 10 of 12 games in April, yet both losses were Cy's—an Opening Day loss in New York and a 2–0 loss to Philadelphia's Rube Waddell on April 25. In the latter game, the Athletics scored twice in the first inning, and won the game as Waddell threw a six-hit shutout, but Young held them scoreless for the final seven innings.

The last day of April saw George Winter start for Boston against Washington, but after Winter yielded three consecutive singles and one run in the third inning, he was pulled and Cy sent in to relieve. There were two men on base and nobody out. Young set the next three batters down, stranding both runners. He allowed only one Senator to reach base in seven innings of relief, and that on an error by Hobe Ferris—seven innings of hitless ball from a pitcher not expecting to enter the game.

Waddell, meanwhile, seemed to have Boston's number. He started the first game of a four-game visit by the Athletics on May 2, and beat Jesse Tannehill with a one-hitter. Young's next start came on May 5, the finale of the four-game set; Waddell hoped to shut out Boston for the third straight time. The game became a showdown between two great pitchers—both future Hall of Famers. Waddell had led the league in strikeouts in both 1902 and 1903 (and was on his way to setting a new record with 349 strikeouts in 1904). Young already had 380 career wins to his credit, more than anyone in history. There was quite a buildup to the game, given Waddell's one-hitter, and Waddell reportedly issued a personal challenge to Young: "I'll give you the same what I gave Tannehill" (Frederick Lieb, *The Boston Red Sox*, p. 54). Waddell was a media favorite in his day, an eccentric character who loved "fire engines, parades, marbles, fishing and drinking" (David S. Neft and Richard H. Cohen, *The World Series*), and on July 1, 1902, had become the first pitcher to strike out the side on nine pitches.

Cy Young

The weather and grounds were both perfect, and more than 10,000 fans turned out, to that point the largest regular-season crowd since the Boston franchise had been founded.

Young handled the A's with aplomb in the first two innings, striking out three of the six men. Waddell did not have as easy a time, as Jimmy Collins doubled in the first, and Freddy Parent singled in the second; both were stranded as Waddell racked up three strikeouts of his own. The duel was on.

The first Athletics batter in the third inning, Monte Cross, lofted a ball behind second base that could have dropped in, but Buck Freeman came tearing in from right field and snagged it. Ossee Schreckengost grounded out, and so did the pitcher, Waddell. After Young struck out to start the third, back-to-back singles by Patsy Dougherty and Collins set up a promising scenario, but Stahl struck out and Freeman flied to left.

Connie Mack, Philadelphia's business-suited tactician, led off the fourth with a pinch hitter—Danny Hoffman, batting for Topsy Hartsel, who had apparently become ill. Hoffman flew out to center. Pickering grounded out to second, and Harry Davis then fouled out to the catcher, Lou Criger, who gathered in the ball just in front of the Boston bench. Cy showed not a crack in his armor.

Boston's Candy LaChance singled to left in the bottom of the fourth, but could not advance. Five hits, but Waddell still held the Boston team scoreless through four.

The fifth inning saw both teams go down 1-2-3, and Young added a couple more strikeouts in the sixth, getting Monte Cross, popping up Schreckengost, and whiffing Waddell. Six innings and still not a man had reached base, yet Boston's offense had been stifled as well.

Chick Stahl sparked some action in the bottom of the sixth as he drove a ball into the crowd in right field for a ground-rule triple. Buck Freeman did the same thing a moment later, and Boston took a 1–0 lead. Parent fouled out to Schreckengost, though, and when LaChance popped a ball into short left field, Hoffman's throw nailed Freeman at the plate.

In the seventh, at the top of the order, Hoffman led off and hit the ball hard into the left-field corner. The ball drifted foul, but Dougherty made a leaping catch and converted the foul into out number 1 of the seventh, number 19 of the game. Pickering puttered a slow roller to Parent at short, who threw to LaChance for the second out. Davis struck out for the second time in the game. Cy was cruising and the anticipation in the crowd was heightened by the slim lead.

Boston added a couple of insurance runs in the seventh when Ferris hit a ball to the warning track embankment in left-center field for a triple. Criger doubled past third and drove in Ferris. Now everyone in the Boston lineup had hit safely but the pitcher. Young tried a sacrifice bunt but popped to short. Cross took it on one hop, but first baseman Davis couldn't handle Cross's throw, and Criger scored all the way from second on the play, making it 3–0 Boston. Dougherty fouled out, Collins flied out, and Young was forced at second on Stahl's ground ball, but now Boston had a three-run cushion, and the Athletics had yet to dent Young.

The crowd realized that Young was working on more than just a shutout. Even though there was no scoreboard at the Huntington Avenue Grounds, the word "no-hitter" had spread. The crowd was alternately dead silent as each batter approached the plate and loud when he was then retired. Six outs to go, and Lafayette Napoleon "Lave" Cross flew out to Freeman in right. Seybold bounced one back to the box, and Young threw him out. Then Murphy sliced a fly ball to right that Freeman was clearly unable to reach. Fortunately, it fell foul and Young's no-hitter was intact. Cy fired one past Murphy to strike him out and end the inning.

The Bostons engaged in some action on the bases in the eighth, but nothing came of it, and the crowd's attention was fully focused on the ninth inning.

Three more outs stood between Young and the no-hitter. James Buckley Jr. in his book *Perfect* speculates that the crowd might not have realized that a perfect game was on the line. Nearly 24 years had passed since Lee Richmond and John Montgomery Ward had each retired all 27 batters without a man reaching first base. Richmond threw the first perfect game on June 12, 1880, for Worcester against the Cleveland Forest Citys, and Ward's perfect game followed just five days later, when he and the Providence Grays beat the visiting Buffalo nine. Buckley writes, "In fact, there was not even a term for what

MAY 5, 1904: PHILADELPHIA AT BOSTON												
Philadelphia A's	AB	R	H	RBI	PO	A	Boston Red Sox	AB	R	H	RBI	PO	A
Hartsel lf	1	0	0	0	0	0	Dougherty lf	4	0	1	0	1	0
Hoffman ph,lf	2	0	0	0	2	1	Collins 3b	4	0	2	0	2	0
Pickering cf	3	0	0	0	1	0	Stahl cf	4	1	1	0	3	0
Davis 1b	3	0	0	0	5	0	Freeman rf	4	0	1	1	2	0
L Cross 3b	3	0	0	0	4	1	Parent ss	4	0	2	0	1	4
Seybold rf	3	0	0	0	2	0	LaChance 1b	3	0	1	0	9	0
Murphy 2b	3	0	0	0	1	2	Ferris 2b	3	1	1	0	0	3
M Cross ss	3	0	0	0	2	2	Criger c	3	1	1	1	9	0
Schreckengost c	3	0	0	0	7	0	Young p	3	0	0	1	0	2
Waddell p	3	0	0	0	0	1	**Totals**	32	3	10	3	27	9
Totals	27	0	0	0	24	7							

Philadelphia A's	IP	H	R	ER	BB	SO	Boston Red Sox	IP	H	R	ER	BB	SO
Waddell (L)	9	10	3	3	0	6	Young (W)	9	0	0	0	0	3

	1	2	3	4	5	6	7	8	9		R	H	E
PHI A	0	0	0	0	0	0	0	0	0		0	0	1
BOS A	0	0	0	0	0	1	2	0	x		3	10	0

Young was about to accomplish. No one called it a 'perfect' game until 1922. The very concept of a game in which no opponent reached base was nearly unheard of. Yes, Ward and Richmond had done it, but that was nearly ancient history, in another time, another place, with different rules."

There was no scoreboard, no radio, no cell phones. Buckley asks us to consider "that fans were watching history in the making but . . . they didn't really know just how historic an event it was." And yet they sensed the gravity of the situation. As each Athletic came to bat, a "deathlike silence" settled over the grounds.

Montford Montgomery "Monte" Cross led off the ninth, fouling off several pitches, before finally taking strike three. Up rose a mighty roar, an "awful din." Sudden silence descended once again. Schreckengost "almost gave the anxious fans heart disease when he hit a grounder toward Parent," but Freddy fielded and threw cleanly to LaChance. "There was no one that had the courage to stir until Parent had sent the ball straight into LaChance's glove, and then a roar even louder than before emitted from the throats of the onlookers" *(Boston Herald)*.

Young had retired 26 batters in a row. Rube Waddell was due up next. As he walked to the plate, many in the crowd yelled out angrily. They wanted to see Young put down a pinch hitter—to beat the best the A's could put up. Why would Connie Mack send up his pitcher, rather than pinch-hitting for him? His team was losing by three runs. There were some good-hitting pitchers—Young had batted .321 in 1903—but Waddell was not one of them. Waddell had averaged just .122 the previous season. As it would happen, he would hit .122 again in 1904. Maybe Reed Browning had it best: "perhaps . . . Mack liked the agonistic drama inherent in seeing whether Young's great mound rival could do what no one else had done that day" (Reed Browning, *Cy Young: A Baseball Life*, p. 143).

He didn't. Young's first offering was wide. Ball one. Rube swung at the second pitch but missed. The crowd remained completely silent, "each spectator was afraid any noise might disturb Young." The third pitch looked good, so Waddell swung and hit a fly ball to Stahl in center. Stahl didn't move an inch, wrote the *Boston Journal*. "I thought that ball would never come down," Stahl said after the game.

The *Boston Post* reported, "A pin drop could have been heard in the grand stand as Stahl waited for the ball to drop. Young followed the flight of the ball; so did every man, woman and child. . . . Never did a single catch mean so much. As it dropped into Stahl's glove a roar as if a hundred cannon had belched forth rocked the stands and bleachers."

"Ten thousand voices, keyed to the highest pitch, went off as if by an electric shock," declared the *Globe*. The *Herald* said that the fans "acted like maniacs just let loose." Fans jumped onto the field and mobbed Young.

"I am proud to be defeated by such pitching," Mack told Young, and Waddell offered his congratulations, too.

The game had taken 83 minutes, from start to finish.

"Young was at his best," the *Boston Globe* wrote, "having fine speed, good curves and perfect control. He was never forced to shorten his preliminary swing [his windup], as there were no bases to watch."

The Boston newspapers were hard-pressed to find similar pitching feats. Though remembering seven innings thrown by Hoss Radbourne, the *Globe* couldn't recall another game in which a runner failed to reach first. "No Quaker Gets Far as First Base" proclaimed a *Globe* headline. "Young's Performance Has No Equal In Baseball History," ran directly under it. The *Herald* recalled the Richmond and Ward games, but Young's perfect game didn't make the front page. "Happy, I should say I was," Young declared. "Things broke beautifully for me. I never felt better in my life. My curves broke well, and my speed seemed a little faster than usual. I am proud as any man could be to be the first to pitch such a game." Young, too, was unaware of any precedent. He shared the credit: "It was not all my doing. I was supported in brilliant fashion, and I am grateful to the other eight players for making it possible for me to establish the record. From the fifth inning I only dreamed of being able to do it. In the seventh I figured on my chances. In the eighth I began to hope so, and in the ninth with the tail end of the batting list I felt confident. I was mighty nervous at the end." He commented on Waddell being the 27th batter. "Waddell is eccentric and erratic. I feared him more than any other. When he hit that ball to center I sighed. As it dropped into Stahl's glove I felt like a colt, and when I gained possession of that ball I was overjoyed. Why didn't the Athletics hit me? That is too much for me to answer. It is up to them. The other Boston players did their share. Criger's judgment for what kind of balls to throw was perfect, and Dougherty's catch against the fence was a beauty" *(Boston Post)*.

Young's brilliance continued throughout the season. Perhaps even more astonishing an accomplishment was the fact that Young's perfecto nestled between two other streaks of note. Most baseball fans have heard of Johnny Vander Meer, who threw no-hitters in consecutive games in June 1938. In all, Vander Meer threw 22 straight hitless innings, yet fell two innings short of Cy Young. Cy threw 24 innings in a row without letting opponents have a hit.

Young didn't give up a hit in either of the last two innings of the game on April 25, then threw seven innings of hitless relief on April 30. Then he threw nine innings of perfect ball in the May 5 game. Six days after his perfect game, he faced Detroit. This time stingy Cy threw another shutout—but it took 15 innings. He didn't allow a hit for the first six frames. Take those six innings, add them to the 18 he had already accumulated, and one gets 24 innings without a hit.

Finally giving up a hit did not cause Young to fall apart. The May 11 game remained scoreless after 14½ innings (Young had yielded five hits and four walks—but not one run). Detroit's Ed Killian was clearly superb as well. Three of the four hits Killian allowed in the first nine innings were made by Young. But Boston won the game, 1–0, in the bottom of the 15th inning. Even after the first hit, Young had kept the Tigers scoreless for nine more innings and thus ran up a streak of 45 consecutive scoreless innings. That streak finally ended on May 17, when he gave up three runs—and even lost the game.

When it came down to the finale of the season, Boston was in a tight pennant race with New York. Young won three of the last nine games, every one of them a shutout, tallying three shutouts in seven days. On October 2, Young beat St. Louis 2–0 at St. Louis, and on October 5, he shut out the White Sox 3–0 in Chicago. On October 8, Jimmy Collins handed Cy Young the ball for the second game of the day's doubleheader, and Cy shut down New York. Young faced 23-game winner Jack Powell. One run by Boston in the fifth was all Young needed. Cy Young won his 26th game, 1–0, his 10th shutout of the season.

He would eventually finish his career with 511 career wins, 150 wins more than his nearest competitors at the time of his retirement. To this day he tops the list, still almost 100 wins ahead of Walter Johnson, who racked up 417. Cy won 30 games in a season five times and was elected to the National Baseball Hall of Fame in 1937.

Extra Innings

- Cy Young's string of 45 consecutive scoreless innings was impressive, but was matched later that year by Doc White of Chicago, with 45 innings racked up between September 12 and September 30. Walter Johnson surpassed that with 55⅔ scoreless innings between April 10 and May 14, 1913. And Orel Hershiser holds the major league record with 59 innings, between August 30, 1988, and September 28, 1988.

October 10, 1904: Boston at New York

Capture the Flag

In which the Olde Towne Team prevails in their first pennant race against their rivals from Gotham

The year 1904 saw Boston look to repeat the feat of capturing the American League pennant, but as the race drew to a close this year there was a new contender, as New York now had a team in the American League ranks. Ban Johnson was the architect of the American League, founded in 1901. Enticing many players from the National League with better salaries, while dropping ticket prices to patrons, the AL made substantial inroads and drew more fans in its very first season. Buoyed by the initial success, Johnson wanted to place a franchise in the metropolitan New York market. After the 1902 season, he arranged to move the Baltimore team to New York. Johnson also wanted the New York team to be a contender, and so influenced a number of player moves that benefited the New York club.

In mid-June Boston traded star left fielder Patsy Dougherty to New York for utilityman Bob Unglaub. In *Red Sox Century* Glenn Stout and Richard Johnson call it "one of the worst trades in [Boston] team history" and say it "precipitated a decline on the field far worse than that which was blamed on the sale of Babe Ruth sixteen years later." Dougherty had begun the 1904 season with a .336 career batting average. New York rapidly became a remarkably stronger team, and challenged Boston for supremacy, running fairly neck-and-neck for the rest of the season. In fact, the 1904 season saw the tightest Boston/New York pennant race for 74 years. The next time the teams would be so close at the wire would be 1978.

New York edged Boston out of first place on September 3. From that point on, the lead shifted 15 times in the final four weeks of the season. New York came to Boston and on the 14th began a stretch of six games in three days (back-to-back-to-back doubleheaders). Two were 1–1 ties, called due to heavy mist and to darkness. Of the games that counted, each team won two, and Boston retained their one-percentage-point lead, but then Philly came to town and Boston booted both games. New York assumed first place in the pennant race. On October 2 Boston was in first (.6096) and New York in second (.6083).

The last five games were head-to-head, in effect a best-of-five matchup. Whichever team took three would win the pennant. Boston lost the first game—and the lead—as Jack Chesbro won his 41st (!) victory of 1904. Four games remained—a doubleheader in Boston and then a doubleheader in New York.

New York's starting pitching was clearly worn thin. Despite going all the way, throwing nine innings on October 7, Chesbro came back again the very next day, pitching on zero days' rest, starting the first game of the double-header—he didn't even wait until the second game. It wasn't a particularly good idea—Boston scored six times in the fourth and the game was effectively over, Big Bill Dinneen holding New York to seven hits. Boston won 13–2 and reclaimed the lead.

Jimmy Collins handed Cy Young the ball for the second game, and Cy shut down New York. Young faced 23-game winner Jack Powell, and it was a lower-scoring affair. One run by Boston in the fifth was all Young needed. Cy Young won his 26th game, 1–0, his 10th shutout of the season.

October 9 was a Sunday, and while players and fans could pray, neither city allowed baseball on Sundays. Should Boston win either of the games scheduled for New York on Monday, October 10, Boston would retain the pennant they'd won the year before.

Dinneen got the start for Boston (he was 22–14), facing—for the third game day in a row—Jack Chesbro. New York's back was to the wall, and this was their ace—he'd already won 41 games. "Happy Jack" was their hottest hurler, regardless of the fact that he'd started on both the seventh and the eighth. Dinneen had started on the eighth himself, yet here he was again, too, taking the hill at Hilltop Park in upper Manhattan.

The first two innings had some fits and starts, but neither team broke through. Boston went out 1-2-3 in the first. Dinneen didn't start well. Dougherty walked on four straight pitches, reached second on Wee Willie Keeler's sacrifice, but was stranded as Big Bill got out of the inning. Both Buck Freeman and Hobe Ferris singled for Boston in the second, but Lou Criger hit the ball right back to Chesbro, who tossed to first for the third out. This time New York went down in order, Freddy Parent making an excellent play at short.

No one reached base for Boston in the top of the third. In the bottom of the inning, when it was Chesbro's first time up, the proceedings were stopped as the great pitcher was presented an "elegant" sealskin fur coat and hat. Perhaps warmed by the presentation, he promptly tripled down the right-field line, but was stranded on third as Dinneen struck out both Dougherty (swinging three times at low pitches) and Keeler.

Neither team reached in the fourth. In the fifth, though Criger walked and took second on a wild pitch, Dinneen fouled out to Keeler to end any threat. The game was half over. New York broke the ice, and scored twice in the bottom of the inning. Two outs, nobody on base, two strikes on the batter when Red Kleinow singled to right. Chesbro slapped his second hit of the game—a shot that caromed off Dinneen. Dougherty—as he so often did—figured in the scoring. Down to his final strike, Pat "slammed a beauty to right and Kleinow crossed the rubber" *(Boston Herald)*. Keeler walked to load the bases, perhaps intentionally, but then Dinneen couldn't find the plate, giving a free pass to Kid Elberfeld, which forced in Chesbro with the second run. Unrattled, Dinneen ably handled Jimmy Williams's bounder for the third out. New York had sent eight batters to the plate and twice loaded the bases, but had only two runs to show for it. New York 2, Boston 0.

In the sixth, Boston put runners on first and second on two errors (one of them Chesbro's), but when Williams settled under Buck Freeman's fly, again "Happy Jack" escaped unscathed. The only Highlander threat came when John Anderson singled in the New York sixth, but he was caught between first and second when John Ganzel struck out. Wid Conroy grounded out, Parent to LaChance.

Chesbro had allowed only two hits over the first six innings, but the bottom of the Boston order tied the game in the top of the seventh. LaChance led off with a drive to second; Williams couldn't handle it and Candy was safe at first. Ferris fired a shot past Williams. Criger moved both runners up a base with a successful sacrifice. Williams had yet another chance as Dinneen hit one to him, but he muffed it with a low throw home, trying to cut down LaChance at the plate. The ball got away and both LaChance and Ferris scored as Dinneen made his way to second. Williams handled the next grounder, Dinneen taking third on the play. Parent was the fielding hero of the game, with several solid plays noted. Now Parent hit the ball hard, but flew out to Dougherty in left. New York was jittery in the field, making three errors to Boston's none.

Now the score was knotted at 2–2. New York's Kleinow singled to lead off the seventh, but was forced at second by Chesbro. Dougherty's bunt attempt resulted in a pop-up to Dinneen. Chesbro himself was forced at second when Keeler hit to Ferris. Boston knocked out three hits in the top of the eighth but failed to score. Stahl singled to left but Collins struck out trying to advance him to second. Freeman singled to center. LaChance hit the ball far to right but Stahl was cut down sliding in at the plate. Duke Farrell was coaching third, and some felt he shouldn't have sent Stahl home. First-ball-hitting, Ferris grounded to third for a 5-3 play. New York went down 1-2-3 in the bottom of the eighth.

The game had reached the ninth inning. A New York win would bring the season down to its final game later that same afternoon. A Boston win would secure a second straight pennant for the "World Beaters." Chesbro took the hill for the final time that season. Lou Criger hit a slow grounder to the shortstop and was safe at first. Dinneen sacrificed him to second, Chesbro throwing to Ganzel at first. One down. Kip Selbach grounded out, short to first, moving Criger to third. Two out. Freddy Parent stepped into the box, 0-for-4 on the afternoon, with the go-ahead run 90 feet from home plate. At this point New York's 41-game winner prepared a spitball, his signature pitch, and uncorked a wild pitch that flew all the way to the press box behind the plate. Red Kleinow scampered after the ball, but there would be no chance to catch Criger coming home. The Boston catcher crossed the plate without incident—Chesbro, instead of running to cover the plate, had turned away, unable to look. He then gave up a hit—Parent singled to center—but escaped further damage when the runner was forced at second by Stahl. Still, the damage was enough. Boston took the field, ahead 3–2, and Chesbro collapsed, disconsolate, on the bench.

And Boston's rooters, a "vociferous army [who] far exceed in noise any body that ever gathered at either baseball park or gridiron," were flush with the scent of victory. Does this kind of support really matter to the team on the field? A. H. C. Mitchell of the *Boston American* was one of many sportswriters who thought so. He wrote, "No wonder the Bostons worked with more snap and vim than has been customary. They knew the value of the support of the rooters in Pittsburgh [in the World Series] and they also realized its worth to-day."

New York still had last ups, though—the bottom of the ninth—and it was do or die. There was, for the first time in the game, a hush. First baseman Ganzel struck out, even though the New York crowd began to try to rattle Dinneen. The *American* said that Criger and Dinneen differed on almost every pitch thrown in the final frame. Dinneen walked Conroy, the third baseman, though at least one Boston writer felt that the umpire had missed what should have been called a strike. "It was a raw piece of work by [home plate umpire] Sheridan but not a word spoke Sir William" *(Boston Globe)*. Kleinow, who already had a couple of singles to his credit, hit a high fly ball, caught by Hobe Ferris at second base. Two outs, a man on first—manager Griffith sent up the veteran Deacon McGuire to hit for the demoralized Chesbro. McGuire was hitting only a bit over .200, but he'd been playing pro ball since 1884, and, indeed, he showed patience at the plate, drawing a base on balls and moving the lead runner into scoring position. Two on, two out.

Dinneen had now walked four batters; Chesbro had walked only one.

Dave Fultz was put in to run for McGuire. It all came down to Pat Dougherty.

Dougherty had resented the trade from this very Boston team to New York, and he'd hit decisively against Boston several times during the season. The *Globe* reporter commented, "Here was the opportunity of a lifetime to win a game that meant disappointment for honest Jimmie Collins, and untold glory for Dougherty. The excitement was intense. . . . The Boston men bent lower and followed the ball like wild cats. Dineen paid little attention to the men on bases. He wanted Patsy and he wanted him very badly."

As Dougherty stepped into the batter's box, he was "cheered to the echo" by the New York crowd. A curveball right over the plate. Dougherty took a look, and strike one. Dinneen again threw a curve, low and inside, and Dougherty swung and fouled off the pitch. 0–2. A roar went up from the Royal Rooters. Inside and high came the next pitch. Ball one. Another one, this time high and outside. 2–2. Dinneen checked the count with Sheridan behind the plate. Yes,

OCTOBER 10, 1904: BOSTON AT NEW YORK													
Boston Americans	**AB**	**R**	**H**	**RBI**	**PO**	**A**	**New York Yankees**	**AB**	**R**	**H**	**RBI**	**PO**	**A**
Selbach lf	5	0	0	0	0	0	Dougherty lf	4	0	1	1	1	0
Parent ss	5	0	1	0	3	5	Keeler rf	2	0	0	0	2	0
Stahl cf	5	0	1	0	0	0	Elberfeld ss	3	0	0	1	1	5
Collins 3b	4	0	1	0	0	1	Williams 2b	4	0	0	0	3	2
Freeman rf	4	0	2	0	1	0	Anderson cf	4	0	1	0	0	1
LaChance 1b	4	1	2	0	13	1	Ganzel 1b	4	0	0	0	13	1
Ferris 2b	4	1	1	0	3	2	Conroy 3b	3	0	0	0	1	2
Criger c	2	1	1	0	6	1	Kleinow c	4	1	2	0	6	0
Dinneen p	3	0	0	0	1	7	Chesbro p	3	1	2	0	0	3
Totals	**36**	**3**	**9**	**0**	**27**	**17**	McGuire ph	0	0	0	0	0	0
							Fultz pr	0	0	0	0	0	0
							Totals	**31**	**2**	**6**	**2**	**27**	**14**

Boston Americans	**IP**	**H**	**R**	**ER**	**BB**	**SO**	**New York Yankees**	**IP**	**H**	**R**	**ER**	**BB**	**SO**
Dinneen (W)	9	6	2	2	5	7	Chesbro (L)	9	9	3	1	1	5

	1	2	3	4	5	6	7	8	9	R	H	E
BOS A	0	0	0	0	0	0	2	0	1	3	9	0
NY A	0	0	0	0	2	0	0	0	0	2	6	3

2 and 2. A decent hit could have tied, or won, the game. Criger came out to the mound and conferred with Dinneen for quite some time, then repositioned himself behind the plate. "Dineen started with a short, slow preliminary motion, his arm gaining in speed as it circled his head for the second time, and with all the power in his body he shot that ball across Dougherty's waist over the inside corner of the plate, and watched Patrick miss it by six inches, and go down in history as the last man out in the most important game of ball ever played. The New York players acted as if tied to the ground for several seconds, then they started for the bench. The New York fans were as silent as the grass" *(Boston Globe)*.

Behind the Boston bench, the band of Boston faithful struck up "Tessie" once again. Mighty Dougherty had struck out.

"The Boston rooters fairly hugged each other in the exuberance of their joy. Louis Criger tossed his cap in the air as he ran off with the ball" *(Boston Herald)*. Collins looked spent. Unglaub filled in for him in game two and backup catcher Tom Doran subbed for Criger. Though the pennant had been decided, and the Royal Rooters presumably were as hoarse as can be, there was another game to play. Only five minutes' rest were taken between the two games. There had been the tension, the release, for Boston the exultation—and then just five minutes to calm down and start another game. There was some worry that darkness might prevent a full game from being played, but it was a brisk, well-pitched matchup between George Winter and Ambrose Puttmann. Most of the crowd stayed for the second game—a remarkable tribute to the New York fans who had nothing to gain and were no doubt fully deflated. It was an exciting game, which saw the two pitchers both throw nine scoreless innings in just 66 minutes. In the bottom of the tenth, New York's Conroy singled, reached third on McGuire's out, and scored when LaChance's throw across the diamond to Unglaub at third sailed past the third baseman. The whole 10-inning game took an hour and 12 minutes (1:10, according to the *Times*). What would otherwise have been a stunning New York 1–0 extra-inning triumph was, instead, almost a footnote to the 1904 season and one of the greatest pennant races of the last 100 years.

Extra Innings

- The American Association race in 1883 and the National League pennant in 1889 were both decided on the last day of the season (in '89, New York beat Boston), but in neither case was it a head-to-head confrontation, as it was in 1904—when it came down to that one final strikeout.

- Though Boston won the pennant, they did not meet the Giants in the World Series. John McGraw's Giants refused to play the American League entry. After much public outcry, World Series play resumed in 1905, when the Giants faced Philadelphia.

- Since 1900, only a handful of pitchers have hit a home run on their birthday. Jack Chesbro did it on June 5, 1906. It was the fifth of the five home runs he hit during his major league career.

July 29, 1911: St. Louis at Boston

Throwing Smoke

In which Howard Ellsworth Wood achieves mound mastery

Just 21 years old in 1911, "Smoky Joe" Wood was an exceptionally good pitcher on a mediocre Red Sox team. The 5'11" right-hander had broken in late in the 1908 season and through 1910 had compiled a record of 24–21. In 1910 he'd won 12 but lost 13 despite an ERA of only 1.69. This was a man who seemed poised to break out.

Boston had just come back to its home Huntington Avenue Grounds ballpark from a 19-game road trip on which they'd lost seven of the last nine games. Back in Boston, though, they swept a three-game series from the visiting White Sox and prepared to host the woeful St. Louis Browns (26–64) for five games. Boston was playing just over .500 ball (47–45).

Wood had lost the last game of the road trip, but was the starting pitcher for the first game of the July 29 doubleheader. Starting for St. Louis was Joe Lake, a competent journeyman pitcher in the midst of a six-year major league career. Lake had been St. Lou's best pitcher in 1910, leading the team in ERA and their only starter to notch double-digit wins.

Wood had broken in with Boston just as Cy Young was bowing out, and was described in the *Boston Herald* as "Cy Young's successor hereabouts." A fastball pitcher (hence the nickname "Smoky," for the smoke he threw) who could hit his spots, Wood only mixed in a curveball once in a while to make his fastball seem even faster. Walter Johnson, the preeminent fastball pitcher of his day, was reported to have said, "Can I throw harder than Joe Wood? Listen, my friend, there's no man alive can throw harder than Smoky Joe Wood." On July 7, in the very first game of the long road trip, Wood had faced Lake in Sportsman's Park and shut down the Browns with 8⅓ innings of no-hit pitching. Wood, called the "Kansas Cyclone" by the *Boston Journal,* struck out 15 Browns batters but tired a bit in the bottom of the ninth and lost both his no-hitter and his shutout when Burt Shotton singled in one run. Boston won, 6–1.

Shotton was the leadoff hitter for the Browns on July 29. Wood missed with his first three pitches; despite being granted a 3–0 count, Shotton struck out. Third baseman Jimmy Austin flew out to Tris Speaker in center and Al Schweitzer (this particular Albert Schweitzer went by the nickname "Cheese") struck out, too. In the second inning, Wood was helped by his defense as Larry Gardner made a terrific stop of a grounder and threw to first for one out. Wood walked Happy Hogan, but Jim Stephens flied out to the shortstop Steve Yerkes on a hit-and-run, and Yerkes was easily able to double Stephens by throwing to Hack Engle at first base.

Boston got a gift run in the second when first baseman John Black fielded Heinie Wagner's grounder and tossed a "weird heave" *(Boston Post)* toward Lake, who was a little late covering first. Wagner took second on the error. The catcher, Stephens, snapped a throw to second to try to pick off Wagner, but the throw sailed into center, and Wagner took third. The infield played in, but catcher Bill Carrigan singled in the run with a hit past the shortstop.

After two outs in the third, Lake walked because the sole umpire working the game (Silk O'Loughlin) missed a swing, but was left stranded at first. Happy Hogan was hit by Wood's pitch to lead off the fifth, and moved up to second on a sacrifice. He advanced to third on a grounder, but Wood bore down and struck out the veteran Bobby Wallace, who served as St. Louis's manager as well, to end the threat.

JULY 29, 1911: ST. LOUIS AT BOSTON													
St. Louis Browns	AB	R	H	BB	PO	A	Boston Red Sox	AB	R	H	PO	A	
Shotton cf	4	0	0	0	1	0	Hooper rf	4	0	0	0	0	
Austin 3b	4	0	0	0	1	4	Engle 1b	4	0	2	8	1	
Schweitzer rf	3	0	0	0	1	0	Speaker cf	3	1	1	2	0	
Laporte 2b	3	0	0	0	3	2	Wagner 2b	4	1	0	0	2	
Hogan lf	1	0	0	1	1	0	Carrigan c	4	1	1	14	0	
Stephens c	2	0	0	0	4	2	Gardner 3b	4	1	1	0	2	
Black 1b	3	0	0	0	10	2	Riggert lf	3	0	1	1	0	
Wallace ss	3	0	0	0	1	2	Yerkes ss	3	1	1	1	1	
Lake p	1	0	0	1	2	3	Wood p	3	0	0	1	2	
Criss ph	1	0	0	0	0	0	Totals	32	5	7	27	8	
Totals	25	0	0	2	24	15							

St. Louis Browns	IP	H	R	ER	BB	SO	Boston Red Sox	IP	H	R	ER	BB	SO
Lake (L)	8	7	5	4	2	4	Wood (W)	9	0	0	0	2	12

	1	2	3	4	5	6	7	8	9	R	H	E
STL A	0	0	0	0	0	0	0	0	0	0	0	4
BOS A	0	1	0	0	1	2	0	1	x	5	7	0

Smoky Joe Wood

A single, a fielder's choice, and another single brought in another Red Sox run in the fifth inning. Boston got two more in the sixth, the big blow being a triple by Gardner. Speaker's home run into the left-field bleachers provided a fifth and final run in the eighth.

And all the while, Smoky Joe cruised. The last man to reach base against him had been Hogan, in the fifth. The large Saturday crowd of 17,596 cheered each out Wood recorded through the seventh and eighth, the ovations increasing in volume as each Brownie came up to bat and was sent back hitless.

Dode Criss pinch-hit for Lake to lead off the ninth. He swung on an 0–2 count and tapped out on a weak bounder. Shotton flew out to the left fielder, Joe Riggert, for the second out. Wood was really in command; the fly ball was only the third ball hit out of the infield.

The final man to step into the batter's box against Smoky Joe that day was Jimmy Austin, just one man between him and the sort of baseball immortality that comes with pitching a no-hitter. The crowd, which had been boisterous and loud, quieted down, "almost holding their breath," according to Herman Nickerson of the *Boston Journal*. Wood got two strikes on Austin, and he was just one pitch away. Wood wound up and fired the ball home. Austin swung at the pitch but swung through it, the ball going into and bounding out of Carrigan's glove—a foul tip. Still two strikes. "He just loved to throw the ball as hard as he could," his son Bob Wood told interviewers years later. Wood wound up again and put just a little more on the pitch. Austin swung again, and missed. Joe Wood had a no-hitter, and a permanent place in Red Sox lore.

In all, Smoky Joe struck out 12 St. Louis batters, even though several times early in the game, the Browns only whiffed after being staked to 3–0 counts. Wood walked two and hit one batter. Given his one-hit masterpiece on July 7, Smoky Joe had now yielded but one hit to St. Louis over 18 consecutive innings. It was the fifth no-hitter for a Boston pitcher. Cy Young had a perfect game in May 1904, and Jesse Tannehill had a no-hitter in August of the same year. Bill Dinneen threw one in September 1905 and Cy Young threw another in June 1908. Of the 13 no-hitters in early American League history, Boston now boasted five.

Joe Wood finished the year well. He was a 23-game winner with a fifth-place Boston team that barely cracked .500. The Red Sox' record was 78–75. Wood was 23–17 with a 2.02 ERA and 231 strikeouts, good for second on the list behind Big Ed Walsh and ahead of Walter Johnson, despite the fact that Johnson pitched 40 more innings.

The following year, 1912, was Smoky Joe's stellar season. He won 34 games and lost only five, struck out 258 opponents, and posted a 1.91 ERA, second only to Walter Johnson in both categories. Joe also reeled off 10 shutouts as part of a streak in which he won 16 decisions in a row. He won three more games in the World Series.

◆ Extra Innings

- Howard Ellsworth "Smoky Joe" Wood broke into professional baseball in his hometown of Ness City, Kansas, by playing with the Bloomer Girls in 1906. He was paid $35 for three weeks' playing time. Later that winter, in 1906, he signed with Cedar Rapids in the Illinois-Indiana-Iowa (Three-I) minor league.

- Joe Wood's son Joseph Frank "Joe" Wood pitched in three games for the Red Sox in 1944.

6

October 12, 1912: New York at Boston
Taking the Fifth

In which a rookie bests the Christian Gentleman

Boston fans were discouraged; the Red Sox hadn't won a pennant for seven long years. After winning back-to-back flags in 1903 and 1904, the team plunged to mediocre in '05 and to last place in '06. The next five finishes were mired in mediocrity. But 1912 brought new ownership and a new ballpark—Fenway Park opened in April.

John I. Taylor had sold off or traded many of the ball club's best players, and early in 1912 he sold the club itself to former ballplayer James McAleer. "It was no secret," write Glenn Stout and Richard Johnson in *Red Sox Century*, "that McAleer was only the front man in the deal. Most of the money was [league president Ban] Johnson's. Despite their play, Boston was the most lucrative franchise in the league and he wanted in on it." These sorts of shenanigans were not that surprising in those days, but what did surprise everyone was the play of the 1912 Red Sox. They fielded virtually the same starting nine as the year before, when they'd finished 24 games behind Connie Mack's repeating world champion Philadelphia Athletics.

The biggest addition to the squad was Hugh Bedient on the mound. He debuted in April and went 20–9. With 15 wins, Charley "Sea Lion" Hall almost doubled his win total of eight from the previous year, but that's what can happen when a team begins firing on all cylinders. Buck O'Brien surprised everyone with 20 victories, as he'd previously appeared in only six games. The most dramatic contribution, though, came from Smoky Joe Wood, who'd won 23 games the year before, but lost 17. In 1912 he would end up with a 34–5 record.

The new ownership had brought Jake Stahl out of retirement and installed him as manager and first baseman. Stahl hit .301. The outfield trio of Tris Speaker in center, flanked by Duffy Lewis in left and Harry Hooper in right, shared stellar years. Speaker added nearly 50 points to an already outstanding 1911 season, and hit .383. Lewis dipped under .300 in average but drove in 109 runs. Hooper fell off sharply in average to just .242, but ranged far and wide in right field. Not too many balls got past the Red Sox outfield. Boston won 105 games, and Mack's Athletics finished third, 15 games back, a game behind the Washington Senators. The Sox clinched on a road trip and arrived home at South Station on September 23, welcomed by more than 100,000 people who crowded the roads leading from the train station to Boston Common, where Mayor John F. Fitzgerald gave the team keys to the city.

Although the Red Sox were the clear pick of the pundits, the World Series against John McGraw's New York Giants proved to be a battle, with every game hard fought. Game One was at the Polo Grounds in New York. New York scored first, with two runs in the third off Joe Wood. Boston didn't even manage a hit off Jeff Tesreau until the sixth, but scored once in the sixth and three times in the seventh to take a 4–2 lead. The Giants scored a run in the ninth and had runners on second and third with two out. Smoky Joe ran the count to 3-and-2 before reaching back and blazing a fastball past the last Giant for his 11th strikeout and the victory.

Game Two was in Boston. In those days, the Series switched cities for each game if the teams were nearby enough to allow it, with a coin toss determining where the Series would start. Boston got three runs in the first off Christy Mathewson, but the Giants took a 5–4 lead in the top of the eighth. Boston answered with one, and the game remained tied at 5–5 until New York scored a single run in the 10th. With one out in the bottom of the 10th, Tris Speaker hit the first pitch he saw and banged it off the wall in left-center field. Streaking to third, he rounded the bag and—when he saw the second baseman fumble the relay—he headed for home. He seemed a sure out, but catcher Art Wilson dropped the throw to the plate and Speaker was safe. The 6–6 tie had to be called on account of darkness after 11 innings of play. Hugh Fullerton of the *New York Times* dubbed it "the greatest world's series game ever played."

Game Three was a 2–1 squeaker, Rube Marquard over O'Brien. Boston was down by one run, but had two men on base in the bottom of the ninth with two out when Hick Cady drove a ball deep into right-center field that looked a sure game-winner. Outfielder Josh Devore, just 5'6" tall, was "legging it like mad back across the sward in deep right, reached up and clutched a win away from the Red Sox in the last second" *(Boston Herald).* Game Four was another Wood vs. Tesreau match, won by Wood 3–1 and characterized by Sox shortstop Heinie Wagner's spectacular play in the field.

Game Five featured 13-year veteran Christy Mathewson against the 22-year-old rookie Hugh Bedient. John McGraw had been led to expect that Boston manager Jake Stahl would start Ray Collins, but Stahl craftily bid Bedient take the ball just minutes before game time. "Four hundred and twenty years ago today Mr. Columbus discovered America," wrote Hugh Fullerton in a special report to the *Chicago Tribune,* "and some . . . New Yorkers discovered to their

OCTOBER 12, 1912: NEW YORK AT BOSTON

New York Giants	AB	R	H	RBI	BB	SO	PO	A	Boston Red Sox	AB	R	H	RBI	BB	SO	PO	A
Devore lf	2	0	0	0	2	1	0	0	Hooper rf	4	1	2	0	0	0	4	0
Doyle 2b	4	0	0	0	0	0	0	3	Yerkes 2b	4	1	1	1	0	0	3	3
Snodgrass cf	4	0	0	0	0	1	2	0	Speaker cf	3	0	1	1	0	0	3	0
Murray rf	3	0	0	0	1	0	0	1	Lewis lf	3	0	0	0	0	0	1	0
Merkle 1b	4	1	1	0	0	1	15	0	Gardner 3b	3	0	0	0	0	1	2	2
Herzog 3b	4	0	0	0	0	0	2	3	Stahl 1b	3	0	0	0	0	0	7	0
Meyers c	3	0	1	0	0	0	2	0	Wagner ss	3	0	1	0	0	1	2	1
Fletcher ss	2	0	0	0	0	0	2	2	Cady c	3	0	0	0	0	0	5	0
McCormick ph	1	0	0	0	0	0	0	0	Bedient p	3	0	0	0	0	0	0	0
Shafer ss	0	0	0	0	0	0	1	1	Totals	29	2	5	2	0	2	27	6
Mathewson p	3	0	1	0	0	1	0	3									
Totals	30	1	3	0	3	4	24	13									

New York Giants	IP	H	R	ER	BB	SO	HR	Boston Red Sox	IP	H	R	ER	BB	SO	HR
Mathewson (L)	8	5	2	2	0	2	0	Bedient (W)	9	3	1	0	3	4	0

	1	2	3	4	5	6	7	8	9	R	H	E
NY N	0	0	0	0	0	0	1	0	0	1	3	1
BOS A	0	0	2	0	0	0	0	0	x	2	5	1

astonishment that the Boston Americans possess more than one pitcher." Bedient came to the attention of major league baseball in 1908 while pitching for a semipro team in Falconer, New York. In a game against Corry, Pennsylvania, that lasted 23 innings, he struck out 42 men, for what is still considered a world record. When the newspapers picked up the story, 19 major league clubs came knocking on his door. Now four years later he was pitching in the World Series, and facing one of the most highly respected men in the game in Mathewson.

Red Sox fans had begun to gather outside the gates at midnight, and the Saturday Columbus Day game drew well. The crush from the crowd caused Fenway's center-field fence to break down just before game time, but police maintained order and held back the spectators. Bedient took the hill amid the hubbub and walked leadoff batter Josh Devore on four straight pitches, but thanks to a high fly ball and a quick double play, the moment of wildness proved harmless. Mathewson and Bedient traded places. Harry Hooper hit Mathewson's first pitch for a single. Speaker singled, too, but there was an out sandwiched between, and Matty got the next two batters. In the second, Bedient again walked the first batter up on four pitches. Again he escaped any further damage.

The first scoring came in the Sox half of the third inning. Harry Hooper had "a beautiful whack . . . hard whanged into the uttermost confines" *(Boston Herald)* that got by Buck Herzog at third base. Normally the ball would have been scored a home run, but as it rolled between the side bleachers and the stands, it stayed in sight of umpire Bill Klem and so remained in play. Steve Yerkes pounced on the next pitch and drove it between outfielders all the way to the center-field stands for another triple. Speaker was first-pitch hitting, too, and he hit a routine grounder—but the ball went straight through Giants second baseman Larry Doyle and drove Yerkes in with the second run. Speaker was thrown out trying to reach second on Doyle's error. Mathewson then shut Boston down, retiring the next 17 batters he faced. Not a single Red Sox batter reached first base for the rest of the game. But two Sox had already crossed the plate, and there was no undoing the damage.

The Giants offense tried to make their own mark against Bedient, but New York mustered only a single by Mathewson in the third and another by Chief Meyers in the fifth. In the seventh they nicked him finally. Fred Merkle kicked off New York's half of the inning with a double that just missed being a home run. He had to hold, though, as the next batter, Herzog, hit a towering fly ball, snagged by Heinie Wagner on the mound. Chief Meyers hit a very long drive to center, but Speaker reeled it in and almost threw out Merkle going to third. Pinch hitter Moose McCormick grounded to Larry Gardner at third, but Gardner let it go right through him, and Merkle scored easily. But he would be the only Giant to cross the plate. Bedient set down the final seven batters and had a three-hit win to his credit. The Red Sox had only five hits in all, but won the game, 2–1.

The Red Sox were up three games to one, and Hugh Fullerton noted the reaction of the Boston boosters. "Such a scene as that which followed the Red Sox victory today had never been seen in Boston. Men and women rushed on to the field and fell in line behind two brass bands and paraded around and around singing, shouting and roaring over the victory of the home team. They howled and yelled at Bedient; they rushed to the Boston bench and tried to get him so they could carry him on their shoulders, but he was hurried away to the clubhouse" (*New York Times*, October 13, 1912). Fullerton reckoned that "This man Columbus missed a lot by visiting the country as early as he did, because he did not see this world's series, with the two evenly matched teams clawing and scrapping at each other for dear life."

The Sporting News termed the game "the beginning of the end of the Series," though as events transpired, there were three games left to play.

◆ Extra Innings

- "The hold of baseball on the public mind is not to be condemned as unwholesome" (*New York Times* editorial, October 9, 1912).

- After the game, Walter Johnson gave Mathewson some advice, in an article he wrote for the *Boston Herald*: "Every time that Harry Hooper has faced Mathewson, he has hit the famous pitcher hard and safe, and yesterday was no exception. 'Hoop' came through with a single and a triple, both of which were solid drives. Mathewson has always made the mistake of pitching Hooper high balls on the outside, for Hooper's weakness is a low ball and high ones on the inside."

October 16, 1912: New York at Boston

To Err Is Human

In which Fred Snodgrass etches his name in baseball parlance

Before Game Six, with a 3–1 lead in the 1912 World Series (and one tie game), the Boston papers had been supremely confident in an ultimate Red Sox triumph. That morning, the *Boston Journal* titled their story, "Red Sox to Clinch World Championship in the Battle Today." The *Herald* headlined, "Red Sox on Edge to Make Series a Rout." It wasn't just the hometown scribes who felt that way. Hugh Fullerton of the *New York Times* expected Game Six to be the finale as well. After Game Five, Christy Mathewson said he threw his arm out and was done for the duration, and Rube Marquard said his arm was sore.

Marquard took the mound, however, and went the distance, scattering seven hits and holding the Sox to two runs. The Giants scored five times in the bottom of the first inning off Buck O'Brien, and for all intents and purposes the game was over at that point. Ray Collins took over for O'Brien in the second and didn't allow a run, but the final score stood 5–2. Observers quietly suggested that Red Sox management and Buck O'Brien had conspired to let the Giants win Game Six. The *New York Times* reported that Joe Wood and O'Brien had gotten into a fight aboard the train from New York back to Boston, perhaps due to words Wood had uttered regarding O'Brien's dismal performance. The *Times* suggested that the fight had hurt Wood's effectiveness on the mound in Game Seven. O'Brien's poor performance hatched a number of conspiracy theories.

Boston tried to wrap up the championship the following day, but New York battered Joe Wood for six runs in the first inning; the final score was 11–4. Given Smoky Joe's regular-season ERA of 1.91, that one inning alone produced as many runs as any three complete games. Stahl took him out early so he might have some gas left if needed in a final, deciding game. Perhaps Wood had been affected by the incident on the train or perhaps by the odd events that transpired just before the game.

Wood had warmed up, but the starting time was set back about 15 minutes when a near-riot broke out as the Royal Rooters found that the seats they'd expected to occupy had been sold by the ball club. They were placed behind a barrier in left field, but began to climb the fence to charge the grandstand. Herded in by mounted police, they pressed against the fence, which was knocked flat. These were true fans, however, and when at last order was restored, the Royal Rooters helped to hold the fence in place throughout the game. In a guest column for the *Boston Herald*, Walter Johnson wrote that Wood being stuck on the mound throughout all this was chilled and stiffened by the cold wind of the day. Third baseman Larry Gardner simply said, "It is doubtful if any club that ever figured in a World's Series gave such a wretched exhibition as we did" *(Boston Herald)*.

The mayor of Boston denounced the Boston ball club's secretary Robert McRoy for his failure to look after the Royal Rooters.

Thirteen pitches later, and Wood was gone. By the seventh-inning stretch the score reached 10–1 and many Boston fans headed home. One of the newspapers noted that the Royal Rooters had not sung "Tessie" and declared that many fans attributed the loss to this failure *(Boston Herald)*. Other papers berated Boston's "stupid baserunning."

Somehow Boston had gone from a commanding 3–1 lead in the Series to a 3–3 tie and now faced a do-or-die Game Eight. Momentum seemed to be on the side of the Giants. The Sox stopper, Smoky Joe Wood, had been the one who was routed. John McGraw told the *Journal*, "The Red Sox have broken and are on the run. With the same aggressive attack tomorrow the Giants will be carried to victory." Jake Stahl disagreed. "All clubs have form reversals, but the rebound is always violent. Tomorrow will tell another story for the Red Sox," he said. The stage was set for Game Eight, in Boston. The game would reprise Game Five, pitting Bedient against Mathewson.

Boston fans were discouraged by the back-to-back defeats, and maybe more than a little fatigued. Angry because the ball club had not supported them the day before, the Royal Rooters boycotted the game, though individuals among them were probably present. Attendance was down dramatically, the park only about half-full, with 17,000 fans.

Christy Mathewson, despite having felt his arm was "done" after Game Five, took the mound for the Giants in Game Eight. Matty hadn't walked a batter yet in the Series, but he was indeed tired and issued five free passes in Game Eight. Bedient had walked four and passed a fifth harmlessly in the first inning, but it was his walk of the leadoff man in the third that allowed the Giants to draw first blood. After Josh Devore reached on four pitches, Bedient induced

Larry Doyle to ground to Larry Gardner at third base, who bobbled the ball long enough that he had to throw to first rather than get the lead runner. With Devore on second, Fred Snodgrass grounded to first, and Devore moved up yet another base, taking third. Murray drove a ball deep to left-center field; Speaker ran hard but could only get his fingertips on it. The ball fell just beyond his reach; he retrieved it quickly and held Murray to a double, but Devore had scored. The Giants had a run, and one run loomed large. Bedient got hit hard a couple of times in the fifth, with the first batter banging one off his shin, and the second batter hitting a ball so deep to right that Hooper had to run full tilt with his back to the ball, then leap high to haul it back in—with his bare hand. Hooper held on to the rail to keep himself from falling over the fence with the ball. The *Boston Journal* front-page story declared, "Old-time players, men whose names are legion for great work, all declare that this catch was the greatest thing of its kind they ever saw." The sparkling play got Bedient out of hot water, and the Sox looked to even the score.

But Mathewson, with his impeccable control and tricky "fadeaway" (screwball) pitch, was not so easy to dent. In the fourth, with one out, Gardner doubled past Snodgrass in center. Gardner got a little greedy, though, and a perfect relay by Doyle cut him down trying to stretch the two-bagger into a triple. The veteran right hander needed only three pitches to set down the Sox in the fifth, and a brewing threat was snuffed in the sixth when Yerkes was caught off third. So when the Red Sox came to bat in the bottom of the seventh, the score remained 1–0.

Gardner's luck was no better on this at-bat, as he led off the seventh with a soft, easy fly to Snodgrass in center. Jake Stahl hit a Texas Leaguer that dropped safely in left-center, falling among three hesitating Giants: Art Fletcher, Red Murray, and Snodgrass. Mathewson walked Wagner, then got the catcher, Hick Cady, to pop up to the shortstop. Stahl called on Olaf Henriksen to pinch-hit for Bedient, who was 0-for-6 at the plate. Born in Denmark, Henriksen was known as "Swede" by geographically challenged American ballplayers. Henriksen doubled hard, the ball hitting the third-base bag and traveling right down the third-base line. Stahl scored from second. With men on second and third, Harry Hooper drove a ball deep, but it was caught for the third out. The score was tied 1–1.

Stahl had saved Smoky Joe for just such an emergency, so Wood was brought in to pitch for the Red Sox. He retired the Giants in the eighth and ninth. Mathewson kept Boston at bay, and the 1912 World Series had proved to be so hard fought that it took not only eight games to bring it to a conclusion but extra innings on top of that.

OCTOBER 16, 1912: NEW YORK AT BOSTON

New York Giants	AB	R	H	RBI	BB	SO	PO	A	Boston Red Sox	AB	R	H	RBI	BB	SO	PO	A
Devore rf	3	1	1	0	2	0	3	1	Hooper rf	5	0	0	0	0	0	4	0
Doyle 2b	5	0	0	0	0	0	1	5	Yerkes 2b	4	1	1	0	1	1	0	3
Snodgrass cf	4	0	1	0	1	0	4	1	Speaker cf	4	0	2	1	1	1	2	0
Murray lf	5	1	2	1	0	0	3	0	Lewis lf	4	0	0	0	1	1	0	0
Merkle 1b	5	0	1	1	0	1	10	0	Gardner 3b	3	0	1	1	1	0	1	4
Herzog 3b	5	0	2	0	0	1	2	1	Stahl 1b	4	1	2	0	0	1	15	0
Meyers c	3	0	0	0	1	0	4	1	Wagner ss	3	0	1	0	1	0	3	5
Fletcher ss	3	0	1	0	0	1	2	3	Cady c	4	0	0	0	0	0	5	3
McCormick ph	1	0	0	0	0	0	0	0	Bedient p	2	0	0	0	0	0	0	1
Shafer ss	0	0	0	0	0	0	0	0	Henriksen ph	1	0	1	1	0	0	0	0
Mathewson p	4	0	1	0	0	1	0	3	Wood p	0	0	0	0	0	0	0	2
Totals	38	2	9	2	4	4	29	15	Engle ph	1	1	0	0	0	0	0	0
									Totals	35	3	8	3	5	4	30	18

New York Giants	IP	H	R	ER	BB	SO	HR	Boston Red Sox	IP	H	R	ER	BB	SO	HR
Mathewson (L)	9.2	8	3	1	5	4	0	Bedient	7	6	1	1	3	2	0
								Wood (W)	3	3	1	1	1	2	0
								Totals	10	9	2	2	4	4	0

	1	2	3	4	5	6	7	8	9	10	R	H	E
NY N	0	0	1	0	0	0	0	0	0	1	2	9	2
BOS A	0	0	0	0	0	0	1	0	0	2	3	8	4

Wood secured the first out in the 10th, but then Murray hit a ball "over the head of Speaker into the left field stands. It is a home run hit, but ground rules limit it to two bases" *(New York Times)*. The temporary stands built in left and in foul territory along the third-base line to accommodate the World Series crowd required an alteration of the ground rules. Among the oddities that these makeshift bleachers created was a gap behind the stands that was considered still in play—a ball hit into that area would not be considered a home run if the umpire could still see it. Harry Hooper had hit a ball into the gap earlier in the Series and got a triple out of it, at which point John McGraw insisted the umpires make a ground rule limiting these hits to doubles. Before Game Two, umpire Silk O'Loughlin also ruled that one of the sets of stands "encroached so far [onto the field of play] that hits into the stand were limited to two bases" *(New York Times)*. So Murray stood on second; he would soon score, regardless. When Merkle singled to center, Speaker charged the ball to grab it and make one of his patented throws to the plate, but he was too aggressive and overran the ball. Murray scored easily, and Merkle took second. With four pitches, Wood bore down and struck out Buck Herzog, then got Chief Meyers to line right back to him on the mound. Wood knocked it down with his pitching hand, but threw Meyers out at first base. The damage was done, though. New York had taken a 2–1 lead in the top of the 10th.

Mathewson came out to finish off the Red Sox and seal the championship. Wood was due up first, and though an excellent hitter with a career .283 mark, his hand had swollen badly from Meyers's liner. Stahl sent in Hack Engle to hit for the pitcher. Engle had hit .234 in 1912. The hometown crowd was not happy, but his routine high fly ball to right-center was caught two-handed by Fred Snodgrass in center—and then, quite simply, dropped. Engle reached second base on Snodgrass's muff and his wide throw to second. "Engle was sitting on second base before I could get [the ball] back to the infield," Snodgrass told interviewer Larry Ritter in *The Glory of Their Times*. Hooper failed at a couple of sacrifice attempts, then followed with a hard-hit liner to center, which Snodgrass snagged out of the air. Engle tagged and took third. Yerkes walked on four pitches, none of them close; was Mathewson thinking about the error? The newspapers had largely blamed his Game Five loss on the Giants' poor defense. Matty looked at the batter. First and third, one out, with Boston's best hitter—Tris Speaker—at the plate. Speaker lifted a high foul ball to first base. Merkle could have caught it easily. So could the catcher, Meyers, and so could Mathewson. Three more hesitating Giants watched as once again a ball dropped among them. Walter Johnson later wrote that Merkle had "choked." Fullerton said, "I could have jumped out of the press box and caught it behind my back—but Merkle quit. Yes, Merkle quit cold." Given new life, Speaker shot a single to right field to tie the game, as Engle scored. Yerkes took third base, and Speaker took second on Devore's throw to the plate. Mathewson was visibly agitated both on the Snodgrass muff and the untouched foul fly by first base. He walked Duffy Lewis intentionally. Larry Gardner, up with the bases loaded and the outfield playing in to keep a single from tying the game, gauged Mathewson's 27th pitch of the long inning and drove a ball over Devore's head in right. Devore ran back hard and caught it, but before his "despairing heave" reached Meyers, Yerkes had scored on the sacrifice fly. The Red Sox had won the game and the World Series, 3–2.

The victory set off no immediate citywide celebrations. Expected to win in a walk, the Red Sox had just barely held on to win. Mismanagement of the relationship with their most loyal fans, combined with suspicions that Game Six might have been rigged to prolong the competition, really robbed Boston fandom of some of their customary passion. There were no intimations that any game other than Game Six might have been compromised, but it was nevertheless a dispirited ending for an otherwise great World Series. All was forgiven, though, and the following day the Royal Rooters led a victory parade of thousands down Tremont Street and to Boston's Faneuil Hall.

◀Extra Innings

- Christy Mathewson lost two games in the Series, despite an ERA of 1.26, and pitched a tie, as well. Both losses came on unearned runs, due to the Giants' unreliable defense. He might have won Game Two, the tie game, but another unearned run deprived him of that honor, too. The Boston fans applauded his work. Walter Johnson noted, "Never has a losing pitcher received such an ovation as was given Matty as he slowly forced his way through about a thousand fans."

• Joe Wood's bad inning hurt him badly; he won three games but finished the Series with a 3.68 ERA. Boston's best pitcher was young Bedient, with a 0.50 ERA over 18 innings of work. The entire Giants staff held the Red Sox to 1.59 earned runs per game, well below the 2.67 ERA the Sox staff posted. The Giants also topped the Red Sox in team batting average, .270 to .220. The unearned runs and their defensive lapses did them in.

• Hugh Bedient stayed with the Red Sox through 1914 and then left the major leagues, though he continued to play in pro and semipro leagues through 1925.

• Feel sorry for Snodgrass?

Ever since October 1912, "Snodgrass's muff" has been a catchphrase for a World Series blunder. Snodgrass appeared in the World Series for three straight years with the Giants (they lost all three Series) and was a decent ballplayer, but by no means a linchpin of the team. One sympathizes with a ballplayer at whose feet can be laid the responsibility for defeat in a World Series game, though inevitably there are many contributing factors. (Tell that to Bill Buckner, though!)

Christy Mathewson was generous to his teammate after the game. "I don't blame Snodgrass for the loss of the game," he said, "although his error was a heart-breaker. Such a muff was likely to happen in any game. It is only unfortunate that it occurred when it did." An anonymous columnist in *The Sporting News* was not so forgiving. Apparently Mr. Snodgrass carried some baggage in this writer's eye. "That a chain is no stronger than its weakest link was demonstrated to Manager McGraw of the Giants, when Snodgrass, center fielder for the New York team, dropped a fly ball in the final game of the World's Series at Boston, and allowed the Boston Red Sox to defeat Christy Mathewson after one of the finest exhibitions of pitching ever given by a pitcher. . . . To Snodgrass alone must the blame be given, and he is entitled to every bit of condemnation that may be heaped on his youthful shoulders. When a player tries to spike a man in one World's Series, as has been charged this player for his attempt to disable Frank Baker last year, and when that same player deliberately throws a ball with all his power at a boy over-eager to capture a souvenir baseball which he would prize many times more than Rockefeller his money, there is no excuse for any misplay he may make, or sympathy he may desire. Snodgrass deserves everything that he may receive from press, public, and members of the New York base ball team."

A subhead in a neighboring column reads, "Error by Snodgrass Beats Masterly Pitching of Mathewson."

October 9, 1915: Boston at Philadelphia

Foster Home

In which a pitcher allows three hits and tallies three of his own

The Red Sox dropped off dramatically in 1913, sinking to fourth place as the Philadelphia Athletics resumed their winning ways. In 1914 the Sox climbed back to second place but still trailed the Athletics by 8½ games. That was the last year of Connie Mack's dynasty—the A's had won four of five pennants. Boston and Philadelphia met in the 1914 World Series, at Fenway Park, but it was the Philadelphia A's versus the Boston Braves. It is ironic that the only world championship the Boston Braves ever won was won at Fenway. Braves Field had not yet been built, and the "Miracle Braves" were offered the use of the Red Sox home field instead of their usual, smaller home, the South End Grounds. In 1915, the Red Sox reasserted themselves while Philadelphia plunged from first to last—the most precipitous drop in the history of baseball, brought about because Connie Mack dismantled his team. They finished the season 58½ games behind the resurgent Sox.

With the A's down and out, the 1915 race was between Boston and the Detroit Tigers. The Red Sox fielded virtually the same team they had in 1914, but got better results. The pitching staff had five 15-game winners in Rube Foster, Ernie Shore, Babe Ruth, Dutch Leonard, and Joe Wood. Shore's 19–8, 1.64 ERA made him an ace among aces. In the field, no one was going to crack the outfield of Duffy Lewis, Tris Speaker, and Harry Hooper. All had exceptional speed and cannons for arms, and among the three of them, they amassed 59 assists. Speaker led the offense with a .322 average, but the strength of the team lay in its pitching and defense. Red Sox batters, collectively, hit 14 homers. Three position players (Speaker, Lewis, and Dick Hoblitzell) had two apiece, and the young pitcher, Ruth, led the club with four home runs.

The Sox took first place during a 13–7 road trip in July and never let go. Though they faltered a bit around Labor Day, the Sox went on a 14–2 tear. There were some heated confrontations with Ty Cobb and the Tigers in mid-September. Detroit crept within one game, but the Red Sox knocked them back for the final time by taking three of a four-game series.

Though the loss of four key players—Home Run Baker, Chief Bender, Jimmy Collins, and Eddie Plank—did in Philadelphia's American League team, the City of Brotherly Love was still represented in the World Series: the Phillies took the National League flag by seven games over Boston's National League entry.

Home field for Boston in the 1915 World Series was Braves Field. Reciprocating the loan of Fenway in 1914, the Braves invited the Red Sox to use their new park, which accommodated some 15,000 more ticket buyers.

Grover Cleveland Alexander was Philadelphia's ace, 31–10, with a 1.22 ERA, 36 complete games, and 12 shutouts. Erskine Mayer had 21 wins, with a 2.36 ERA. The Phillies had a couple of power hitters—Gavvy Cravath had set the modern single-season home run record with 24, and Beals Becker hit 11. The Phillies' 58 homers dwarfed the 14 hit by the Red Sox. The Red Sox manufactured runs, though, and scored 669 to Philadelphia's 589, which still made Philly an offensive powerhouse in their league. No National League team scored more than 600 runs that season, and the Phillies led the league in runs scored per game.

The first game of the Series was played at a very soggy Baker Bowl in Philadelphia. The park was not sold out, but back in Boston thousands of

OCTOBER 9, 1915: BOSTON AT PHILADELPHIA

Boston Red Sox	AB	R	H	RBI	BB	SO	PO	A	Philadelphia Phillies	AB	R	H	RBI	BB	SO	PO	A
Hooper rf	3	1	1	0	2	2	2	0	Stock 3b	4	0	0	0	0	0	0	2
Scott ss	3	0	0	0	0	1	0	3	Bancroft ss	4	0	1	0	0	2	2	2
Henriksen ph	1	0	0	0	0	0	0	0	Paskert cf	4	0	0	0	0	0	1	0
Cady c	0	0	0	0	0	0	3	0	Cravath rf	3	1	1	0	0	2	1	0
Speaker cf	4	0	1	0	0	0	3	0	Luderus 1b	3	0	1	1	0	1	9	1
Hoblitzell 1b	4	0	1	0	0	0	8	3	Whitted lf	3	0	0	0	0	0	3	0
Lewis lf	4	0	1	0	0	2	1	0	Niehoff 2b	3	0	0	0	0	1	4	1
Gardner 3b	4	1	2	0	0	0	0	2	Burns c	3	0	0	0	0	1	6	3
Barry 2b	4	0	1	0	0	1	0	3	Mayer p	3	0	0	0	0	1	1	3
Thomas c	3	0	0	0	0	0	6	0	**Totals**	**30**	**1**	**3**	**1**	**0**	**8**	**27**	**12**
Janvrin ss	1	0	0	0	0	0	1	0									
Foster p	4	0	3	1	0	1	3	0									
Totals	**35**	**2**	**10**	**1**	**2**	**7**	**27**	**11**									

Boston Red Sox	IP	H	R	ER	BB	SO	HR	Philadelphia Phillies	IP	H	R	ER	BB	SO	HR
Foster (W)	9	3	1	1	0	8	0	Mayer (L)	9	10	2	1	2	7	0

	1	2	3	4	5	6	7	8	9	R	H	E
BOS A	1	0	0	0	0	0	0	0	1	2	10	0
PHI N	0	0	0	0	1	0	0	0	0	1	3	1

people followed the progress of the game on a large, electrically operated board set up outside the offices of the *Boston Journal*. Five thousand more seats were available inside the Boston Arena, where patrons could watch the "Coleman Life-Like Baseball Players" act out each play moments after it occurred.

Both managers—first-year skipper Pat Moran for the Phillies and Bill Carrigan for the Sox—led with their best pitchers: Alexander versus Shore. There wasn't a single extra-base hit by either side. Alexander gave up eight singles but distributed them well—no more than one in any given inning. Shore yielded only five hits, and only one of the five went out of the infield—a short Texas Leaguer just over Dick "Hobby" Hoblitzell at first base that he probably could have handled had the ground not been so saturated. Shore also walked four batters. He may have pitched a better game, but luck was on the side of the Philadelphians. Four of the five hits figured in the scoring. The Phillies scored one run in the bottom of the fourth on a two-out grounder to Jack Barry at second base that George "Possum" Whitted just barely beat out, while Dode Paskert scored from third. The Sox tied it up in the top of the eighth on a walk, a ground out, and a Duffy Lewis single, but Moran's crew bunched two singles and two walks and broke the tie in the bottom of the eighth. Shore might have gotten out of the inning, but when Barry barehanded a grounder, he found that Everett Scott was late to cover second. The Phillies now had two runs, both of them on grounders sensationally fielded by Jack Barry, but in vain. "Scott's Bonehead Play" read the headline in the *Journal*. Sox players, according to the *Post*, agreed that Scott was surprised that Barry had even gotten to the ball; Scott was moving to cover third base. The next hitter, Fred Luderus, hit one right back to Shore, but it struck a pebble and bounced a foot or two away, just far enough to allow another run to score. The game ended with a 3–1 win for the hometown Phillies.

Game Two featured Mayer against Boston's Rube Foster (19–8, 2.11 ERA). Among those present was the first president of the United States to attend a World Series game, Woodrow Wilson, and what a great game he witnessed. He didn't have to wait long to see some action, as Harry Hooper walked to lead off the game. Everett Scott tried to sacrifice, but popped up to the first baseman instead. Catcher Ed Burns called for a couple of pitchouts, but Hooper wasn't fooled. As soon as Mayer put one over, Speaker rapped a single to right and Hooper raced around to third base. Dick Hoblitzell took one strike. Speaker took off on Mayer's next throw—another pitchout—and was thrown out at second base, Ed Burns to Bert Niehoff at second, but it was either a delayed double steal or a play Hooper lucked out on. He broke for home and—even though Niehoff made a strong return throw to Burns—Hooper slid by untouched, but missed the plate. Burns bobbled the throw and Hooper quickly crawled back just before the catcher could put down the tag; 1–0, Boston. Mayer settled down and kept it to that—though his counterpart, Foster, touched him for a double in the fifth.

Foster didn't let a single Quaker reach base through the first four, but let down his guard just a bit in the fifth and it cost him. With no one out, back-to-back doubles by Cravath to left field and by Luderus to right-center tied the score at 1–1. Foster nearly shut the Phillies down from that point forward; the only other hit of the game was a sixth-inning single by Dave "Beauty" Bancroft.

The Red Sox loaded the bases in the seventh but couldn't score. The score stood 1–1 after eight innings. Larry Gardner led off the ninth with a solid single to left field. Barry flied out. Hal Janvrin laid down a nice bunt, which Mayer fielded and threw to first. The umpire called it an out; the Boston papers didn't agree. Two down, but Gardner was now on second. Rube Foster was up. The 5'7" pitcher already had a double and a single. "What do you think he said to me as he came in from the box at the beginning of the ninth inning?" Carrigan asked rhetorically in the *Boston Post*. "As I went to slap him on the shoulder, he yelled, 'Let's go for them now, Bill. Just get a man on the bases, and I'll win your old ball game for you.' And I guess he did, didn't he?"

Carrigan's faith was rewarded as Foster singled sharply to center. With two out, Gardner was off on contact and raced for home. Paskert fielded the ball well and launched a "mighty heave to the plate," but it was wide and Gardner scored.

Foster had as many hits (three) as he doled out to the opposition, and now he had driven in the go-ahead run for the Red Sox. Foster took second on the throw-in, but Mayer got Hooper to strike out, and Foster strolled over to take the mound. A fly ball to Duffy Lewis, a strikeout of Bancroft, and Foster faced Dode Paskert with two out and the game on the line. Grover Alexander noted in a bylined story for the *Philadelphia Public Ledger* that Paskert had "slammed three on the nose, and twice he caused the Sox outfielders to make good catches to prevent home runs." One of those was the final drive of the day, as he hit a long fly ball to Speaker in center. Speaker ran hard, all the way back to the center-field seats, and snared the ball just before it fell among the spectators. He then "put the ball in his hip pocket as he raced to the clubhouse." Foster got a big send-off by the several hundred Royal Rooters who'd made the trip to Philly, and President Wilson "smiled his appreciation at the Boston man's work." The Red Sox had tied the series at one game apiece.

Extra Innings

- George "Rube" Foster pitched for the Red Sox from 1913 to 1917, the entirety of his short major league career. He credited Smoky Joe Wood with teaching him how to throw the fastball that served him so well in the 1915 World Series and in tossing a no-hitter against the Yankees on June 21, 1916, at Fenway Park. It was the first no-hitter at Fenway.

- Rube Foster of the Red Sox is not to be confused with contemporary Andrew "Rube" Foster, known as the "Father of Negro League Baseball." Andrew Foster was 6'2" and 200 pounds, while the Sox' Foster was listed at a mere 5'7" and 170 pounds.

October 13, 1915: Boston at Philadelphia

Cinched Tight

In which Harry Hooper is the hitting hero

The 1915 World Series was the lowest-scoring Series to date. The Red Sox 2–1 victory in Game Two was followed by a 2–1 victory in Game Three and a 2–1 victory in Game Four. Without benefit of a shutout, the Red Sox held a 3–1 edge despite scoring a total of only seven runs in four games.

A total of 42,300 fans jammed the new Braves Field (lent to the Sox for the occasion) for Game Three—the largest crowd in baseball history up to that point. They were eager to see their hometown Red Sox play their third World Series in the franchise's 15-year history.

With Grover Cleveland Alexander on the mound again, the Phillies felt good about their chances, and the veteran pitcher breezed through the first three innings without a hitch, a single by Duffy Lewis down the line in left and a walk to Carrigan accounting for the only two base runners Boston had. Meanwhile, though Boston's Dutch Leonard kept the Phillies quiet for two innings with his spitball and an aggressive fastball, they nicked him for a run in the third. Speaker tripled and scored in the fourth for Boston. Not another run crossed the plate through eight innings, and the two teams entered the ninth tied 1–1. Leonard had pitched perfect ball from the fourth through the ninth inning, not letting a single Phillie reach base. Boston would take the win in Game Three when Harry Hooper singled off Alexander, then moved over

Harry Hooper

on a sacrifice and a ground out. Perched on third, he scampered home with the winning run when, swinging at the first pitch, Duffy Lewis hit the ball so hard it was described as "a report like that of a Winchester rifle."

In Game Four, Lewis was once again the hero. Ernie Shore was pitching again for Boston, and George Chalmers toed the rubber for Philadelphia. Milt Stock, leading off for the Phillies, singled down the left-field line, but Lewis hustled over and fired to second base, getting an assist and wiping out an early scoring opportunity. Lewis was there in the third, too, ranging far back to the fence to haul in Cravath's drive to end the inning. Boston scratched a run in the bottom half of the third.

In the sixth, Dick Hoblitzell singled and Lewis hit a double that rolled to the wall in left, driving in the second run for the Red Sox. Gavvy Cravath tripled in the top of the eighth with a ball that hit hard in front of Speaker and bounced all the way over his head. Fred Luderus singled him home, but that was the only run for Philadelphia. They were now down three games to one as the Series went back to Baker Bowl.

A loss in Game Five would wipe out the Phillies. George "Rube" Foster started again for the Red Sox, but Philadelphia struck early. With the second pitch he threw, Foster hit Stock. Rather than lay down the predictable bunt, Dave Bancroft singled to center. Dode Paskert bunted and seemed to have been routinely thrown out at first, but the umpire called him safe. Bases loaded, nobody out. Babe Ruth and Carl Mays both started loosening on the side. The power hitter Cravath was up—the hitter who'd set a new single-season mark with 24 home runs in 1915. He swung hard, but hit just a "puny grounder" to Foster, who cut down Stock at the plate. Pinch Thomas then fired to Hobby at first and the Sox had themselves a nice double play. Luderus banged out a two-bagger, though, and the Phillies had a 2–0 lead.

Boston got one run back in the second when Larry Gardner hit a two-out triple off Erskine Mayer. His slide into third tore his pants, requiring immediate repairs. Jack Barry singled over third base, and the Sox were on the board. They tied it up when Harry Hooper, hitting first, hit a ground-rule homer on a ball that bounced into the center-field bleachers. (We'd call it a ground-rule double today, but the two teams had agreed, as was common then, that a ball bouncing out of the park would count as a home run.) After two more deep drives, one caught and the other a long single, Eppa Rixey relieved Mayer with the score tied at 2–2.

In the fourth inning Luderus joined the home-run parade with a solo shot over the scoreboard, and Philadelphia retook the lead. After Possum Whitted

OCTOBER 13, 1915: BOSTON AT PHILADELPHIA

Boston Red Sox	AB	R	H	RBI	BB	SO	PO	A	Philadelphia Phillies	AB	R	H	RBI	BB	SO	PO	A
Hooper rf	4	2	3	2	0	0	2	0	Stock 3b	3	0	0	0	0	0	0	1
Scott ss	5	0	0	0	0	0	2	2	Bancroft ss	4	1	2	0	0	0	3	6
Speaker cf	5	0	1	0	0	1	3	0	Paskert cf	4	1	2	0	0	0	3	0
Hoblitzell 1b	1	0	0	0	0	0	1	0	Cravath rf	3	0	0	0	1	2	1	0
Gainer ph,1b	3	1	1	0	0	0	9	0	Dugey pr	0	0	0	0	0	0	0	0
Lewis lf	4	1	1	2	0	0	0	0	Becker rf	0	0	0	0	0	0	0	0
Gardner 3b	3	1	1	0	1	0	2	3	Luderus 1b	2	1	2	3	1	0	12	2
Barry 2b	4	0	1	1	0	0	1	0	Whitted lf	4	0	0	0	0	0	2	0
Thomas c	2	0	1	0	0	0	4	3	Niehoff 2b	4	1	1	0	0	2	2	2
Cady ph,c	1	0	0	0	1	0	2	1	Burns c	4	0	1	0	0	0	3	1
Foster p	4	0	1	0	0	1	1	3	Mayer p	1	0	0	0	0	1	1	0
Totals	36	5	10	5	2	2	27	12	Rixey p	2	0	1	0	0	0	0	1
									Killefer ph	1	0	0	0	0	0	0	0
									Totals	32	4	9	3	2	5	27	13

Boston Red Sox	IP	H	R	ER	BB	SO	HR	Philadelphia Phillies	IP	H	R	ER	BB	SO	HR
Foster (W)	9	9	4	3	2	5	1	Mayer	2.1	6	2	2	0	0	1
								Rixey (L)	6.2	4	3	3	2	2	2
								Totals	9	10	5	5	2	2	3

	1	2	3	4	5	6	7	8	9		R	H	E
BOS A	0	1	1	0	0	0	0	2	1		5	10	1
PHI N	2	0	0	2	0	0	0	0	0		4	9	1

popped out to third baseman Gardner, Bert Niehoff singled and then Ed Burns singled to right. Hooper's throw from shallow right bounced and got by third baseman Gardner, hitting the barrier. Gardner recovered the ball and threw to Pinch Thomas at the plate, but Thomas couldn't make the play: Niehoff scored. The score was now 4–2 in the Phillies' favor, their two-run lead restored.

All this scoring must have fatigued the two teams. Neither team scored in the fifth, sixth, or seventh innings. In the top of the eighth, though, the Red Sox made a move. Del Gainer had taken over for Hoblitzell at first base and singled off Rixey. Up came that man again, Duffy Lewis. He hit a home run into the center-field stands. The score was retied, 4–4. The next three Boston batters were retired. Then with two out in the home half of the inning, Foster walked Cravath and then hit Luderus, but Philly's mini-rally was stifled when Whitted bounced the ball right back to the mound. Foster threw to first for the final out, escaping trouble again.

In the top of the ninth inning, despite the nine hits and four runs Foster had surrendered, Carrigan let the young pitcher hit for himself. He was, after all, 4-for-7 in the Series. As it happens, Foster fanned on a "horse-shoe curve." Harry Hooper was up. He already had two hits, a home run and a single, but Rixey got two quick strikes on him, also on curves. Then the unfortunate pitcher sent one in straight over the plate. Hooper did not miss it, and hit another ground-rule homer, this time to straightaway center. No one had hit a home run in the first four games. In all of 1915, in his 566 at-bats in 149 games, Hooper had hit two home runs. In Game Five there were four homers, and two of them were Harry Hooper's, both high hoppers that bounced into the stands, a lucky fact of the ground rules. The Sox now had a one-run lead, and if they could hold the Phillies for one more inning, the championship would be theirs. Foster buckled down and struck out Niehoff. Burns hit a roller to Gainer at first, who stepped on the bag for the second out. Red Killefer pinch-hit for Rixey but grounded out, short to first. Game over. The Red Sox were once again champions of the world.

Extra Innings

- The 1915 World Series was won by the Red Sox with a total of 12 runs to their opponent's 10. The next time a Series was that close? In 1918, when the Sox scored only nine runs.

- Joe Wood never appeared in the Series. Babe Ruth pinch-hit once, but without a hit.

An estimated 12,000 to 16,000 thronged downtown Boston on October 16. A parade, yes, but it was a parade for women's suffrage. The "suffs" invited the victorious Red Sox to join them in the parade, but the Sox chose instead to head off for hunting and fishing at Squam Lake in New Hampshire. The party included Tris Speaker, Ernie Shore, Carl Mays, and other members of the team, and also sportswriters Paul Shannon of the *Boston Post* and Tim Murnane of the *Boston Globe.* Maybe these early Sox teams could have offered some advice to Ted Williams on how to get along better with the knights of the keyboard.

10

October 9, 1916: Brooklyn at Boston

Leftist Duel

In which a big southpaw must record 42 outs to earn a World Series win

Boston won the pennant again in 1916, by just two games over the White Sox and four over the Tigers. The World Series home games were again held at Braves Field, but this time the Red Sox faced the Brooklyn Robins (later, Dodgers). The Sox presented a similar but not identical team to the previous year. Bill Carrigan remained as manager, but Tris Speaker was traded away, and Smoky Joe Wood was injured. George Herman Ruth emerged as the ace on the pitching staff (23–12, 1.75 ERA), while both Dutch Leonard and Carl Mays won 18 games. All in all, the staff ERA was 2.48, slightly worse from the 2.39 of the previous year. Team batting was off marginally, too—the 1915 team average was .260 (.336 OBP), while in 1916 it dipped to .248 (.317 OBP), decent numbers in the era of the dead ball. Run production dropped from 669 to 548. Still, they had done what they needed to do: they won the pennant.

Babe Ruth

This was an overconfident team, and there was talk in the papers about the Sox sweeping Brooklyn.

OCTOBER 9, 1916: BROOKLYN AT BOSTON																
Brooklyn Robins	AB	R	H	RBI	BB	SO	PO	A	Boston Red Sox	AB	R	H	RBI	BB	SO	PO	A
Johnston rf	5	0	1	0	1	0	1	0	Hooper rf	6	0	1	0	0	0	2	1
Daubert 1b	5	0	0	0	1	1	18	0	Janvrin 2b	6	0	1	0	0	0	4	5
Myers cf	6	1	1	1	0	1	4	1	Walker cf	3	0	0	0	0	0	2	1
Wheat lf	5	0	0	0	0	0	2	0	Walsh ph,cf	3	0	0	0	0	0	1	0
Cutshaw 2b	5	0	0	0	0	1	5	5	Hoblitzell 1b	2	0	0	0	4	0	22	1
Mowrey 3b	5	0	1	0	0	0	3	5	McNally pr	0	1	0	0	0	0	0	0
Olson ss	2	0	1	0	1	1	2	4	Lewis lf	3	0	1	0	1	0	1	0
Miller c	5	0	0	0	0	0	4	1	Gardner 3b	5	0	0	0	0	0	2	8
Smith p	5	0	1	0	0	0	1	7	Gainer ph	1	0	1	1	0	0	0	0
Totals	43	1	6	1	3	4	40	23	Scott ss	4	1	2	0	1	0	1	8
									Thomas c	4	0	1	0	0	0	5	4
									Ruth p	5	0	0	1	2	2	2	4
									Totals	42	2	7	2	6	2	42	32

Brooklyn Robins	IP	H	R	ER	BB	SO	HR	Boston Red Sox	IP	H	R	ER	BB	SO	HR
Smith (L)	13.1	7	2	2	6	2	0	Ruth (W)	14	6	1	1	3	4	1

	1	2	3	4	5	6	7	8	9	10	11	12	13	14		R	H	E
BRO N	1	0	0	0	0	0	0	0	0	0	0	0	0	0		1	6	2
BOS A	0	0	1	0	0	0	0	0	0	0	0	0	0	1		2	7	1

Game One opened in Boston. Ernie Shore against Rube Marquard (who'd opposed the Sox in the 1912 Series for the Giants), now pitching for Brooklyn. The early innings were tight going and the score was 2–1 in the Sox' favor when Boston looked to put the game out of reach, scoring three runs in the bottom of the seventh and adding another in the eighth to establish a 6–1 lead. They would need every run, as the game almost slipped away. In the top of the ninth, Shore tired. Casey Stengel and Zack Wheat both scored on an error by infielder Hal Janvrin. After Brooklyn sent a third man across the plate, Carl Mays came in in relief and gave up an infield single that scored the fourth run of the frame. Brooklyn was one run away from tying the game, the bases were still loaded, and Jake Daubert was up for the second time in the inning. Mays got him: Daubert grounded to Scott at short and just barely preserved Boston's victory.

Game Two pitted Red Sox ace Ruth against Sherry Smith, a matchup of two southpaws. Ruth's 1.75 ERA had led the American League. Smith was 14–10, with a 2.34 ERA. Brooklyn batted first and didn't wait long to put a run on the board. After Ruth retired the first two Robins, center fielder Hi Myers drove a ball between Tilly Walker in center and Harry Hooper in right, sparking a Keystone Cops moment. Hooper dove, but the ball rolled all the way to the fence in center. Then Walker also fell trying to field the rebound off the wall. Myers legged all the way around the bases for an inside-the-park home run.

Brooklyn's moundsman Smith doubled to right field with one out in the top of the third and was waved toward third, but Hooper threw the ball to Walker, serving as a cutoff man; the center fielder fired a strike all the way to third and cut down Smith. The score remained 1–0 Brooklyn.

Boston tried to answer in their half of the inning. Everett "Deacon" Scott led off with a triple to the cement wall in right field. He had to hold on Pinch Thomas's grounder to George Cutshaw at second. Ruth grounded to Cutshaw, too, but this time the second baseman bobbled the ball. Though Ruth was thrown out on the play, Scott scored to even things at 1–1. After that, both teams put men into scoring position at times, but neither brought them home. In the fifth, Brooklyn's shortstop Ivy Olson was accused of tripping Pinch Thomas as he rounded second, and the umpire awarded Thomas third base on interference. But Thomas languished there when Ruth struck out.

In the eighth, Brooklyn again feinted. Harry "Mike" Mowrey singled, moved to second on a sacrifice, and moved up when Otto Miller singled, but Walker fired so fast to the plate that Mowrey had to stop at third, though Miller took second on the throw. With runners at second and third and just one out, the pitcher Smith grounded to short and Scott luckily caught Mowrey in a rundown between third and home, Ruth making the tag. Now it would take a hit. Jimmy Johnston hit a high bounder and Ruth leaped to grab it, threw to first, and snuffed the threat.

So it came to the bottom of the ninth. If Boston could push across just one run, they would win the game. Janvrin doubled to lead off for a promising start. Jimmy Walsh pinch-hit for Walker but managed only a comebacker. Smith fielded the ball, tossed to Mowrey to cut down the lead runner, but Mowrey dropped the ball and Janny was safe. With runners on first and third and no one out, the crowd was on the edge of their seats. A run seemed certain, as even a fly ball could score Janvrin. Dick Hoblitzell got that fly to center, but Myers' throw home erased Janvrin, two outs on one play. After an intentional walk to Duffy Lewis, Larry Gardner fouled out to send the game into extra innings, still tied 1–1.

The Red Sox escaped a couple of potential problems in the top of the 10th as a deflected grounder was converted into an out and a walk went for naught, and looked once again to push across that one crucial run. Scott singled to lead off and Thomas moved him up with a sacrifice. Ruth swung hard three times but missed three times for the second out. Hooper hit a ball down the third-base line; as it went off his glove, Mowrey knew Hooper had it beat but feigned a throw to first. The decoy worked, and Scott overran third. Olson scooted over from shortstop and took Mowrey's throw, nabbing Scott as he tried to get back to the bag. The scorer credited Hooper with a single, but the side was retired.

Neither team had particularly good chances in the 11th or 12th innings, and the sky was growing dark. If the game were called because of darkness, it would go into the scorebook as a tie. Neither team wanted to waste a great pitching performance, but they were running out of time.

So to the 13th. Brooklyn's first batter, Mowrey, reached base when Gardner's throw pulled Hoblitzell off the bag. The Robins sacrificed to move Mowrey to second, but Miller popped up to the catcher for out number two. Smith, still pitching for Brooklyn, almost dropped one into short left, but Lewis made a "phenomenal" *(Boston Globe)* catch and the Sox were out of the 13th. Tim Murnane of the *Boston Globe* felt sure that Lewis had saved a run. "Tearing along as if it was a case of life or death, he made one final reach while twisting his neck like a seagull and managed to reach and hold the ball." The game had been characterized throughout by exceptional fielding for both teams. Smith quickly retired all three of Boston's batters, and the game entered the 14th inning.

Babe Ruth had not given up a hit since the eighth inning. He set them down again 1-2-3 in the top of the 14th. The Sox came up in the bottom half and Smith walked Hoblitzell, the fourth time in a row that Hobby had worked a walk. Lewis sacrificed the walking man to second, first-pitch bunting. A hit now could win the game. Larry Gardner was due up, but he was 0-for-5 on the day and Carrigan decided to try something different. He put the speedy Mike McNally in to run for Hobby and sent up "Sheriff" Del Gainer (a .254 hitter in 1916) to pinch-hit for Gardner (.308 in the regular season, and 1-for-4 in Game One, and reached on an error). Despite his overall better numbers, Gardner had struggled against the left-hander Smith, and Gainer hit portsiders at a .295 clip. The switch paid off. Gainer singled, a low liner to left, and Wheat had to play it on one hop and hope the throw home could beat McNally. Not a chance. McNally burned around the bases and crossed the plate. The Red Sox had their one run and the game.

The 14-inning game stood for 89 years as the longest in World Series history until it was matched in 2005 by the Astros and White Sox. After Myers' freak inside-the-park home run back in the first inning, Babe Ruth had held the National League champions scoreless and earned the complete-game victory.

The Series would be over in five games. Game Three saw Brooklyn take one from the Red Sox 4–3, but the Red Sox handled the Robins by a 6–2 score in Game Four (Larry Gardner's three-run inside-the-park homer in the second inning being the decisive blow). They won the World Series, their fourth, the second in a row, and the third in five years, with a 4–1 triumph the next day, Ernie Shore allowing just three hits and picking up his second win.

A lengthy *Globe* editorial rhapsodized about how the Athens of America followed in the Greek tradition of the Olympics being justly proud of the manly prowess of its sons. Carrigan, who had caught Game Four, went 2-for-3, and managed the club, was dubbed "another Ivanhoe, less brutal and more civilized, less romantic than Scott's fictional hero, but more skillful." The confidence the Sox had carried into the Series had been justified.

Extra Innings

- The *Globe* reported a long line waiting for bleacher tickets as of midnight the evening before the Series. First in line was David Cohen of East Boston, who had literally raced against "Samuel Averett, 17, colored, of 64 Richdale Av., North Cambridge." They had come on the same streetcar at 2:00 p.m. the day before, to get in line 24 hours early. "Hardly had the motorman thrown open the door of the car before each was running at top speed down Gaffney St., but by virtue of a quicker start and longer legs, Cohen reached the ticket office goal first." Needless to say, both secured tickets. It's an old tradition that still adheres. In December 2004, the first fans in line to buy tickets for the 2005 Red Sox season camped out beginning on the Wednesday before the Saturday sale date.

- T. H. Murnane of the *Boston Globe*, a former ballplayer himself, excelled at the era's colorful style of sports writing. His wonderfully flamboyant lead paragraph before Game One read: "The same sun that looked down on the old Roman gladiators sent on the open arena to fight for their lives will pass down the western sky this afternoon while the ball players, young American athletes trained to the hour, strive to win the honors for their respective leagues."

- In a tragedy attendant on Game One, a Brooklyn resident who rooted for the Red Sox was killed in a barroom brawl. As reported in the *Boston Globe*: "An argument over the relative merit of the Brooklyn and Boston baseball teams resulted tonight in the death of William Sickles, 39 years old, a letter carrier. Sickles engaged in a dispute in a Brooklyn saloon with an unidentified man who was a rabid partisan of the home team. The debate continued until a blow on the jaw felled the letter carrier, whose skull was fractured when he struck the floor. He died 20 minutes later. His assailant escaped."

- Bill Carrigan, only 33 years old and lionized as a hero for bringing back-to-back championships to Boston, decided to retire from baseball after the 1916 season. He and his wife, who was pregnant, moved to the woods of Maine. He returned in 1927 to manage the Red Sox again, but with less stellar results, as he had little talent to work with and did not adjust well to the lively-ball era.

11

June 23, 1917: Washington at Boston

What a Relief!

In which the Carolina professor picks up the ball the Babe dropped

Two young pitchers arrived together in Boston in 1914, lefty Babe Ruth and righty Ernie Shore. Jack Dunn, owner of the minor league Baltimore Orioles, sold the hurlers (along with catcher Ben Egan) to the Sox for a reported $25,000 in cash. From that moment on, their careers would intertwine curiously.

Shore got off to a hot start in 1914, first holding Cleveland to two hits in his Fenway Park debut, losing the next one, and then reeling off three more wins in a row. The 24-year-old Ernie would earn the start in the opener of the World Series versus Philadelphia in 1915 and give up only one run through seven innings before being bested, 3–1, by Grover Cleveland Alexander. Ruth would make his only appearance in the Series pinch-hitting for Shore in the game (and grounding out). Slated to start on Opening Day 1916, Shore was scratched; Ruth replaced him and won 2–1 over the A's. Later in the year, Shore would relieve Ruth on a day when the southpaw went 2-for-2 at the plate, including his third homer in three games, but tired after 5⅓ innings.

But Shore's most memorable relief job of Ruth came on June 23, 1917. Fenway Park was sunlit that day, the riot of advertisements painted all over the left-field wall as bright and colorful as the crowd of 16,158 who turned out to see a doubleheader against Washington.

Ruth took the hill and faced the spark plug of the Senators' offense, 5'8", 155-pound Ray Morgan. Behind the plate was umpire Brick Owens, a man of formidable size and prowess described by J. V. Fitz Gerald in the *Washington Post* as a man who could "lick his weight in wild cats"—that is, hold his own in a fight. Owens called Ruth's first pitch a ball, and Ruth erupted vociferously. The next offering

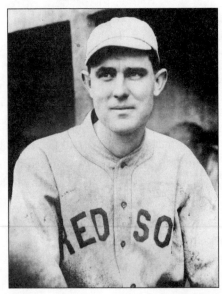

Ernie Shore

JUNE 23, 1917: WASHINGTON AT BOSTON

Washington Senators	AB	R	H	BB	PO	A	Boston Red Sox	AB	R	H	BB	PO	A
Morgan 2b	2	0	0	1	5	2	Hooper rf	4	0	1	0	0	0
Foster 3b	3	0	0	0	1	3	Barry 2b	4	0	0	0	2	1
Leonard 3b	0	0	0	0	0	1	Hoblitzell 1b	4	0	0	0	12	2
Milan cf	3	0	0	0	1	0	Gardner 3b	4	1	1	0	2	1
Rice rf	3	0	0	0	3	0	Lewis lf	4	0	3	0	2	0
Gharrity 1b	0	0	0	0	0	0	Walker cf	3	1	1	0	4	0
Judge 1b	3	0	0	0	10	1	Scott ss	3	0	0	0	1	5
Jamieson lf	3	0	0	0	0	0	Thomas c	0	0	0	0	0	0
Shanks ss	3	0	0	0	1	2	Agnew c	3	1	3	0	2	1
Henry c	3	0	0	0	1	0	Ruth p	0	0	0	0	0	0
Ayers p	2	0	0	0	2	8	Shore p	2	1	0	0	2	6
Menoskey ph	1	0	0	0	0	0	**Totals**	**31**	**4**	**9**	**0**	**27**	**16**
Totals	**26**	**0**	**0**	**1**	**24**	**17**							

Washington Senators	IP	R	H	ER	BB	SO	Boston Red Sox	IP	R	H	ER	BB	SO
Ayers (L)	9	4	9	4	0	0	Ruth	0*	0	0	0	1	0
							Shore (W)	9	0	0	0	0	2
							Totals	**9**	**0**	**0**	**0**	**1**	**2**
							*faced Morgan in the 1st						

	1	2	3	4	5	6	7	8	9	R	H	E
WAS A	0	0	0	0	0	0	0	0	0	0	0	3
BOS A	0	1	0	0	0	0	3	0	x	4	9	0

produced the same result, Ruth arguing again. Words became heated; Owens told Ruth to clam up or risk ejection. Ruth reportedly replied that if he were tossed, he would give Owens a licking on his way out. When ball four was called, Ruth attempted to make good on his boast, but only managed to nick Owens on the ear as catcher Pinch Thomas held the big lefty back.

Ruth was dragged off the field by policemen and Sox player-manager Jack Barry. Morgan went to first on the base on balls, while Thomas went to the clubhouse. Though not officially ejected from the game, the catcher had to act as Babe-sitter. The Red Sox turned to Shore to fill in, and Ernie hopped up on the mound without much preamble. Sam Agnew came on to catch, and his first duty was to catch Morgan stealing. A ground out and an easy fly ball later, and Shore was back in the dugout, having faced the minimum and recorded no runs, no hits, no errors, and no men left on base.

In his next inning of work, Shore fielded two comebackers and also covered first on a ground ball to the right side, accounting for three more outs. Boston, meanwhile, put a run on the board in the bottom of the inning, off one of Washington's best pitchers, Doc Ayers. Larry Gardner started the action with a single to right. Duffy Lewis dropped down a bunt that took a bad bounce and he reached safely. Tilly Walker sacrificed them both along. Everett Scott couldn't cash them in with his soft pop, but Agnew, who had expected to be on the bench that day, singled past third, scoring Gardner and putting men on the corners. Ayers then faced Shore, squelching the threat by striking the pitcher out; 1–0 Boston. Ruth made his way into the stands to watch the game and converse with fans, complaining that two of the called balls were strikes, but did not stay long—his part in the day's events was over.

With one run to work with, Shore almost allowed a hit to Howie Shanks, but shortstop Scott snared the "nasty bounder" *(Boston Globe)* and nipped him at first. Shore struck out John Henry and retired Ayers easily on an infield grounder, eight men in a row retired since Morgan was picked off—nine in succession since Shore took the hill.

The pesky leadoff man came up again in the fourth, this time hitting a ball deep in the shortstop hole, but Scott's long throw was still in time to nab the speedy runner. A foul pop and another comebacker made it 11 outs in a row. Three more went down in the fifth, although Charlie Jamieson almost reached when Shore deflected his line drive, but Everett Scott was there once again, getting the ball to first in time. Another close call came in the sixth, this time Scott making a high throw that Hoblitzell leaped and brought down on the bag to get Shanks. And there was one deep drive in the seventh, which Duffy Lewis ran up onto the embankment bordering the left-field wall—so aptly called "Duffy's Cliff"—to snare.

The Sox added three to their tally in the bottom of the seventh, allowing Shore to breeze the rest of the way, until Henry hit one more sinking drive in the ninth, which Duffy raced in to snare. "[Shore] is indebted to Scotty and Duffy . . . for making his record," wrote Edward F. Martin in the *Globe*. "It was the best pitching seen in this city since 1904 when Cy Young put over a similar feat, the only difference being that Uncle Cyrus pitched to every batter, while the Carolina professor did not get into the exercises until after [one man had walked]."

"After Morgan . . . the Senators did not know that there was a first base on the field," wrote John J. Hallahan in the *Boston Herald.* "The good-natured Shore did not realize he had earned a niche in the hall of fame until it was all over." The Sox won the game 4–0, and then, to ice the cake, beat Walter Johnson 5–0 in the second game of the doubleheader. Ruth was handed a nine-game suspension and a $100 fine, while Shore earned a place in the record books: 27 up and 27 down in a complete nine-inning game was considered a perfect game for the pitcher. Major League Baseball changed the rules regarding perfect games and no-hitters in 1991, removing Shore's name from the official list, but the improbable nature of Shore's pitching perfection will never be forgotten.

◀Extra Innings

- Ernie Shore would be traded to the Yankees after the 1918 season, and be joined there by Ruth in 1920.

- One of the umpires working the game was former Red Sox pitcher Bill Dinneen, who twirled a no-hitter himself in 1905. Dinneen's no-hit game was spun September 27, a 2–0 victory in Boston against the White Sox. Dinneen walked two and hit a batter but allowed not a hit. It was the first game of a doubleheader; Boston lost the second game, 15–1.

12

September 5, 1918: Boston at Chicago

Wartime

In which a lone run is all the Babe needs

The first four times the Red Sox had gone into a World Series, they had emerged victorious each time. They brought home flags in 1903, 1912, 1915, and 1916 (and won the pennant in 1904, a year there was no World Series, since the Giants refused to participate). The club had slipped a bit in 1917, though, finishing second, nine games behind the Chicago White Sox. By 1918, with World War I sapping the talent pool, the Sox looked like the team to beat. Babe Ruth, pitching and batting ninth, won on Opening Day, and the club got off to a 12–3 start.

With talent scarce, manager Ed Barrow began to take advantage of Ruth's prowess at the plate and began to convert him into more of an everyday role than merely pitching every few days, by starting him at first base and in the outfield in 72 games. The New York Yankees were impressed with the young player's ability to pitch and slug, and offered owner Harry Frazee $150,000 for him. Frazee declined. Ruth, too, became enamored of hitting, and refused to pitch for a while, but eventually returned to the rotation "for the good of the club." By the end of the season, Ruth was tied for the league lead in homers (11), and led the league in slugging average at .555. With the war-shortened season, the Sox managed only a 75–51 record, but that was 2½ games better than Cleveland. Although Cleveland's offense garnered most of the records that season, Boston's pitching led the league in complete games and shutouts, allowed the fewest hits, and tied for the fewest home runs allowed.

Boston's opponent in the World Series would be the Chicago Cubs, who had cruised to a 10½-game lead for the pennant over the Giants. Chicago had done it with pitching, as Hippo Vaughn (22–10) had the league's lowest ERA (1.74), Lefty Tyler (19–8) came in at 2.00, and the 20–7 Claude Hendrix topped out at 2.78. Vaughn led the league in most other pitching categories as well, with 148 strikeouts and 22 wins, eight of them shutouts. And this in a

SEPTEMBER 5, 1918: BOSTON AT CHICAGO																	
Boston Red Sox	AB	R	H	RBI	BB	SO	PO	A	Chicago Cubs	AB	R	H	RBI	BB	SO	PO	A
Hooper rf	4	0	1	0	0	0	4	0	Flack rf	3	0	1	0	0	1	2	0
Shean 2b	2	1	1	0	2	1	0	3	Hollocher ss	3	0	0	0	0	0	2	1
Strunk cf	3	0	0	0	0	0	2	0	Mann lf	4	0	1	0	0	0	0	0
Whiteman lf	4	0	2	0	0	1	5	0	Paskert cf	4	0	2	0	0	1	2	0
McInnis 1b	2	0	1	1	1	0	10	0	Merkle 1b	3	0	1	0	1	0	9	2
Scott ss	4	0	0	0	0	0	0	3	Pick 2b	3	0	0	0	0	1	1	1
Thomas 3b	3	0	0	0	0	2	1	1	O'Farrell ph	1	0	0	0	0	0	0	0
Agnew c	3	0	0	0	0	0	5	0	Deal 3b	4	0	1	0	0	0	1	3
Ruth p	3	0	0	0	0	2	0	1	McCabe pr	0	0	0	0	0	0	0	0
Totals	**28**	**1**	**5**	**1**	**3**	**6**	**27**	**8**	Killefer c	4	0	0	0	0	0	7	2
									Vaughn p	3	0	0	0	0	1	3	5
									Totals	32	0	6	0	1	4	27	14

Boston Red Sox	IP	H	R	ER	BB	SO	HR	Chicago Cubs	IP	H	R	ER	BB	SO	HR
Ruth (W)	9	6	0	0	1	4	0	Vaughn (L)	9	5	1	1	3	6	0

	1	2	3	4	5	6	7	8	9	R	H	E
BOS A	0	0	0	1	0	0	0	0	0	1	5	0
CHI N	0	0	0	0	0	0	0	0	0	0	6	0

season shortened by the demands of the war. Baseball's healthy players were allowed to avoid the service until September 1, those in the Series until September 15. Thus the season ended on Labor Day, and the World Series was played not in October but in September.

The Cubs worried about Ruth's power with the bat, and opted to move their home games out of cozy Weeghman Park (later called Wrigley Field) and into Comiskey Park, which also had a larger seating capacity. Comiskey's right-field fence was a good 50 to 75 feet farther from the plate, but when Ruth stepped in for batting practice prior to the first game, he sent the first pitch he saw into the right-field seats. The Cubs also dropped the right-handed Hendrix from the rotation to favor the left-handers Tyler and Vaughn.

Most observers at that point expected that Barrow would play Ruth in left—benching the veteran George Whiteman, who'd had an up-and-down season—and give the start to "Bullet" Joe Bush (15–15, but with a strong 2.11 ERA). Barrow refused to name his starter; so did Fred Mitchell of the Cubs, who had both Vaughn and Tyler warm up before the game to maintain the secrecy. No one was surprised when Vaughn was tabbed, but everyone was when Barrow went with Ruth (13–7, 2.22 ERA), batting him ninth and Whiteman fourth.

Both Vaughn and Ruth scuffled on the mound in the early going. Ruth retired the first two men he faced easily, but loaded the bases on successive singles and a walk. Charlie Pick, the Cubs' second baseman, then looped a sinking liner into left, and Whiteman bailed Ruth out by snaring it. Vaughn gave up a hit an inning but kept turning the Red Sox away until the fourth, when he walked the leadoff man, Dave Shean. Amos Strunk hit a comebacker, bringing up George Whiteman. Whitey dinked a single, moving Shean to second. Barrow put on the hit and run and Stuffy McInnis executed it to perfection, scoring Shean.

Whiteman and McInnis were stranded, but Boston led 1–0.

Ruth did not allow another hit until the sixth, a one-out single to Dode Paskert, quickly followed by another from Fred Merkle. But Pick grounded out and Charlie Deal flew to left, another chance for Whiteman, who barely caught up to the ball and snared it with the minimum amount of glove.

"From the ball player's standpoint it was a great game," wrote I. E. Sanborn in the *Chicago Daily Tribune*, "[but] from the rooter's viewpoint it was tame and monotonous." James Crusinberry in the same paper opined it was "perhaps the quietest [World Series game] on record." The combination of Ruth and Whiteman was too much for Chicago, and the Cubs were shut out the rest of the way. Ruth earned the 1–0 victory, and with the six-hit shutout stretched his World Series scoreless innings streak to 22⅔, but George Whiteman was the hero of the hour. Whitey was given the start in left the next day, while Ruth was benched.

Extra Innings

- Army planes flew exercises in the vicinity during the game. "At one time there were six planes almost over the field," reported the *Chicago Tribune*. "Occasionally one of them would do a nose dive or a tail spin just to let us know they were ready for a flight to Berlin."

- For Ruth, the game was the start of a shutout pitching streak in World Series play that would eventually run to 29⅔ innings. Lefty Whitey Ford would eventually snap that record in 1961, the same year that Roger Maris broke Ruth's single-season home-run record.

13

September 11, 1918: Chicago at Boston

Bittersweet

In which Boston seals a fifth championship under dire circumstances

Wartime had already shortened the baseball season, forced the World Series into September, and curtailed the crowds because of high travel costs and the lack of young men in the stands. It also necessitated that the Red Sox and the

SEPTEMBER 11, 1918: CHICAGO AT BOSTON

Chicago Cubs	AB	R	H	RBI	BB	SO	PO	A	Boston Red Sox	AB	R	H	RBI	BB	SO	PO	A
Flack rf	3	1	1	0	1	0	1	0	Hooper rf	3	0	0	0	0	0	1	0
Hollocher ss	4	0	0	0	0	0	0	4	Shean 2b	3	1	0	0	1	1	2	4
Mann lf	3	0	0	0	0	0	2	0	Strunk cf	4	0	2	0	0	0	0	0
Paskert cf	2	0	0	0	1	0	6	0	Whiteman lf	4	0	0	0	0	0	2	0
Merkle 1b	3	0	1	1	0	1	8	2	Ruth lf	0	0	0	0	0	0	1	0
Pick 2b	3	0	1	0	0	0	3	1	McInnis 1b	4	0	1	0	0	0	16	1
Deal 3b	2	0	0	0	0	0	2	1	Scott ss	4	0	1	0	0	0	3	3
Barber ph	1	0	0	0	0	0	0	0	Thomas 3b	2	0	0	0	1	0	1	2
Zeider 3b	0	0	0	0	0	0	0	0	Schang c	1	0	0	0	2	0	1	2
Killefer c	2	0	0	0	0	0	2	2	Mays p	2	1	1	0	1	0	0	6
O'Farrell ph,c	1	0	0	0	0	0	0	0	**Totals**	**27**	**2**	**5**	**0**	**5**	**1**	**27**	**18**
Tyler p	2	0	0	0	0	0	0	3									
McCabe ph	1	0	0	0	0	0	0	0									
Hendrix p	0	0	0	0	0	0	0	0									
Totals	**27**	**1**	**3**	**1**	**2**	**1**	**24**	**13**									

Chicago Cubs	IP	H	R	ER	BB	SO	HR	Boston Red Sox	IP	H	R	ER	BB	SO	HR
Tyler (L)	7	5	2	0	5	1	0	Mays (W)	9	3	1	1	2	1	0
Hendrix	1	0	0	0	0	0	0								
Totals	**8**	**5**	**2**	**0**	**5**	**1**	**0**								

	1	2	3	4	5	6	7	8	9	R	H	E
CHI N	0	0	0	1	0	0	0	0	0	1	3	2
BOS A	0	0	2	0	0	0	0	0	x	2	5	0

Cubs travel together on a single train from Chicago to Boston. So it was that the players, "the Boys of September," were all together when they received the news that their traditional World Series share would be curtailed, too.

The owners had voted months earlier to change from distributing 60% of the gate receipts of the first four games to the players on the two participating teams to further subdividing the share among players on the second-, third-, and fourth-place clubs. They knew that if they did so, they could reduce salaries even more for players across the league by promising a "bonus" without reducing their own take of the World Series money one bit. Thus each Cub and Red Soxer who had expected to receive $3,000 to $4,000 was suddenly looking to pocket only about $1,000.

The players banded together and forced a meeting in Boston with the league officials, threatening not to play if their demands were not heard. The three commissioners—American League president Ban Johnson, National League president John Heydler, and chairman August Herrmann—would have none of it, placating the players with promises of future meetings while planning to ignore all demands. The start of Game Five was delayed as the players tried to reassert their demands, resulting in jeers from the fans who knew little of the conflict and perceived the players as wartime slackers.

"All chances for a continuation of yesterday's players' strike was dispelled this noon when the [players] conferred with the club owners, who promised to use their influence with the national commission . . . to increase the players' pool," reported the *Chicago Tribune*. So it was that on September 11, 1918, the players took the field at Fenway Park for Game Six in front of a mere 15,238 disgruntled fans. At the time it looked as if there might be no 1919 season because of the war; a Sox win might make it the final ball game for a long time, yet the fans had bigger things, such as the war, on their minds.

Carl Mays took the hill for the Red Sox. He had been the Sox ace all year, going 21–13 (2.21 ERA), with his underslung delivery baffling batters. He was opposed by Lefty Tyler, the Cubs' number-two man. The pitching had been strong all Series, no team scoring more than three runs in a game. In the previous five games, Boston's cumulative score was 7, Chicago's 9, though Boston held the 3–2 advantage in wins.

With scoring at such a premium, Boston could be said to have won it in the third inning. Here Tyler faced Mays to lead off the inning, and walked him. Harry Hooper sacrificed him to second, and with first base open, Dave Shean worked out a walk. Amos Strunk grounded out, moving the runners to second and third for George Whiteman. Whitey had continued to play strong defense since Game One, and at .250 was among the Sox leaders in batting average in this pitching-dominated Series. This time he smacked a liner to right, which Max Flack gloved but dropped. "The hands and feet of Max Flack were a potent factor [in the game]," concluded the *Chicago Herald*. Mays and Shean both scored, the runs unearned, but that was little consolation to the Cubs.

Flack tried to set things right in the fourth when he singled, took second on a ground out, stole third, and came in on a hit by Fred Merkle. But one man is only one run, and that was the only crack in Mays's armor until the eighth. Turner Barber stepped in to pinch-hit for Charlie Deal and whacked a liner to left. Whiteman charged in, gloved the ball, and somersaulted in a move that the *Examiner* described as "unhinged his neck in a circus diving catch." The crowd's ovation for Whiteman went on for several minutes while he tried to recover from the maneuver. He stayed in for one more out, but was too unsteady to remain in the game; Ruth replaced him, barely noticed in the applause for Whiteman's heroics.

After that, it was up to Carl Mays, jealously guarding the 2–1 lead for the final four outs. Chicago did not get another man to first base, and when Les Mann grounded to Shean, the Red Sox became the champions of the world for the fifth time in five tries.

There was no victory parade, and the winners received a measly $1,108, while the losers got only $671 each, the lowest postseason payout then or since. In a final act of spite, despite promises not to take punitive action against the players sworn in front of Boston's mayor, the commissioners refused to award commemorative medallions to each player (the equivalent of today's championship rings) because of the Game Five strike. The fans had already put the season behind them.

"The general feeling for the last six weeks that playing ball was not helping much in winning the war practically killed interest in the annual series," reported the *Tribune*. Boston rooters could reasonably expect that their club would be in the mix often in the coming years, and surely a better, more carefree time would bring a more satisfying championship to the city soon.

They would wait until 1946 for their next chance, and until 2004 to finally win another world championship.

◢Extra Innings

- The commemorative medallions due the players were never awarded by the commissioners. In 1993, after much prompting by local writer Glenn Stout, the Red Sox gave them to the players' surviving relatives on the 75th anniversary of the 1918 world championship—at the time the commissioner's office was vacant.

- George Whiteman was considered by many to be the Series MVP, a designation not awarded in this era. He got some key hits and made some key plays, though he batted only .250 in the World Series. He had an unusual major league career, debuting in four games with the Red Sox in late 1907, then next appearing with the Yankees in 11 games some six years later, in 1913. After four more years out of the majors, he resurfaced with the Sox in 1918. He got himself into 71 games, batting .266, but he never really distinguished himself either in the field (.935 FA) or at the plate—until he made his major contributions in the World Series. He never turned up in the major leagues again.

- The Red Sox team batting average in the Series was .186. When did a team with a lower batting average win the World Series? Answer: never. In 1906, the Chicago White Sox batted only .198, but they defeated the Cubs, who batted only .196. In 1930, the Philadelphia A's won while hitting only .197. The Indians beat the Braves in '48 with only a .199 average, as did the Yankees over the Giants in 1962.

14

September 5, 1927: New York at Boston

New York Marathon

In which fans crash the gates to see the home-run race and are treated to an 18-inning marathon

By the latter part of the Roaring Twenties, the Red Sox found themselves in the cellar. Bill Carrigan, who had managed the team to back-to-back world championships in 1915 and 1916, returned to Boston to try to turn the team around. "He is on top of everything . . . [and] does not delegate his various duties to a flock of subordinates. He is patient, yet when he finds that the boys are not giving their best, he chases the staller," wrote *The Sporting News* in praise of the manager's job in 1927, lamenting, "But the Carrigan methods were strange to this generation of ballplayers. Bill really had to educate his players [about] his own aggressive, hustling ideas." Attendance sagged while the team struggled, but rose a bit when Carrigan's fighting spirit began to be reflected on the field.

On September 5, though, the turnout for the holiday doubleheader went beyond the expected. Babe Ruth, Lou Gehrig, and the rest of "Murderers' Row" had come to town, and the throngs eager to see Ruth face his old team overwhelmed ticket takers and the park's infrastructure. "The weak spots in the wooden barricade on the Ipswich Street side of the park were rushed and several holes made through which the human flood poured in a merry torrent," wrote Burt Whitman in the *Boston Herald*. Paid attendance was listed at 34,385, but "hundreds stormed the gates after ticket sales were stopped" (Associated Press), and the spillover of spectators onto the field had to be pressed back against the outfield wall by a mounted policeman and then roped off. Photographs showed the people 15 to 20 rows deep on the grass. Any ball hit into the horde would be considered a ground-rule double.

The *New York Times* put the estimate of those inside at about 36,000, "the largest to attend a ballgame at Fenway Park in twelve years"—that is, since the 1915 World Series. (The *Times* writer either did not realize that the 1915 World Series was played at Braves Field rather than Fenway Park, or was referring only to regular-season games.) The *Boston Herald* inflated the number to 38,000 in a front-page headline, and counted the number turned away at 40,000. "There were pathetic scenes around, as there always must be when fans are disappointed by the tens of thousands. Men said they came all the way from Northern Maine or the tip of Cape Cod, leading little freckle-faced kids by the hand," Whitman reported.

"Ostensibly, the crowd had turned out to see Babe Ruth and Lou Gehrig continue their great struggle in the Great American Home Run Derby," wrote John Drebinger in the *Times*. "But as the Sox bobbed up with a surprising amount of energy . . . interest gradually shifted from the derby to the game itself." The Yankees came out swinging, loading the bases in the first inning. But Carrigan's boys were not going to let the New Yorkers run away with things. On the hill, the Sox had Charley "Red" Ruffing, a righty who was one of the first pitchers to perfect the slider. He fanned Tony Lazzeri to end the sacks-full threat, and the Sox came roaring back, scoring three runs in the bottom of the inning.

Murderers' Row mashed out six runs over the next few innings, one on Lou Gehrig's 44th homer of the year, which put the Iron Horse and Ruth in a dead heat for the home-run title. But the Sox took the lead in the fifth, 8–6, and as the ninth inning rolled around, it looked as if they might hang on to win. But with two out, Ray Morehart pinch-hit for Joe Dugan and walked. Another pinch hitter, Ben Paschal, followed and doubled to left. Earle Combs came

SEPTEMBER 5, 1927: NEW YORK AT BOSTON

New York Yankees	AB	R	H	PO	A	Boston Red Sox	AB	R	H	PO	A
Combs cf	10	2	5	5	0	Rothrock ss	7	1	1	3	4
Koenig ss	10	3	3	5	4	Myer 3b	8	2	3	4	3
Ruth lf	7	1	1	2	0	Flagstead cf	8	1	2	5	1
Gehrig 1b	6	1	4	24	0	Regan 2b	9	1	3	8	4
Meusel rf	8	1	3	0	3	Tobin rf	8	2	3	2	0
Lazzeri 2b	9	0	2	2	11	Shaner lf	7	3	3	1	0
Duran 3b	3	0	0	1	2	Todt 1b	8	1	3	16	3
Morehart ph	0	1	0	0	0	Hofmann c	5	1	1	13	2
Gazella 3b	3	0	0	1	0	Hartley c	1	0	0	0	0
Bengough c	3	0	0	6	2	Moore c	1	0	1	0	1
Durst ph	1	0	1	0	0	Ruffing p	5	0	0	2	6
Collins c	3	1	1	5	1	Wiltse p	1	0	0	0	1
Pipgras p	2	0	0	0	1	**Totals**	**70**	**12**	**20**	**54**	**25**
Giard p	1	0	0	0	2						
Shawkey p	0	0	0	0	1						
Paschal ph	1	1	1	0	0						
Moore p	3	0	0	1	7						
Hoyt p	0	0	0	0	0						
Totals	**71**	**11**	**21**	**52**	**34**						

New York Yankees	IP	H	R	ER	BB	SO	Boston Red Sox	IP	H	R	ER	BB	SO
Pipgras	3+	8	7	7	3	2	Ruffing	15	16	8	8	12	12
Giard	3	3	1	1	1	0	Wiltse (W)	3	5	3	3	2	0
Shawkey	2	2	0	0	0	0	**Totals**	**18**	**21**	**11**	**11**	**14**	**12**
Moore	8+	3	2	2	2	3							
Hoyt (L)	1.1	4	2	2	0	1							
Totals	**17.1**	**20**	**12**	**12**	**6**	**6**							

	1	2	3	4	5	6	7	8	9	10	11	12	13	14	15	16	17	18		R	H	E
NY A	0	0	4	2	0	0	0	0	2	0	0	0	0	0	0	0	3	0		11	21	2
BOS A	3	0	0	4	1	0	0	0	0	0	0	0	0	0	0	0	3	1		12	20	5

next and popped a ball foul that would surely have been the third and final out if the overflow crowd had not gotten in the way. On the next pitch he lifted a fly ball into left, another one that Wally Shaner could have easily hauled in if not for the people on the grass. This one landed in the crowd fair, though, and the ground-rule double allowed the tying runs to score.

Thus the game went into extra innings, and the two teams stayed in their 8–8 deadlock inning after inning for almost two more hours.

In the 17th inning the Yankees looked like they would prevail. Harold "Hal" Wiltse, who had come on to pitch after Ruffing's removal for a pinch hitter, walked Pat Collins to begin the trouble. A sacrifice and an Earl Combs single brought him in—Combs's fifth hit of the day. Mark Koenig doubled into the crowd in center, and Ruth was walked, both advancing on an error when Wiltse muffed catching the throw back to the mound. Gehrig singled, tallying his fourth hit of the day and two RBI.

"That 11–8 lead looked as big as the Park Square building," read the *Herald* story, but Carrigan's boys rallied back. In the bottom half of the inning, to the delight of the huge crowd, they tied the score. Wilcy Moore had been pitching for the Yankees since the ninth inning, and had allowed only three hits, but after Regan doubled off the left-field wall and Tobin singled, Moore was yanked in favor of Waite Hoyt.

Hoyt gave up two fly balls, the first by Shaner almost clearing the wall in left, but then falling into the crowd for a double. Then young Bill Moore, a backup catcher, went in to pinch-hit and sent a fly to right, but between the crowd and the sun Bob Meusel did not have a chance, and Moore was credited with a double, tying the score at 11.

The Yankees could not answer in the top of the 18th, and in the bottom of the inning the Sox put more balls into play in the treacherous outfield. "Myer [*sic*] just popped another double into center and Flagstead dropped another into right and the game was over" *(New York Times)*. The Red Sox had prevailed, 12–11, and the record crowd had seen an exceptional game.

Extra Innings

- The Sox would draw a total of 305,275 fans to the park in 1927. On September 5, they drew more than 10% of their total for the year.

- With the game starting late because of crowd control problems, and then running for almost 4½ hours, the second half of the doubleheader was played in haste and called on account of darkness after five innings (only 55 minutes) at 5–0, in favor of the Yankees. Wiltse, who had earned the win in game one, stayed on the mound for game two and lost.

● Red Ruffing had only one toe on his left foot, the others having been lost in a mine accident when he was a youngster. He had a reputation for wearing out his arm after five or six innings, but in this game he pitched until he was lifted for a pinch hitter in the 15th. The Yankees traded for him in 1930, and Yankee manager Bob Shawkey helped him to adjust his pitching motion to put less strain on his arm. Ruffing pitched 16 years with the Yankees and was elected to the Hall of Fame in 1967.

● Babe Ruth would eventually be the victor in the home-run race, setting the record at 60 that would stand until 1961, when Roger Maris hit 61.

15

September 12, 1931: Detroit at Boston

Bullheaded

In which a curveballing Carolinian completes a contest

Almost nothing at all good happened for the Sox in the 1920s. The closest they got to first place was 23½ games behind the first-place team. In 1927 they were 59 games out, and they were in undisputed control of the cellar in most other years. In 1924 the White Sox earned the distinction by half a game. Both teams lost 87 games, but Boston played one more and won it. There weren't any no-hitters for Boston pitchers, and nothing else to get excited about. So when James O'Leary of the *Boston Globe* called the game of September 12, 1931, "the best game seen this season," he might as well have said, "of the decade." All thanks to one Eddie Durham.

The predictably nicknamed "Bull" Durham had been 4–15 in his first full year, 1930. He walked more batters than he struck out. In 1931 his ERA improved a bit (from 4.69 to 4.25) and his walks and strikeouts evened out. This skinny right-handed native of South Carolina was up against Art Herring of the Tigers on September 12, and the only hint that anything unusual might have been about to occur was the abysmal batting of the Detroiters the day before. Danny MacFayden had shut them out on just three hits. (The Somerville High graduate was the Sox standout that year—the shutout was his 14th win.)

Not much happened in the first four innings as Durham scattered five hits. And the Red Sox managed only four. The 0–0 game wound into the bottom of the sixth, when Bill Sweeney and Marty McManus hit back-to-back singles,

Ed Durham

but Earl Webb hit into a double play and Tom Oliver popped up to Mark Koenig at second. They tried again for a run in the eighth. Jack Rothrock had tripled to lead off for Boston, but Sweeney grounded to shortstop Billy Rogell, and McManus bounced back to Herring, who caught Rothrock off third.

The game passed into extra innings with no suggestion that either starter would leave the game. In those days before pitch counts and relief specialists, complete games were not as rare as they are now, but even still, going into extra innings with a 0–0 score and both pitchers in the game was rare. Durham had handled the Tigers without much trouble—those five hits they had in the first four innings were all they had, and he had not walked a man. Boston, by contrast, had 10 hits and got four walks, but left 11 men on base and didn't score through 12 innings.

The Tigers mustered nothing more through 13, and Boston's Bill Sweeney (a former Tiger) lifted a ball into right-center to lead off the bottom of the

13th. Roy Johnson had time to make the catch and camped under the ball, but just then a flock of pigeons helped bring the game to a conclusion. Perhaps bored with all the goose eggs, the pigeons suddenly flew up in front of Johnson, blocking his vision, and the ball ticked off his fingertips and bounced over to center fielder Hub Walker. Walker was only in the game at that point because his brother Gee had been tossed in the top of the inning for calling home plate umpire Bill Guthrie a "fathead" for ruling him out on strikes in the top of the inning. Walker's throw-in was hurried and wild and went into the Detroit dugout, so Sweeney took third. Up came McManus with a great opportunity to get the winning run in just by making contact with the ball, but he struck out. Earl Webb was intentionally walked; Webb had 59 doubles at this point, eight short of the major league record he would set later in September at 67.

Johnson was playing in close in right, hoping to cut down any play at the plate. Red Sox center fielder Tom Oliver lashed a low liner to Johnson, who made a remarkable shoestring catch, came up, and fired the ball home on one bounce, right into the hands of catcher Muddy Ruel—but it bounced high, and as Ruel stretched up to make the catch, the swift Sweeney had time to run back to third, tag up, and scoot across the plate. And so the final score stood 1–0 on Ed Durham's 13-inning complete-game masterpiece.

This was a suddenly competitive Boston Red Sox. The next day, they lost game one of a home doubleheader with the White Sox, 6–5, and battled to a 2–2 tie in 14 innings during game two. By the time the season was over, the Red Sox were 45 games out of first (62–90)—but they finished in sixth place, better than either Detroit or Chicago.

SEPTEMBER 12, 1931: DETROIT AT BOSTON

Detroit Tigers	AB	R	H	PO	A	Boston Red Sox	AB	R	H	PO	A
Johnson rf	5	0	0	4	0	Rothrock lf	6	0	2	8	0
Koenig 2b	5	0	1	4	4	Sweeney 1b	6	1	2	12	0
Stone lf	5	0	1	3	0	McManus 2b	5	0	2	4	4
Alexander 1b	5	0	1	11	0	Webb rf	5	0	1	2	0
G. Walker 1b	5	0	1	5	0	Oliver cf	6	0	1	4	1
H. Walker cf	0	0	0	0	0	Miller 3b	5	0	0	1	1
Rogell ss	5	0	0	3	6	Rhyne ss	4	0	1	4	4
Richardson 3b	5	0	0	1	0	Connolly c	4	0	1	3	1
Ruel c	4	0	0	7	1	Durham p	4	0	0	1	2
Herring p	4	0	1	0	5	Totals	45	1	10	39	13
Totals	43	0	5	38	16						

Detroit Tigers	IP	H	R	ER	BB	SO	Boston Red Sox	IP	H	R	ER	BB	SO
Herring (L)	12.2	10	1	0	4	7	Durham (W)	13	5	0	0	0	1

	1	2	3	4	5	6	7	8	9	10	11	12	13	R	H	E
DET A	0	0	0	0	0	0	0	0	0	0	0	0	0	0	5	2
BOS A	0	0	0	0	0	0	0	0	0	0	0	0	1	1	10	2

Extra Innings

- Ed Durham's tenure with the Red Sox ended after the 1932 season, when he and Hal Rhyne were traded to the Chicago White Sox. In return Boston received four players: Fats Fothergill, Bob Seeds, Urban Hodapp, and Greg Mulleavy. Durham would win a career-high 10 games in Chicago in 1933, his final year before health troubles ended his playing days.

16

September 28, 1941: Boston at Philadelphia

Splendid

In which the greatest hitter who ever lived stakes his claim

Legend has it that Red Sox manager Joe Cronin talked to his star hitter Ted Williams before the doubleheader on the final day of the 1941 season. Williams, who had just turned 23 a few weeks before, was hitting .39955—and that would round off to .400. Cronin asked the Kid if he wanted to sit out. If Ted took the day off, he'd preserve his .400 batting average for the season and forever be a member of one of baseball's most exclusive circles. If he played, he might well drop below the magic mark.

Ted had hit over .400 most of the season. He was hitting .413 with 14 games to play, but in those final games his average began to slip. With only his 27th strikeout of the year, he had fallen under .400 (just barely) the day before. It was a bit of a slump; he'd now made just three hits in his last 14 at-bats going into the final day of the season—a doubleheader against the Philadelphia Athletics in Shibe Park. It was a common enough practice to take a seat to preserve your average. Wally Moses of the A's planned to do just that today—he was batting .301 and sat out the doubleheader. In 1921, Rogers Hornsby was hitting .39966 going into the final game. Hornsby played, failed to get a hit in conditions so miserable the game was called after five innings, and saw his season average forever posted at .397.

Williams was worried. He knew the pressure was on, but he didn't want to hit .400 by the rounding off of a number. Ted spent a few hours the night before just walking and walking, restlessly, and talking with his clubhouse buddy, Johnny Orlando.

Ted recalls Sox manager Cronin as having told him, "You don't have to play. You're .400 officially." Ted's reaction? "I was dumbfounded to hear him talking that way because I never even had an ounce of an idea that I wasn't going to play. 'No!' I said, 'Hell, I'm going to play!'" He told *The Sporting News*, "I want to have more than my toenails on the line." So Ted went out, played both games of the doubleheader, and made history.

So says the legend, but it didn't happen quite that way. Yes, Williams was batting .39955, but there was never any chance he wasn't going to hit. He didn't really have a choice. The notion that a batting average could be rounded up just didn't cut it with the newspapers or the public. On the very morning of the final day, the *Boston Herald* had a front-page story by Burt Whitman headlined, "Williams Dips Below .400." Ted had gone 1-for-4, and even though it was a double, he was "below .400." The story noted that it was the first time since July 25 that Williams had gone below .400, and that even if Ted were to go 2-for-5 on the final day, he'd still hit only .39959. The *Boston Globe* subhead read, "Average Now Is .399"—the *Globe* was *not* rounding up. The other papers followed suit, the *Boston Post* citing a number below .400 and the *New York Times* headline putting Ted at .3996.

Ted might have rested on his laurels a day earlier. Had he sat out the September 27 game he could have rested the final day, too, and finished with a noncontroversial mark of .4009. In fact, he could have sat down after the last home game, almost a week before the season's end. The final six games were road games, meaningless ones. Cronin went to Williams and told him it was fine with the ball club if Ted wanted to take off the final six games. The pennant was long since decided, with Boston securely in second place. But Williams said he wanted to play. Ted went 1-for-3 on Tuesday against the Senators, and then went only 1-for-7 in a Wednesday twin bill. He was in the worst slump he'd been in all season long. The Philadelphia Athletics didn't care whether they won or lost, either; they had no chance to escape last place. Cronin again asked Ted if he might prefer to watch the last three games from the bench. The fans would understand. League officials would raise no objection. As Al Hirshberg wrote in the *Post*, Ted had nothing to gain by playing—either for himself or for the Red Sox—and he had everything to lose. But Teddy Ballgame wanted to play. "Give credit to the Kid," wrote Hirshberg. "He did it the hard way."

After dipping under .400, Williams had to go for it. Phil Marchildon, a pitcher for the A's, said that Ted had said before the three-game series, "I want to hit over .400, but I'm going to play all three games here even if I don't hit a ball out of the infield. The record's no good unless it's made in all the games." Marchildon also explained the slump, writing in his autobiography that Ted "didn't consider it an advantage to be facing our rookie pitchers. His average dropped steadily during September, mainly, he said, because he was seeing a steady diet of youngsters whose pitching styles he hadn't had a chance to study." (Marchildon, *Ace*, p. 82) Much of hitting was informed guesswork, outwitting the pitcher. Williams hit better against pitchers who were more familiar to him, and he knew it.

Ted batted cleanup, but the Red Sox were set down 1-2-3 in the top of the first and left him in the on-deck circle. Ted led off the second inning facing left-hander Dick Fowler, whose major league debut had been a couple of weeks earlier, on September 13. Ted didn't know him. There was a little recognition of the moment in the batter's box as Williams stepped in to get set. Frankie Hayes, the Philadelphia catcher, told the .39955 hitter, "Ted, Mr. Mack told us if we let up on you he'll run us out of baseball. I wish you all the luck in the world, but we're not giving you a damn thing." The umpire, Bill McGowan, called time and started dusting off the plate with his whisk. Williams wrote in his autobiography, "Without looking up, he said, 'To hit .400 a batter has got to be loose. He has got to be loose.'"

Fowler's first pitch missed low and outside. Ball one. Ted took ball two, inside. Down 2–0 in the count, Fowler was going to have to try to get one over, and of course Williams knew it. Ted cracked a single. A "fierce, low grounder" *(Boston Herald)*, it shot to the right of first baseman Indian Bob Johnson, and pumped Ted's average solidly over .400, at .402. Joe Cronin said afterward, "I never came closer to bawling right out loud on a baseball diamond than when

SEPTEMBER 28, 1941: BOSTON AT PHILADELPHIA

Boston Red Sox	AB	R	H	RBI	PO	A	Philadelphia A's	AB	R	H	RBI	PO	A
DiMaggio cf	5	1	3	0	4	0	Collins rf	5	2	2	1	3	0
Finney rf	4	1	0	0	3	0	Valo lf	5	3	2	2	2	0
Flair 1b	5	2	1	2	5	0	Richmond 3b	5	2	3	1	0	3
Williams lf	5	2	4	2	3	0	Johnson 1b	4	1	2	2	15	1
Tabor 3b	4	2	2	1	1	2	Chapman cf	5	0	2	1	1	0
Doerr 2b	5	3	2	3	3	3	Davis 2b	4	1	1	1	2	6
L. Newsome ss	3	0	1	1	2	2	Suder ss	5	1	2	0	2	4
Foxx ph	0	1	0	0	0	0	Hayes c	3	0	0	0	1	0
Carey ss	0	0	0	1	0	0	Fowler p	2	0	0	0	0	2
Pytlak c	4	0	1	0	6	1	Miles ph	1	1	1	0	0	0
H. Newsome p	2	0	1	0	0	1	Vaughn p	1	0	0	0	1	0
Wagner p	3	0	1	2	0	0	Shirley p	0	0	0	0	0	2
Totals	40	12	16	12	27	9	McCoy ph	1	0	0	0	0	0
							Totals	41	11	15	9	27	18

Boston Red Sox	IP	H	R	ER	BB	SO	Philadelphia A's	IP	H	R	ER	BB	SO
Newsome	4.2	12	11	8	3	5	Fowler	5	8	3	3	0	0
Wagner (W)	4.1	2	0	0	2	0	Vaughn	1.2	5	7	6	3	0
Totals	9	14	11	8	5	5	Shirley (L)	2.1	3	2	0	2	0
							Totals	9	16	12	9	5	0

	1	2	3	4	5	6	7	8	9	R	H	E
BOS A	0	0	0	0	3	1	6	0	2	12	16	3
PHI A	0	0	2	0	9	0	0	0	0	11	15	3

Ted got that hit. I really filled right up. I was so happy that the Kid had done the trick without asking or getting any favors."

Philadelphia scored a couple of runs, Boston's hitters did nothing, but the score was of little consequence on this day. The next time Ted came up was the fifth inning, and Fowler fell behind again. On a 1–0 count, Ted banged a long home run over the right-field wall right onto 20th Street, a drive of a good 440 feet. That kicked off the scoring for the Sox. A couple of other runs came in later, and Boston took a 3–2 lead. It was Williams's 37th homer of the year, the most by any hitter in the majors.

Fowler was lifted for a pinch hitter in the bottom of the fifth. The A's scored nine runs in the fifth to overtake the Red Sox and post an 11–3 lead. Another lefty, Porter Vaughan, took over mound duties for the A's, and in the sixth started off Ted the same way Fowler had, with a 2–0 count, both curveballs. "I'd faced Ted once before, in 1940," Vaughan explained in an interview. "Ted came up in the bottom of the ninth with the score tied and two outs, at Fenway Park. Ted singled in the game-winning run. It was a curveball. He hit it three feet over my head into center." This time, Ted hit the curve again. Crash Davis was playing second for Philadelphia, and playing in the hole between second and first, but Ted still hit it by him. Ted was now 3-for-3 on the day and not done yet.

In the seventh inning, still facing Vaughan, Ted singled on a 3–2 count, "a clean drive over the first-sacker's head, well into right field" (Burt Whitman, *Boston Herald*). Four straight hits. Slump over. Vaughan would later comment: "I felt very fortunate to hold him to two singles!" The Red Sox scored six runs off Vaughan and had made a game of it again. With the one they'd manufactured in the sixth, in part thanks to Ted, the score was now 11–10 in Philly's favor.

In his final at-bat of the game, facing his third pitcher of the game, right-hander Tex Shirley, another rookie with less than five innings of major league experience, Williams hit the ball hard a fifth time. The second baseman couldn't handle it, and was charged with an error. "Fair scoring," wrote the *Herald*'s Whitman, but the Associated Press reported that Williams was "robbed," that it should have been scored a hit.

Williams was loose enough. He'd gone 4-for-5, and might arguably have been a perfect 5-for-5. Boston scored two runs in the top of the ninth. Ted's roommate, Broadway Charlie Wagner, pitched after relieving Dick Newsome and got the 12–11 win.

The second game was the last major league start for Boston's Lefty Grove. He'd pitched for nine seasons with the Athletics, four times leading the league in wins, and then thrown eight seasons for the Red Sox. His record was 300 wins and 140 losses. Philadelphia hosted a "day" in his honor, and Grove was presented a chest of silver between games. Taking the same stance he'd taken regarding Ted's quest to hit .400, Connie Mack wasn't going to let his players ease up on Grove, either. The A's hit him for three runs in the first, and that put the sad ending to a Hall of Fame career. Grove took the 7–1 loss.

Ted Williams, though, kept on hitting. In the second game, Ted led off the second inning again. The pitcher was Fred Caligiuri, a right-hander who was pitching in just his fifth game since debuting earlier in the month. On a 2–0 count, Ted pulled the ball again, hitting it on the ground between first and second, his fifth hit of the day. Then Ted faced another 2–0 count, this time in the fourth. Asked what he'd thrown Ted, Caligiuri described the hit more vividly than the pitch: "He could hit most fastballs, and the only way to get him out is to change speeds on him. We tried to change up on him. In Shibe Park, there was a kind of a megaphone sits up on top of the wall, and that ball went a line drive right into that megaphone and fell back into the park for a double. I suppose that megaphone was at least maybe two feet across and it kept it in the ballpark. If it had been a few feet left or right, it would have gone out." The ball hit the speaker horn so hard it had to be replaced over the winter.

The day was getting dark ("dim, even murky," wrote Whitman), and Caligiuri finally retired Williams on a 1–1 fly ball to left field.

Williams's 6-for-8 showing closed as splendid a season as a player ever had with as much drama as one could have scripted. In the clubhouse after the game, Ted "laughed like a kid," according to Frank Yeutter of the *Philadelphia Bulletin.* He yelled to teammate Jimmie Foxx, "Just think—hitting .400. What do you think of that, Slug? Just a kid like me hitting that high?"

No one has done it since.

◢Extra Innings

- After both games were over, Ted's manager, Joe Cronin, proclaimed, "If there's ever a ballplayer who deserved to hit .400, it's Ted. He's given up plenty of chances to bunt and protect his average in recent weeks. He wouldn't think of getting out of the lineup to keep his average intact. Moreover, most of the other stars who have bettered the mark before were helped by no foul strike rules or sacrifice fly regulations." In 1941, a sacrifice fly was counted as an out, and the batter was also charged with an at-bat. Ted hit six sac flies in 1941. None of the other .400 hitters suffered under this short-lived rule. Had the sacrifice fly rule we're familiar with today been in force—a rule that applied before 1941 as well—Williams would have hit .411 on the season.

* The late Harvard University professor Stephen Jay Gould did a study that argued that—when measured relative to the performance of other hitters in the league—Ted's .406 season was far superior to that of any other .400 hitter. Hornsby hit .424 in 1924—but in the 1920s the marks set by league-leading hitters averaged .392 in the AL and .390 in the NL. That was a decade when many players hit for high averages. Hornsby's .424 was 33 points above the average batting leader of the decade. Sisler's .420 in 1922 was 29 points higher. When Ted hit .406 in 1941, he did so in a decade when the top AL average was .349 and the NL best was .354. That puts Ted's .406 a full 52 points above the NL average and a large 57 points above the AL average. Relative to those who hit during his time, Ted's achievement was far above that of the others in the exclusive .400 Club.

* Lefty Gomez: "I helped Ted get in the Hall of Fame. I don't believe there's any secret when a guy hits .400. You'd try to keep him from pulling the ball. They'd say, 'Why don't he bunt?' I'd be tickled to death if the guy bunted against me. At least you'd know where he'd stop: at first base" (quoted in *The Last .400 Hitter* by John Holway).

17

September 13, 1946: Boston at Cleveland

Round-Tripper

In which a home run is a run home and a pennant clincher at the same time

It seemed to take forever for the 1946 Red Sox to clinch the pennant. There was little question that they would, but closing the deal was something that dragged on and on before it finally happened in a most unexpected fashion.

With all their star players back after World War II, the '46 Sox jumped out to an early lead and never looked back. They won their first five games, and through May 10 had still only lost three times (21–3). They didn't post double-digit losses until June 12, at which point they were 41–10. After winning eight in a row to close August and open September, Boston held an ever firmer grip on first place. After Jim Bagby shut out the Senators 1–0 on September 5, the second-place New York Yankees were a full 16½ games behind, and the Tigers a couple of games behind New York. Boston had a record of 96–40; New York's was 78–55. Tom Yawkey ordered three cases of champagne.

SEPTEMBER 13, 1946: BOSTON AT CLEVELAND											
Boston Red Sox		**AB**	**R**	**H**	**PO**	**A**	**Cleveland Indians**	**AB**	**R**	**H**	**PO**	**A**
DiMaggio cf		3	0	0	1	0	Mackiewicz cf	3	0	0	4	0
Pesky ss		3	0	1	2	5	Ross 3b	4	0	0	1	2
Williams lf		3	1	1	1	0	Seerey lf	3	0	1	1	0
Doerr 2b		4	0	0	3	4	Edwards rf	4	0	0	3	0
York 1b		3	0	0	10	1	Fleming 1b	4	0	0	8	3
McBride rf		4	0	0	6	0	Boudreau ss	3	0	0	0	2
Wagner c		4	0	0	4	0	Mack 2b	3	0	1	3	1
Gutteridge 3b		2	0	0	0	0	Hegan c	3	0	0	6	0
Hughson p		3	0	0	0	3	Embree p	2	0	1	1	3
Totals		**29**	**1**	**2**	**27**	**13**	**Totals**	**29**	**0**	**3**	**27**	**11**

Boston Red Sox	**IP**	**H**	**R**	**ER**	**BB**	**SO**	**Cleveland Indians**	**IP**	**H**	**R**	**ER**	**BB**	**SO**
Hughson (W)	9	2	1	1	2	4	Embree (L)	9	3	0	0	4	3

	1	2	3	4	5	6	7	8	9	R	H	E
BOS A	1	0	0	0	0	0	0	0	0	1	2	0
CLE A	0	0	0	0	0	0	0	0	0	0	3	0

It was accepted as a foregone conclusion that the Red Sox would win it. The only question was: When would they clinch?

They fought hard to win the September 6 game in Washington, but lost it in the 11th, 3–2. The Sox played in Philadelphia on the seventh behind Boo Ferriss, going for his 13th consecutive win, but lost 4–2 as the last-place Athletics dealt Ferriss his first loss since July 4. Philadelphia won again the following day, 5–3, as war hero Phil Marchildon beat Boston's Tex Hughson. Ted Williams had homered on July 7, and his two doubles were among just five hits off Marchildon, but the effort was not enough.

At this point, all the Red Sox needed was one win or one Yankee loss to eliminate the Yankees. The Yankees lost to the Indians on September 10, leaving the Tigers as the only challenger. Detroit still had a mathematical chance to win, but all it would take to count them out was one Red Sox win and one Detroit loss, and the two teams played head-to-head, in Detroit, on the 10th and 11th. Mickey Harris just didn't have it, though, and neither did the Boston bullpen. The Tigers won a convincing 9–1 victory, with Dick Wakefield's three-run homer in the first effectively sealing it. It was the fourth straight loss for the Bosox. Ted Williams hit his 36th home run into the third deck for the only Red Sox run off Fred Hutchinson. After the loss, Al Hirshberg wrote in the *Boston Post* that the Red Sox locker room was "disconsolate." He quoted one of the players: "We can't work ourselves up into a will-to-win pitch. Our trouble is that we know that if we don't clinch today, maybe we'll clinch tomorrow, and if we don't do it then, maybe we will the next day. . . . Nobody seems to be able to give it the old college try."

In the meantime, well over 150,000 postal money orders for World Series tickets had already flooded into the Red Sox ticket office by the 10th. The tickets had been printed in Philadelphia, but a trucking strike in New York was holding up delivery to Boston. New Englanders were hungry for their first Series since 1918.

Denying the Sox the chance to clinch in face-to-face competition, the Tigers won yet again on the 11th, 7–3, despite Ted Williams having a 4-for-4 day and hitting his 37th homer. The champagne cases were loaded back on the train and Boston headed on to Cleveland, while the Yankees arrived in Detroit. Once more, the champagne was unloaded and brought into the League Park visitors' clubhouse, again put on ice before the game on the 12th. Once more, the Red Sox lost, their sixth loss in a row, and the Tigers hung in there, beating New York. Cleveland beat Boston, 4–1, behind Bob Feller's eight-hitter. Lou Boudreau put on his famous shift against Ted Williams, who hit a fluke pop-fly double to left field for one of his two hits on the day. Ted was cut down twice trying for extra bases.

The six losses represented the longest losing streak of the season for the Red Sox, just as they were on the brink of claiming the pennant. Joe Cronin shuffled the lineup a bit. Bill Cunningham noted in the *Boston Herald* that the Red Sox looked worn out. They were "stumbling and staggering. . . . Getting on top isn't the hard trick. It's staying up there that's really tough. When you're fighting among the crowd, competition is divided and there's no ganging on you. Furthermore there's the thrill of competition to needle you." There was even some dissension reported, including the notion that Williams and Johnny Pesky were not speaking. Williams denied it, saying that he never socialized with his teammates. He always kept to himself, he explained, and always would. "I get sick of looking at 'em out there," he said.

The Red Sox squared off against the Indians once more on September 13, the bottles back on ice again as the Indians took the field to open the game. Tex Hughson (17–11) was to be on the mound again for Boston, and the Sox faced Cleveland's Red Embree (8–11). Embree (no relation to recent Red Sox reliever Alan Embree) was known for his red hair and his curveball.

Dom DiMaggio led off and grounded to Don Ross at third. Pesky struck out. This brought up Ted Williams, and player-manager Boudreau had his fielders shift to the right side to defend against the pull-hitting Williams. Cleveland's League Park was roomy in left and left-center—375 feet down the line in left, 415 feet in left-center—but the fielders all shifted to the right. Boudreau had reiterated his thinking after the game: "Concentrating my defense in right field enables us to pitch inside and make Williams try and pull the ball. We gang up on him and we have gotten him out and will continue to get him out by playing the same way."

Left fielder Pat Seerey took a rather shallow stance in left, in part to guard against the unlikelihood of Ted bunting and trying to take two bases on a hard bunt down the third-base line. Williams ran the count to 3–1 before he found the pitch he wanted. He pounded the ball well over Seerey's head, and it rolled all the way to the base of the left-field bleachers in straightaway left. Seerey, described by Al Hirshberg as a "fat . . . notoriously slow runner," couldn't get there in time, nor could center fielder Felix Mackiewicz from well over in right-center. Hirshberg painted a picture of Seerey and Williams in motion: "a frantic, side-splitting race which looked like a sprint between a hippopotamus and a giraffe. Williams bounded around the bases in his typical gallop, while Seerey huffed and puffed in the opposite direction after the ball." By the time Seerey got to the baseball, he had difficulty picking it out of the shallow gutter at the base of the wall about 400 feet from home plate. Ted kept legging around the bases. Mackiewicz fired it in to Boudreau, but the relay was a little off and Ted beat it by about a yard, sliding across the plate for an inside-the-park home run, the only one he ever hit in his long career. Doerr grounded to third base to end the first inning, but the Red Sox had a 1–0 lead thanks to Ted.

After that, a long string of zeroes followed. Hughson handled the Indians, walking two but allowing just three hits all day—one of them to the pitcher, Embree. Meanwhile, Embree, who was not known as a dominating pitcher, did even better. After the inside-the-parker, he did not allow another hit until Pesky singled in the eighth. As the game wore on, the tension in the Sox dugout mounted. Would Ted's one run be enough?

Yes. At the end of nine, Embree had thrown a two-hitter, but Ted's first-inning home run won the game and clinched the pennant for the Red Sox. Finally.

Was it another fluke hit, like the double Ted had hit the day before? No, Ted explained to the *Boston Globe*. "I deliberately hit the ball into left field. I've been planning for weeks to beat the crazy defense Cleveland used against me. When I stepped up in the batter's circle, I noticed Red Embree had a terrific breaking curve. I knew the best place for me to hit the ball would be in left field. . . . I didn't think I'd make it, but I kept on running. . . . I was tired but happy when I hit the plate." Boudreau said he'd continue to play Williams the same way. "We're still way ahead of Ted," he said. Ted concurred: "I'm still not even with the Indians."

Joe Cronin had a few words to say: "It was the way I wanted to win. Hughson pitching a three-hitter, and Williams hitting a home run" *(Boston Post)*.

Now that the Sox had a win, all it would take was a Tiger loss to sew things up. The Red Sox game ended at 2:59 p.m. The Yankees/Tigers game began at

3:00. In that game the Yanks beat Detroit, 5–4, as Joe DiMaggio hit a two-run homer in the seventh, breaking a 3–3 tie. That clinched it. The Sox were set to go to the World Series for the first time in 28 years, the first time since 1918.

◆ Extra Innings

- After the game, Bobby Doerr, Tex Hughson, and Dom DiMaggio sent a telegram to Dom's brother Joe: "Thanks a lot for that home run, pal."

- In *My Turn at Bat*, Williams says that someone once asked him if it was the easiest homer he ever got. "Hell, no," Ted replied. "It was the hardest. I had to run."

- There was some predictable controversy when the press noted that Ted Williams skipped the postgame celebration. Wasn't that carrying the notion of keeping to himself a little too far? Actually, Williams had a good explanation and one the *Boston Globe* headlined with: he had honored a prior commitment to visit a dying World War II veteran. Hy Hurwitz wrote that Williams "had sneaked out to an army hospital to sit at the bedside of a dying veteran who had requested that the 'Kid' visit him. Williams ducked a nation-wide radio broadcast to perform a charitable act." Actually, Hughson couldn't be found, either, nor could Pesky, and Yawkey elected not to break open the champagne, saying, "I want to toss a party, but I don't want to have it unless all the players can be present." It took traveling secretary Tom Dowd four hours to round up enough players for a party in Yawkey's suite, and the celebration got under way, but it was hardly the wild sort with champagne poured on each other's heads we see today.

18

October 6, 1946: Boston at St. Louis

Glory Days

In which Boston returns to the championship stage after a 27-year absence

In 1946, the Red Sox had not won, or even appeared in, a World Series since 1918, almost 30 years. Now the long drought was over. As all the teams reassembled their full rosters in the wake of World War II, the Red Sox found themselves with a superb team and jumped out to a strong start. They were 21–3 by May 10, and had taken first place on April 28. They never looked back. The only hiccup came in the last month of the season. After Jim Bagby's

1–0 win over Washington on September 5, they needed just one win to clinch the pennant. They lost the next six games in a row, before finally winning another 1–0 game, courtesy of the only inside-the-park home run of Ted Williams's career. More than half a million fans swamped the Red Sox ticket office with requests for World Series tickets.

The early clinch left the Red Sox marking time. As they played out the regular-season schedule, they inevitably lacked some of the fire that characterized the St. Louis Cardinals, who fought the Brooklyn Dodgers right to the final day—and then some. The Cards and Dodgers tied and had to fight it out in a best-of-three playoff for the pennant, while Boston sat and waited to learn which team would be their opponent. St. Louis won.

Irving Vaughan of the *Chicago Tribune* Press Service declared that the Sox "had such a formidable lead that they merely had to stumble into a pennant" but that they should therefore be in a "delightfully relaxed state." Too relaxed, some players thought. "We kind of let down a little bit," recalled veteran infielder Don Gutteridge. "We had to wait three or four more days, and that really hurt us."

To try to stave off just such a letdown, the Sox played an exhibition game against a collection of American League all-stars, recruited to help them keep in form. But the plan backfired when in the fifth inning of the game, Mickey Haefner's first pitch hit Ted Williams in the elbow. "It swelled up like a hard-boiled egg after I came in the clubhouse," Ted told reporters. X-rays proved negative, but team physician Dr. Ralph McCarthy told the press, "Ted will be able to start the Series, but he won't have the proper use of his elbow for at least another week."

Even with Ted's injury, odds were cited at 11:5 in favor of the Red Sox. The Series opened in St. Louis. Cardinals manager Eddie Dyer decided to throw his southpaws, with Howie Pollet (21–10, league-leading 2.10 ERA) drawing the Game One start against Joe Cronin's ace Tex Hughson (20–11, 2.75). Hughson had a dizzying array of pitches, all of which moved, including a sinking fastball, both a hard curve and a slider, and he would mix in a screwball or a knuckleball a few times a game.

The game got under way in unseasonably warm weather at 82 degrees, and the Sox scored first with a run in the top of the second, taking advantage of a Pollet pitch that hit Rudy York and a walk to Bobby Doerr on a 3–2 count that moved York into scoring position. Third baseman Pinky Higgins singled to center to drive in York.

Enos Slaughter tripled with two out in the fourth, and even rounded third heading for home when shortstop Johnny Pesky fumbled the relay from Dom

DiMaggio in center. But Pesky got hold of the ball, and Slaughter retreated to third. Some reporters thought Slaughter might have made it home, and the official scorer said later that it would have been ruled an inside-the-park home run with no error if he had scored on the play. Slaughter was stranded at third.

The Cardinals did not score until the bottom of the sixth, when Red Schoendienst singled, took second on a bit of a bumble by Hughson (scored a fielder's choice), and then cruised home on Stan Musial's double off the right-field wall at Sportsman's Park—all to the delight of the largest crowd in park history. Musial took third on Tom McBride's wild throw-in. Slaughter was walked intentionally, and Hughson hit Whitey Kurowski, loading the bases, but rookie catcher Joe Garagiola struck out, and the one run was all they tallied.

St. Louis kept the pressure on in their next time at bat, when Harry Walker walked and Marty Marion sacrificed him to second. Pollet whiffed, but Schoendienst beat out an infield hit and Walker took third. Schoendienst then stole second, with Sox catcher Hal Wagner electing to throw to third rather than second, hoping to catch Walker off the bag. Now there were two men in scoring position, with two out. Hughson was unfazed. Moore flew out deep to Ted Williams in left. The score remained tied, but St. Louis would not let up.

The Redbirds broke the 1–1 tie in the bottom of the eighth. With two out, Kurowski singled down the third-base line. Garagiola drove a high fly ball deep to DiMaggio in center field, but Dominic lost sight of the ball. "The sun had nothing to do with it," Dom said after the game. "There was a funny haze between home plate and the infield." When he saw the ball and chased it

OCTOBER 6, 1946: BOSTON AT ST. LOUIS

Boston Red Sox	AB	R	H	RBI	BB	SO	PO	A	St. Louis Cardinals	AB	R	H	RBI	BB	SO	PO	A
McBride rf	5	0	1	1	0	1	1	0	Schoendienst 2b	5	1	2	0	0	0	2	5
Moses rf	0	0	0	0	0	0	1	0	Moore cf	4	0	0	0	0	1	3	1
Pesky ss	5	0	0	0	0	0	0	3	Musial 1b	5	0	1	1	0	0	13	0
DiMaggio cf	5	0	2	0	0	0	1	1	Slaughter rf	4	0	1	0	1	0	3	0
Williams lf	3	0	1	0	2	0	4	0	Kurowski 3b	3	1	1	0	0	1	1	4
York 1b	4	2	1	1	0	0	10	0	Garagiola c	4	0	1	1	0	1	4	0
Doerr 2b	4	0	1	0	1	1	4	4	Walker lf	2	0	1	0	1	1	3	0
Higgins 3b	4	0	2	1	0	0	2	0	Dusak ph,lf	1	0	0	0	0	0	0	0
Gutteridge pr	0	1	0	0	0	0	0	0	Marion ss	3	0	0	0	0	1	1	3
Johnson p	1	0	0	0	0	0	0	2	Pollet p	4	0	0	0	0	1	0	0
Wagner c	3	0	0	0	0	0	6	1	Totals	35	2	7	2	2	6	30	13
Russell ph,3b	1	0	0	0	0	0	0	0									
Hughson p	2	0	0	0	1	0	0	1									
Partee ph,c	1	0	0	0	0	1	1	0									
Totals	38	3	9	3	4	3	30	12									

Boston Red Sox	IP	H	R	ER	BB	SO	HR	St. Louis Cardinals	IP	H	R	ER	BB	SO	HR
Hughson	8	7	2	2	2	5	0	Pollet (L)	10	9	3	3	4	3	1
Johnson (W)	2	0	0	0	1	0									
Totals	10	7	2	2	2	6	0								

	1	2	3	4	5	6	7	8	9	10	R	H	E
BOS A	0	1	0	0	0	0	0	0	1	1	3	9	2
STL N	0	0	0	0	0	1	0	1	0	0	2	7	0

down, he was just a fraction of a second too late, and the ball ticked off his out-stretched glove. He fired the ball to Pesky, who expertly relayed to Higgins, and Garagiola was cut down at third—before Kurowski crossed the plate. Kurowski was awarded home plate, though, with obstruction called against Higgins for blocking him as he'd come around third. Higgins admitted he'd been in the way, so Cronin's squawk was cut short. St. Louis had a one-run lead to defend heading into the ninth inning. Pollet had given up just four hits and the one run and would be heading out to finish the job.

The Red Sox would need a run to keep their hope of taking the Series opener alive. Bobby Doerr stepped up first but struck out. Next Pinky Higgins hit a ball right to Marion at short, but it scooted through his legs. "It just stuck to the ground," said Cardinals pitcher Red Barrett. The hit was ruled a single, but no matter what the scoring decision, putting a man on at that point was a big break for Boston. Both teams agreed after the game that it was the play that turned things around. Don Gutteridge pinch-ran for Higgins while Cronin sent Rip Russell (.208 on the season) to pinch-hit for Wagner. "That was Russell's forte really," recalled Gutteridge. "He was a better pinch hitter than every-day player the way he produced all the time. He wasn't really a power hitter, more of a line drive hitter. I wasn't looking for a home run, I was looking for something in the gap." Gutteridge limbered up and got ready to run. When Russell ripped a solid single to center, Gutteridge took third. Cronin's third substitution of the inning, Roy Partee, came in to hit for Hughson. "[Cronin] was shooting the works trying to get that run," Gutteridge later said. But Partee struck out. The tying run was 90 feet from home plate, but with two out Cronin was out of options.

Tom McBride was 0-for-4 on the day; he hadn't gotten the ball out of the infield. But he went up to hit, and quickly Pollet had two strikes on him. This time, though, McBride hammered a one-hopper between short and third, and drove in Gutteridge to tie the score. "When I crossed that plate I wanted to jump so high, I was so tickled!" Gutteridge said. Johnny Pesky flew out to Enos Slaughter in right, and the Sox were retired, but they had given them-selves a chance. "The Earl of Emergency"—Earl Johnson—took over for Hughson and set the Cardinals down 1-2-3, sending the game to extra innings. Pollet had given up four hits in the last two innings, and the Sox hoped he was tiring.

In the top of the 10th, Pollet showed he still had some stuff. He got DiMaggio on a grounder to short. Ted Williams was 1-for-2 on the day, a single, and Pollet had walked him twice. In the 10th, though, Ted hit a "towering foul fly" that Musial hauled in. Two out, but the Cardinals feared York as much as

Williams. Earlier in the season, on July 27, York had hit two grand slams on the same day against the St. Louis Browns, in this very same ballpark.

Pollet's first two pitches to the veteran York were both out of the strike zone. Now down in the count, he had to get one over. "It was a fastball, inside," York would recount after the game. "At least that's what I thought it was the last time I saw it. Then I closed my eyes and swung." Cronin thought the pitch was a slow curve. The *Herald*'s Burt Whitman thought it a change of pace. Pollet himself said it was a "fast curve"—the same pitch he'd gotten York on twice before. Whatever pitch it was, York converted it into an arcing shot traveling 410 to 450 feet, and snared one-handed by a "steel-fisted fan." In the dressing room after Game One, York said, "I stopped at second to watch it." York's homer landed in the very last row of the left-field bleachers to give the Red Sox a 3–2 lead. Doerr singled, but Earl Johnson's ground ball forced Doerr at second base. Now if only the Sox could get three more outs!

Johnson didn't have an easy time of it. Pesky erred on Schoendienst's ground ball, and Terry Moore sacrificed Schoendienst to second. With the Cardinals' best two hitters—Stan Musial and Enos Slaughter—coming to the plate, Cronin took McBride out of right field, replacing him with the more experienced Wally Moses. Musial grounded to Doerr, but Schoendienst took third on the play. With two out, Slaughter hit a ball to right-center field, but Moses ran it down for the final out. Boston had scratched out a victory in the first game of the World Series, 3–2, in 10 innings.

In the clubhouse after the game, Hal Wagner jumped on a trunk wearing just his shorts and shouted, "Let's give a little hand to ol' Rudolph!" York took a deep bow to sustained applause. He was one of only three Red Sox with previous Series experience; Gutteridge and Higgins were the other two. (The Cardinals, by contrast, had 15 players with Fall Classic résumés.) York had gone 11-for-54 for the Tigers in two Octobers. The Tigers had given up on him, yet here was York again in another World Series, powering out a game-winning homer. He used a bat that Hank Greenberg had given him.

Earl Johnson won a lot of praise for staying calm and shutting down St. Louis. Johnson was a true war hero who had earned a couple of battlefield medals in the Battle of the Bulge. "That Johnson's not bad for a boy who had 190 straight days of combat," crowed Joe Cronin. With the win, the odds increased, making the Sox 5-to-1 favorites to win the World Series.

Extra Innings

- In the daily column Ted Williams wrote for the *Boston Globe* on October 1, he admitted betting on a World Series game—back in 1931 at age 13, when he'd been rooting for the St. Louis Cardinals. The junior high school student wagered 25 cents on the Cardinals to win, and presumably collected, since they defeated the Philadelphia Athletics, four games to three.

- Dyer pulled an extreme "Cleveland shift" on Ted Williams—moving the third baseman to the other side of the second-base bag but leaving the shortstop in place. The strategy worked in the second inning, but in the sixth Ted singled past the unorthodox defense. He wrote in his column, "I got a single into right field over the third baseman's head. Brother, that's one for the books."

October 15, 1946: Boston at St. Louis

Dash of Bitters

In which the Red Sox are Slaughtered by aggressive baserunning

Though heavy favorites to win the 1946 World Series, particularly after the hard-fought win in Game One, the Red Sox could only seem to win every other game. Boston took Games One, Three, and Five, while St. Louis took the even-numbered games. Game Seven presented itself as a rematch of the Game Three starters, Murry Dickson and Boo Ferriss. During the regular season, Dickson had been 15–6, with a 2.88 ERA, for the best winning percentage in the National League (.714). Ferriss had the best winning percentage in the AL, with a 25–6 mark (.806). His ERA was 3.25. Ferriss had thrown a six-hit shutout in Game Three, Rudy York's three-run homer provided the offense, and Sox fans hoped for similar results.

The team that scored first won each of the first six games. The Red Sox didn't waste time putting a run on the Sportsman's Park scoreboard. Leadoff hitter Wally Moses singled up the middle, and Johnny Pesky hit Dickson's first pitch for another single over second base. Moses took third on Pesky's hit, and scored a moment later on Dom DiMaggio's long fly ball to right. Ted Williams hit an even longer shot, but it was caught, too, and York popped up. The Cardinals tied the score in the bottom of the second when Whitey Kurowski doubled, moved up, then—like Moses—tagged and scored on a fly ball. Neither team scored again until the bottom of the fifth, when St. Louis opened up a lead when the pitcher, Dickson, doubled in Harry Walker. On the next pitch, Red Schoendienst singled to score Dickson. The Cards held the 3–1 lead until the Boston eighth.

Rip Russell, who'd had the key pinch hit in Game One, was called on for the second time in the Series to hit for Hal Wagner, and he came through again, with a single into center field. Joe Dobson was pitching in relief of Ferriss at this point, so Cronin called on another pinch hitter, Catfish Metkovich. The move paid off as Metkovich shot a double into the left-field corner. Russell, perhaps wisely, was held at third base, though he might have made it home. Eddie Dyer changed pitchers, bringing in Harry Brecheen, who had won Games Two and Six. Brecheen blew three pitches by Moses. Pesky hit a sinking liner, but it didn't sink fast enough, and the speedy right fielder, Enos Slaughter, raced in and caught it, holding the runners on the bases. Four outs to go and, against all odds, the Cardinals would win the World Series.

Dom DiMaggio stepped up to the plate. Home plate umpire Al Barlick reportedly told him, "Moses took a strike right down the middle." Dominic banged Brecheen's offering high off the wall over Slaughter's reach in right-center field for a two-base hit, scoring both pinch hitters and tying the score

Johnny Pesky

OCTOBER 15, 1946: BOSTON AT ST. LOUIS

Boston Red Sox	AB	R	H	RBI	BB	SO	PO	A	St. Louis Cardinals	AB	R	H	RBI	BB	SO	PO	A
Moses rf	4	1	1	0	0	1	1	0	Schoendienst 2b	4	0	2	1	0	1	2	3
Pesky ss	4	0	1	0	0	0	2	1	Moore cf	4	0	1	0	0	0	3	0
DiMaggio cf	3	0	1	3	1	1	0	0	Musial 1b	3	0	1	0	1	0	6	0
Culberson pr,cf	0	0	0	0	0	0	0	0	Slaughter rf	3	1	1	0	1	1	4	0
Williams lf	4	0	0	0	0	0	3	1	Kurowski 3b	4	1	1	0	0	0	3	1
York 1b	4	0	1	0	0	2	10	1	Garagiola c	3	0	0	0	0	1	4	0
Campbell pr	0	0	0	0	0	0	0	0	Rice c	1	0	0	0	0	0	0	0
Doerr 2b	4	0	2	0	0	0	3	7	Walker lf	3	1	2	2	1	0	3	0
Higgins 3b	4	0	0	0	0	0	0	1	Marion ss	2	0	0	1	0	2	1
Wagner c	2	0	0	0	0	0	4	0	Dickson p	3	1	1	1	0	1	0	1
Russell ph	1	1	1	0	0	0	0	0	Brecheen p	1	0	0	0	0	0	0	0
Partee c	1	0	0	0	0	0	0	0	**Totals**	**31**	**4**	**9**	**4**	**4**	**4**	**27**	**6**
Ferriss p	2	0	0	0	0	0	0	0									
Dobson p	0	0	0	0	0	0	0	1									
Metkovich ph	1	1	1	0	0	0	0	0									
Klinger p	0	0	0	0	0	0	1	0									
Johnson p	0	0	0	0	0	0	0	0									
McBride ph	1	0	0	0	0	0	0	0									
Totals	**35**	**3**	**8**	**3**	**1**	**4**	**24**	**12**									

Boston Red Sox	IP	H	R	ER	BB	SO	HR	St. Louis Cardinals	IP	H	R	ER	BB	SO	HR
Ferriss	4.1	7	3	3	1	2	0	Dickson	7	5	3	3	1	3	0
Dobson	2.2	0	0	0	2	2	0	Brecheen (W)	2	3	0	0	0	1	0
Klinger (L)	0.2	2	1	1	1	0	0	**Totals**	**9**	**8**	**3**	**3**	**1**	**4**	**0**
Johnson	0.1	0	0	0	0	0	0								
Totals	**8**	**9**	**4**	**4**	**4**	**4**	**0**								

	1	2	3	4	5	6	7	8	9	R	H	E
BOS A	1	0	0	0	0	0	0	2	0	3	8	0
STL N	0	1	0	0	2	0	0	1	x	4	9	1

at 3–3. Three games each, now three runs each in Game Seven. But Dom hoped the Sox could go up 4–3. With thoughts of stretching his hit to a triple, DiMaggio really turned it on, but came up lame. He had to pull up at second and, worse, leave the game. "I knew if I could get to third base they'd have to be very careful how they pitched to Ted, because I'd be ready to score from third even on a passed ball. I tried to dig for a little more speed and I pulled a hamstring heading into second base," Dom recalled. Leon Culberson went in to run for him. The Sox had the tie-breaking run in scoring position and Ted Williams at the plate.

It had been a disappointing Series for Williams, who was 5-for-24 (.208) with just one RBI. He'd walked five times, but also very uncharacteristically struck out five times. The biggest headline he earned in the World Series was when he bunted for a base hit in an earlier game. Ted had two elements working against him, his injured elbow, and the fact that Eddie Dyer had scouted him so carefully. Having noted that the Yankees had held Williams to an average of under .200 on the season, Dyer figured he'd better learn how to do the same. If he could succeed, it wouldn't be the first time a star batter had underperformed in the Series. Honus Wagner hit .222 in 1903, Ty Cobb hit .200

in his first Series (1907), and Babe Ruth was 1-for-11 in the three Series he played for the Red Sox, and only 7-for-33 in his first two Series with New York, a mere .212.

Ted fouled one off Joe Garagiola's hand, and the catcher had to leave the game. He hit another ball, harder, and high in the air, but just to short right, and second baseman Schoendienst made the catch to retire the side.

The Red Sox took the field in the bottom of the eighth. Replacing Wagner behind the plate was Roy Partee, but more significantly, Leon Culberson took DiMaggio's place in center. DiMaggio was one of the best defensive center fielders the Sox have ever enjoyed. Culberson was not. To pitch, Cronin might have chosen Earl Johnson, at least to face Slaughter, who'd hit an even .300 on the season, led the league in RBIs, and was having a good World Series. But the Red Sox manager called on right-hander Bob Klinger to take the mound, despite both leadoff batter Enos "Country" Slaughter and the fourth man due up, Harry "the Hat" Walker, being left-handed hitters. Klinger also hadn't pitched in nearly two weeks since he had left the Sox when his son reportedly contracted polio. He'd started just once all year. The *Chicago Tribune* called Klinger "a National League discard and a second stringer." But Klinger had led the American League in saves in 1946, with nine, and had a 2.37 ERA in 57 innings of work.

Slaughter singled. Kurowski tried to move him to second, but did the Sox a favor and popped up his bunt attempt to Klinger. Del Rice hit a high fly ball to left field, but Ted Williams reeled it in. Now the second left-handed hitter was up, and Walker hit a fairly routine ball into center field, a little shaded over toward left. DiMaggio would almost certainly have caught up to it, with ease, and retired the side. Culberson was no DiMaggio. He angled back a bit, and fielded the ball on one bounce, and lofted the ball ("an unforgivably lazy lob" in the words of the *Washington Post*'s Shirley Povich) to the cutoff man, Johnny Pesky, who came out toward center to take the throw. What no one seemed to have seen was that Slaughter was off before the pitch had left Klinger's hand, and almost at second base by the time of contact. He kept running to third—and then just kept going, streaking for home. By the time Pesky caught the ball, Slaughter was well on his way to the plate. Pesky hurriedly threw home, but Partee had to come up the line maybe eight or nine feet to get to the ball.

Slaughter scored amid a "frenzy of excitement" from the "wildly cheering crowd" *(Boston Herald)* of hometown fans. His "mad dash" gave the Cardinals the go-ahead run, 4–3. Walker's hit was scored a double, but sportswriter Bob Broeg protested the scorer's decision at the time. "Gentlemen, you know what?

By scoring this a double, you've taken the romance out of a great run." Give Slaughter credit for scoring all the way from first base on a routine single. He later added, "I'm very sensitive about that, because it's not fair to Pesky and it's not fair to Slaughter." Walker agreed, but it was a moot point. And the Cardinals were pretty happy, in any event. The Sox walked Marty Marion intentionally to get to Brecheen, who grounded out. But if the Cardinals could get three outs they'd sew up the Series.

The ninth inning started off in promising fashion for the Red Sox. York singled into left field, by the third baseman. Paul Campbell was inserted to run for York. Doerr singled. With men on first and second and nobody out, needing just one run to tie the game, Pinky Higgins laid down a sacrifice bunt to draw Kurowski in from third, but hit it too hard and Kurowski nipped Doerr at second. Nevertheless, Campbell was on third with just one out, and the slow Higgins on first. Partee was catching instead of the .230 hitter Hal Wagner. Partee had hit .315, but only driven in nine runs in his 111 at-bats. On a 1–2 count he fouled out to the first baseman, Stan Musial. Two out. Earl Johnson was due up; Cronin asked Tom McBride (.301) to hit for him.

Brecheen threw a screwball, what he described as "the nicest pitch I think I made all season. . . . It broke nicely so that Tom couldn't do much with it." McBride hit a roller to Schoendienst, who fumbled the ball briefly but recovered and flipped it to Marty Marion covering second base. Higgins was forced out for the final out of the World Series. Brecheen won his third game. Rogers Hornsby expressed what became accepted wisdom: the Sox, he said, "won the pennant too easily and too quickly. They tapered off and Joe Cronin never really got them going again. In contrast, the Cards had to fight for their lives all the way and never lost that fine edge which they carried right into the series and down to the final out." It would be another 21 years before the Sox appeared in another World Series.

◢ Extra Innings

- Did Pesky "hold the ball" and deserve to be branded the goat? Slaughter, interviewed in March 2000 for a book on Pesky, said, "I think Johnny did his job and he did it well. You can't blame him. I blame the second baseman and the third baseman for not letting him know. You can't see nobody out your rear end." Slaughter also explained that an aggressive baserunning strategy had been approved mere days before. "In an early game, I tripled and Mike Gonzalez stopped me at third on the play. We lost that game, and I could have scored easy. So Eddie Dyer, the manager, told me that if I thought I had a chance to score like that, he said for me to go ahead and gamble and he'd be responsible. When I hit second base, I knew I was going to try to score."

- The *Boston American*'s Huck Finnegan agreed with Bob Broeg: "Instead of looking for a goat, however, it would have been wiser simply to credit Slaughter with a daring and imaginative piece of baserunning."

- DiMaggio still wishes he'd been in center field. "Had I been in center field, maybe John would have never had to handle that ball. I don't see how I would have ever thrown the ball to John. Culberson had to back up on the ball. Had he been positioned correctly, it would have made a big difference. I maintained from the beginning that I might have even had a play on Slaughter at third base." Existing films show no definitive hesitation on Pesky's part. The idea that Pesky "held the ball" may have been invented by sportswriters in the press box that day who had not had their eyes on Slaughter and could not imagine how he scampered all the way from first to home on a routine single without some "help" from Pesky.

- Pesky himself said, "When Walker hit the ball I didn't think Slaughter would dare to take more than two bases, not even after Culby fumbled momentarily. I went out to meet the throw and had my back to the infield. I heard Bobby [Doerr] yelling at me. He must have been telling me to throw home, but I couldn't make out what he was saying, because of the noise of the crowd. When I turned and saw Slaughter going all the way, I guess I was dumbstruck. He had six or eight steps on me, I just couldn't seem to make myself throw quickly enough, and when I finally did get rid of it, I knew I couldn't hit him with a .22."

- Any World Series loss produces its possible goats, and when a team doesn't win a World Series for 86 years, the fans look for someone to blame. Ted Williams came in for his share of criticism, too, the injured elbow forgotten. Though he threw out one runner at the plate and another, in Game Seven, at second base, it was with his bat that Ted was supposed to excel. Williams, the 1946 MVP with a league-leading 156 RBIs, batted just .200 and had one RBI. The Cardinals' Stan Musial didn't do that much better; Stan the Man hit .222 but he did drive in four. Talking about Ted, Cards manager Dyer said, "I want to confess I held my breath every time Ted Williams came to bat. He's a great hitter and likely to break up a ball game every time he swings his bat. Fortunately we faced him when he was not going good."

20

August 17, 1947: Boston at New York

Denny's the Menace

In which the workhorse of the staff outpaces New York

Anytime the Red Sox beat the Yankees, it's a great game, but especially when the win comes on the heels of two tough defeats. In 1947, the Sox were reigning American League pennant winners, but by mid-August they were in second place, only mathematically still in the race, lagging about a dozen games behind the Yankees.

New York was particularly hard to beat in Yankee Stadium. The Sox had been swept in a four-game set there at the end of May and had lost six out of their seven games in the Bronx. Returning on August 15, they scored four times in the top of the second, but momentary hopes were soon deflated by the six runs the Yanks put across in their half of the inning. Boston lost again, 10–6. On the 16th, New York's Bobo Newsom held the Sox scoreless through nine innings. The Red Sox started Earl Johnson, the lefty whom the *New York Times* called "the fork-hand flipping Johnson," and he pitched brilliantly, too. When he took the mound to try to close out the ninth, he had thrown 23⅔ straight scoreless innings, but here his string ran out. The Yankees loaded the bases, then won the game 1–0 on Johnny Lindell's sharp single to left through a drawn-in infield.

On the 17th, the two teams met again. The Sox were 13½ games behind the Yankees. The Sox were down, but they hadn't given up. On the way to the ballpark, Sox traveling secretary Tom Dowd saw the bus driver taking an unfamiliar route from the hotel to the Stadium. "Where are you going, Bussy?" he cried. "Down Victory Road!" shouted Birdie Tebbetts.

Vic Raschi pitched for the Yankees and Denny Galehouse went for the Red Sox. Raschi had been 2–0 in 1946, and had been recalled from Portland to help the Yanks for the pennant drive. Help he did; he won his first six decisions. This day he pitched superbly as well, holding Boston to just two hits, without a single walk, in his first nine innings. No Red Sox runner even reached second base in that span.

But Galehouse got the Yankees out, too—four scattered hits were all they could muster in nine innings of work. Denny was a fastball pitcher who came up with the Indians and then spent two years with the Red Sox in 1939 and 1940. After several years with the St. Louis Browns, in 1947 he was sold back to the Sox and was reunited with Browns' teammate Don Gutteridge. In

AUGUST 17, 1947: BOSTON AT NEW YORK											
Boston Red Sox	**AB**	**R**	**H**	**PO**	**A**	**New York Yankees**	**AB**	**R**	**H**	**PO**	**A**
Mele rf	5	1	1	4	0	Stirnweiss 2b	5	0	2	4	3
Pesky ss	5	0	1	0	6	Rizzuto ss	5	0	0	1	1
D. DiMaggio cf	4	0	1	4	0	Clark rf	5	0	0	2	0
Williams lf	5	0	1	4	0	J. DiMaggio cf	5	0	2	0	1
Doerr 2b	4	0	1	1	4	McQuinn 1b	4	0	0	12	1
Jones 1b	4	0	0	18	0	Johnson 3b	4	0	0	3	7
Tebbetts c	4	0	2	2	1	Lindell lf	3	0	2	3	0
Gutteridge pr	0	1	0	0	0	Robinson c	3	0	0	7	0
Partee c	0	0	0	1	0	Raschi p	4	0	0	1	3
Dente 3b	4	1	1	1	2	**Totals**	**38**	**0**	**6**	**33**	**16**
Galehouse p	3	0	0	0	3						
Totals	**38**	**3**	**8**	**33**	**16**						

Boston Red Sox	**IP**	**H**	**R**	**ER**	**BB**	**SO**	**New York Yankees**	**IP**	**H**	**R**	**ER**	**BB**	**SO**
Galehouse (W)	11	6	0	0	2	3	Raschi (L)	11	8	3	3	1	6

	1	2	3	4	5	6	7	8	9	10	11		R	H	E
BOS A	0	0	0	0	0	0	0	0	0	0	3		3	6	0
NY A	0	0	0	0	0	0	0	0	0	0	0		0	6	1

Gutteridge's words, Galehouse was "a workhorse. Even with the old Browns, he didn't want anybody coming out and taking his place. He didn't want nobody taking him out." And after nine innings, no one did. Nor 10, nor 11.

The defense of the DiMaggio brothers had something to do with the lack of scoring. In the bottom of the eighth, with one out, Lindell doubled down the left-field line. Up strode Snuffy Stirnweiss, and he lifted a fly to short left-center that seemed sure to drop in. Both Ted Williams and Dom DiMaggio ran for the ball, but DiMaggio put on an extra burst of speed and "captured the ball off his toe-tops. Even Yankee fans arose and applauded as he came in to the Boston dugout" *(Boston Globe)*. Williams had made a big play in the fourth inning, "perhaps the best catch of his entire career," running down a 400-plus-foot Joe D drive with his back to the plate.

In the 10th, Ted doubled to center, and Bobby Doerr followed with a "harsh ground single" to center, but Joe DiMaggio paid Ted back for the play the Kid had made earlier in the game; he charged the ball "like an infielder, grabbed it and cut loose a dazzling throw to the plate that cut down Williams and prevented a Boston run." Joe's brother Dom said, "That's the best throw I've seen him make in a long time." The Yankees had now shut out the Sox for 23 consecutive scoreless innings. But like Earl Johnson's 23⅔-inning streak, all good things must come to an end.

In the 11th, the Yankee defense crumbled. Birdie Tebbetts doubled straight down the left-field line, inches fair as it shot past third base. Don Gutteridge came in as a pinch runner. Sam Dente bunted between Raschi and third baseman Billy Johnson, and Raschi pounced on the ball with an eye to throwing out the runner at third. With Johnson charging the bunt as well, though, there was no one covering third, and both runners were safe. Galehouse himself now came to the plate with the chance to drive in the go-ahead run, but his heroics for the day were confined to the mound. He moved Dente over to second with a bunt of his own, while Gutteridge held at third, bringing Sox rookie Sam Mele to the plate.

Mele didn't wait. On the first pitch, he singled both runners home, and took second on Lindell's late throw to the plate. Johnny Pesky knocked in Mele from second on a ball hit right through Raschi—but then got picked off first. Dom DiMaggio walked, but Ted Williams struck out to end the inning.

Now it was Galehouse's job to prevent another Yankee uprising. Staked to a 3–0 lead, he yielded a single to Stuffy Stirnweiss but struck out Phil Rizzuto. Allie Clark flew out to DiMaggio in center, and then Joe D also flew out to his brother to close the game. Denny Galehouse had a nice 3–0 complete-game, 11-inning shutout, and the Red Sox a piece of vindication in the Bronx.

Extra Innings

- This win may have affected the route the Red Sox took for years to come. "Ballplayers being superstitious," wrote Herb Ralby for the *Globe*, "it is most probable that from now on the Red Sox will insist upon their special bus taking that new route, when in New York, to the Yankee Stadium."

- Was this game on Joe McCarthy's mind on October 4, 1948, when he needed one pitcher to face the Cleveland Indians in the single-game playoff to determine the winner of the 1948 pennant, and he chose Galehouse? We can't ever know. McCarthy had left the Yankees after 1946, and after a year out of baseball, signed to manage the Red Sox at the end of the 1947 season. Birdie Tebbetts said he made a tape recording telling the true story of that 1948 playoff game and placed it in his attic, and that all would be revealed after he died. Tebbetts's relatives, though, have been unable to locate the tape.

21

October 4, 1948: Cleveland at Boston

Fit to Be Tied

In which the American League flag comes down to winner-take-all

As the 1948 season drew to a close, three teams were still in the hunt for the AL pennant. The Sox had fought hard to climb into contention. It was not impossible, but, in the words of the *Boston Herald*'s Arthur Stratton, it was a "fantastic dream." When September ended, the Red Sox and the Yankees were tied for second place, with two games left on the schedule—against each other.

The Tigers came from behind to beat first-place Cleveland on October 1; the winning blow in the ninth was a single by Little Jimmy Outlaw. On the second, Boston beat New York while Cleveland won, so the Yankees were out of the running. If Boston beat New York again, and the Tigers beat the Indians, there would be a two-way tie at the top. That's precisely what occurred.

The Fenway faithful were scoreboard-watching, attentive to the Cleveland game in progress, and when the "small, unseen man who lives in the scoreboard" took down starter Bob Feller's number 19 and replaced it with a 26, they knew a Tiger rally had driven the Cleveland ace from the mound. "You should have heard that crowd," wrote Red Smith. "Everybody was on his feet, and everybody was screaming." The Tigers won, 7–1. With a five-run third and a four-run sixth, the Sox beat the Yankees 10–5. Many fans simply left their seats after the win over the Yankees and got right in line for the playoff tickets that would go on sale the following morning.

Boston and Cleveland ended the season in a tie, and for the first time in American League history, there would be a single-game playoff—at Fenway Park. Should the Sox win, they would face the Boston Braves in the World Series, for a "streetcar series." The two parks were 1.3 miles apart. This was to be the game of games. "I frankly don't know who I'll pitch," Red Sox manager Joe McCarthy told the *Boston Globe* right after the Yankee game. "I'll have to have time to think, to check up. We had men working in the bullpen all afternoon. I'll have to find out who did what, who's ready, before I can answer that."

The *Globe*'s Harold Kaese reported optimism: the Sox were surging; the Indians were sagging. The Red Sox had a 55–22 home record. Thousands of fans camped out overnight in lines that completely encircled the ballpark, and a near-riot ensued once the ticket windows were thrown open. The Boston City Council canceled its meeting on October 4, since 20 of the 22 councilors were going to the game.

Both managers played the choice of pitchers close to their chests. Cleveland's Lou Boudreau had both Bob Lemon and Bob Feller throwing in the bullpen before the game, but at nearly the last minute unveiled his real choice: the rookie left-hander Gene Bearden, who had already won 19 games and was leading the league in ERA. He'd thrown a shutout just two days before, though, so was pitching on one day's rest. Everyone assumed McCarthy would start either Ellis Kinder (10–7) or the rookie Mel Parnell (15–8). McCarthy chose Denny Galehouse, though, a veteran of 14 years and 109 major league wins. It was a gut call. McCarthy ignored some key data—including the very bullpen data he said he was going to research. In a 1988 interview, Galehouse told Glenn Stout that McCarthy had told him to get loose during the fourth inning the day before, and never called to tell him it was okay to sit down. "So I threw six innings the day before. I don't think people in Boston knew I'd threw for those six innings." McCarthy told Galehouse on Sunday morning, the day of the game, but told him to keep it secret: "Wander around the outfield." The rest of the Red Sox were taken aback, since they knew that both Kinder and Parnell were ready to go.

Joe McCarthy

Galehouse did have a winning record, but not by much. He was 8–7 on the season. He finished the regular season with a 4.00 ERA. This was the biggest game of his life—the game that could get the Red Sox back into the World Series. Much of the 1946 team was still intact and looking forward to redemption after the 1946 loss to the Cardinals.

Galehouse retired the first two Indians, though Dale Mitchell's drive to left backed Ted Williams up against the wall and he had to stretch to haul it in. Then player-manager Lou Boudreau stepped in—and hit the ball on the nose, right off the top of the wall and into the screen in left. Galehouse got the next man out to end the inning down 1–0.

The Sox quickly tied the game when Johnny Pesky doubled deep to right-center in the first and scored on Vern Stephens's single. In the second, the Sox looked to get ahead when Stan Spence walked to lead off the inning, but a strike-'em-out, throw-'em-out double play killed the budding rally as Billy Goodman took a called third strike and Jim Hegan threw to Boudreau covering the second-base bag. Boudreau had both Lemon and Feller warming up at one time or another, but even though the Sox got a single and then Galehouse walked, they couldn't cash in.

Galehouse meanwhile gave up a single in the second and walked the pitcher, Bearden, in the third, but was doing well enough until Boudreau came up to bat again. He led off the top of the fourth with a single to left. Joe Gordon singled to left, too. Next came Ken Keltner, who had dented the wall for a single his first time up. At 2:21 p.m. he "kissed the casaba into the high left-field cordage" (Bill Cunningham, *Boston Herald*)—in other words, he homered into the netting. That was bad news: a three-run homer and a three-run lead for the Indians. McCarthy pulled Galehouse and put in Kinder. Larry Doby greeted him with a double off the wall and scored on a grounder after he'd been sacrificed to third. The Indians had a 5–1 lead.

They added another run in the fifth inning. Boudreau was up again, and he hit another homer well up in the screen: 6–1 Indians. The Boston audience accorded him a round of applause; he'd come through in the clutch. Big time. And Bearden kept bowling down the Bosox. The next time Boudreau came up, he was walked intentionally.

The Sox mounted a rally in the bottom of the sixth. Ted Williams reached on an error; with two out, Bobby Doerr hit a home run high over the wall to bring the score to 6–3. But the Red Sox could not find much traction. In the final three innings, Williams singled and a couple of players walked, but could not score again. Meanwhile, the Indians continued to tack on runs, one coming on an eighth-inning error by Williams (after Larry Doby had again doubled off the wall) and the other on a bases-loaded double play in the ninth. Earlier in the summertime, Indians owner Bill Veeck was said to have threatened to "jump off the highest bridge" in Cleveland if his team didn't win the pennant *(New York Times)*. He was spared the necessity. It was Cleveland's first pennant since 1920, and a few other lives may have been spared as well.

OCTOBER 4, 1948: CLEVELAND AT BOSTON

Cleveland Indians	AB	R	H	RBI	BB	SO	PO	A	Boston Red Sox	AB	R	H	RBI	BB	SO	PO	A
Mitchell lf	5	0	1	0	0	0	1	0	DiMaggio cf	4	0	0	0	0	0	3	0
Clark 1b	2	0	0	0	0	0	5	0	Pesky 3b	4	1	1	0	0	1	3	3
Robinson 1b	2	1	1	0	0	0	9	0	Williams lf	4	1	1	0	0	0	3	0
Boudreau ss	4	3	4	2	1	0	3	5	Stephens ss	4	0	1	1	0	1	2	4
Gordon 2b	4	1	1	0	1	0	2	3	Doerr 2b	4	1	1	2	0	1	5	2
Keltner 3b	5	1	3	3	0	0	0	6	Spence rf	1	0	0	0	2	1	1	0
Doby cf	5	1	2	0	0	1	1	0	Hitchcock ph	0	0	0	0	1	0	0	0
Kennedy rf	2	0	0	0	0	0	0	0	Wright pr	0	0	0	0	0	0	0	0
Hegan c	3	1	0	1	1	2	6	1	Goodman 1b	3	0	0	0	1	2	7	1
Bearden p	3	0	1	0	1	0	0	2	Tebbetts c	4	0	1	0	0	0	3	1
Totals	35	8	13	6	4	3	27	17	Galehouse p	0	0	0	0	1	0	0	1
									Kinder p	2	0	0	0	0	0	0	1
									Totals	30	3	5	3	5	6	27	13

Cleveland Indians	IP	H	R	ER	BB	SO		Boston Red Sox	IP	H	R	ER	BB	SO
Bearden (W)	9	5	3	1	5	6		Galehouse (L)	3	5	4	4	1	1
								Kinder	6	8	4	3	3	2
								Totals	9	13	8	7	4	3

	1	2	3	4	5	6	7	8	9	R	H	E
CLE A	1	0	0	4	1	0	0	1	1	8	13	1
BOS A	1	0	0	0	0	2	0	0	0	3	5	1

Edward Burns wrote that Keltner's home run "probably saved the lives of all the Clevelanders who were planning to wade into Lake Erie until their new fall fedoras floated" *(Chicago Tribune)*. But Lou Boudreau was the clear star of the game. Ed Rumill of the *Christian Science Monitor* summed it up: "All the Cleveland skipper did to help eliminate the Red Sox was hit two home runs and two singles, handle eight shortstop chances in the field and figure in two important double plays. And on the side, of course, he directed the strategy of the club. Could one man do more?"

The Indians collected three home runs, three doubles—13 hits in all—off the Sox staff, and won the game (and the pennant), 8–3. After it was over, Burt Whitman of the *Herald* wrote, "On all sides now you will hear the quick admission that with their pitching staff the Hub Hose were lucky to come so close to the league pennant as a play-off." Bill Cunningham termed it "a miracle to rank beside the Berlin airlift."

Extra Innings

- The following day, Bob Holbrook of the *Boston Globe* explained the choice of Galehouse, referring to a game against Cleveland earlier in the season. On July 30, 1948, Galehouse had been called on to spell Parnell in long relief—and threw 8⅔ innings of one-hit ball. McCarthy remembered that, and wanted a right-hander to pitch to the Indians. The manager's selective memory apparently overlooked the six innings in the bullpen the day before, and disregarded the 9–0 defeat the Indians administered to Galehouse on August 25, not to mention the fact that he'd been pounded in his previous two outings.

- Maybe McCarthy figured he'd confuse Boudreau, catching him so off-guard that he'd be flustered. If that was the strategy, maybe he should have started Ted Williams instead. Williams had been a mound ace in high school, and had even thrown two innings in a 1940 major league game. He gave up one run on three hits, didn't walk a batter, and even struck out Rudy York. His lifetime ERA stands at 4.50. Seeing as how he didn't help much with the bat in the 1948 playoff game (a single in four at-bats, and an error in the field), and seeing as how Galehouse gave up four runs in three innings, it might have at least produced a more memorable outcome.

- Bearden held the Sox to five hits and two runs, only one of which was earned. Boudreau had chosen Bearden the day before, and let him know, but kept the selection from the press to reduce any pressure they might place on him with their questions. He was a rookie, but he was also a war hero who won a Purple Heart in World War II. A machinist's mate, he was among the survivors when three torpedoes hit the USS *Helena* on July 6, 1943. Badly wounded, Bearden was hospitalized for two years, and forever after carried a steel plate in his head.

22

June 24, 1949: St. Louis at Boston

21-Gun Salute

In which Boston delivers a pasting of epic proportions

It started off as just another day in late June. The Red Sox were in fifth place, but with their .533 winning percentage, they had a good shot to be in it right to the finish, so each game counted. The perennially hapless St. Louis Browns were in their accustomed cellar spot, but the Sox knew they weren't automatic pushovers; the Browns had swept the Red Sox in a three-game set in St. Louis earlier in the month.

Mickey McDermott gave out the goose eggs on June 23, though, blanking the Browns 7–0 at Fenway. Then on June 24, Ellis Kinder took on the mound once more, up against "Professor" Joe Ostrowski. Kinder had been knocked out after 1⅔ innings in his St. Louis outing, and the Sox hoped to avoid another lopsided result like the 11–0 drubbing they'd taken that day. "Old Folks" Kinder had not come to the majors until after his 31st birthday, and had pitched his first two years for these same Browns before coming to the Sox. Perhaps the Browns knew his change of pace (his best pitch) and slider too well? He got the first two Brownies out, but then Whitey Platt connected for one of his 13 career home runs, deep to left. But Kinder escaped the inning before further damage could be done when Dick Kokos popped up.

Dom DiMaggio singled to center to lead things off for the Sox. Johnny Pesky upped the ante with a double to right, and Ted Williams trumped that with a three-run homer six rows up into the straightaway-center-field seats. No 11–0 shutout this time! The Red Sox sent nine men to the plate in the bottom of the first, but the three from Ted's homer were all they got. They left the bases loaded when Kinder grounded out to end the inning.

Kinder settled down somewhat, but gave up another gopher ball in the third, when Browns' second baseman Andy Anderson hit one of his two career home runs, also to deep left. But once again, that was all St. Louis did against

Kinder, and in the bottom of the inning, Kinder helped get the run back. With one out, Billy Goodman singled for the Sox. Then Al Zarilla singled and Birdie Tebbetts singled, driving in Goodman. Kinder was up again, and he singled, too, scoring Goodman. Red Sox 5, Browns 2.

From that point on, Kinder was finished with home runs. In fact, he was pretty much finished with hits. There were just two singles off him in the remaining six frames, and the game began to get lopsided, this time in the Red Sox' favor. After Pesky singled and Williams walked to lead off the fourth, Al Papai replaced Ostrowski. Vern Stephens singled. Doerr walked. Goodman singled. After Zarilla grounded out, knocking in the inning's fourth run, Tebbetts was walked intentionally to get to Kinder, who popped up foul to the catcher. Dom DiMaggio, though, who'd hit into a double play to end the third, this time hit a double off the wall to score Goodman. Ray Shore relieved Papai, walked Pesky, but, in an at-bat he surely never forgot, struck out Ted Williams to end the inning. By the end of the fourth, the score stood 10–2 Boston.

The Sox added four more in the fifth—starting with a single, a walk, a single, and a walk. Even the outs produced runs. Tebbetts flew out, but Doerr tagged and scored. After Kinder walked, DiMaggio grounded into a force play at second, but Goodman scored on the play. Pesky walked and then Williams walked, but Vern Stephens forced Williams at second.

Boston added another two in the sixth, on Goodman's double and then another rash of singles. With the score 16–2 at the two-thirds point of the game, St. Louis simply decided to stick with Shore right to the end.

JUNE 24, 1949: ST. LOUIS AT BOSTON

St. Louis Browns	AB	R	H	RBI	PO	A	Boston Red Sox	AB	R	H	RBI	PO	A
Sullivan ss	3	0	1	0	0	5	DiMaggio cf	7	2	4	3	2	0
Spence cf	3	0	0	0	3	0	Pesky 3b	4	3	3	0	3	1
Platt lf	4	1	1	1	1	0	Williams lf	5	4	3	7	3	0
Kokos rf	4	0	0	0	2	0	Stephens ss	7	2	3	1	2	4
Stevens 3b	4	0	0	0	0	1	Doerr 2b	4	2	1	1	3	3
Lollar c	3	0	1	0	5	0	Goodman 1b	7	4	5	3	8	0
Graham 1b	3	0	0	0	6	1	Zarilla rf	5	3	2	2	3	0
Anderson 2b	3	1	1	1	6	2	Tebbetts c	4	0	2	2	3	0
Ostrowski p	1	0	1	0	0	1	Kinder p	5	1	2	1	0	1
Papai p	0	0	0	0	1	0	**Totals**	**48**	**21**	**25**	**20**	**27**	**9**
Shore p	2	0	0	0	0	2							
Totals	**30**	**2**	**5**	**2**	**24**	**11**							

St. Louis Browns	IP	H	R	ER	BB	SO	Boston Red Sox	IP	H	R	ER	BB	SO
Ostrowski (L)	3+	11	7	7	2	1	Kinder (W)	9	5	2	2	1	2
Papai	0.2	3	3	3	2	0							
Shore	4.1	11	11	11	8	3							
Totals	**8**	**25**	**21**	**21**	**12**	**4**							

	1	2	3	4	5	6	7	8	9		R	H	E
STL A	1	0	1	0	0	0	0	0	0		2	5	1
BOS A	3	0	2	5	4	2	1	4	x		21	25	0

After the seventh-inning stretch, Ted Williams led off and got his revenge, homering off Shore to deep right field. In their final frame (there was no need for Boston to bat in the bottom of the ninth), Kinder started the hitting with a one-out single to center. DiMaggio singled, and Pesky walked to load the bases for the Kid. Williams singled, driving in two runs. Vern Stephens struck out, but on the play Williams stole second while Pesky stole home. Nothing like padding the cushion a little bit. Bobby Doerr singled, driving in Ted. It was 21–2 Red Sox. Kinder set St. Louis down in order in the top of the ninth, completing a string of the final 13 men in a row.

Shore was saddled with 11 earned runs, former Red Sox farmhand Ostrowski with seven, and Papai with three. Kinder gave up two runs on five hits, striking out two and walking one. The Sox scored 21 runs but also left 15 runners on base. The Browns left only three. Boston boasted 25 hits. Every member of the starting (and finishing) nine had two or more hits, save Bobby Doerr, who had to settle for just one hit (and one RBI), in the eighth. Ellis Kinder had two hits. Billy Goodman banged five straight, the same number as the whole St. Louis lineup, but had lunged at a bad 3–1 pitch since he "didn't want a walk." The Red Sox worked Browns pitchers for 12 walks, anyway. Ted Williams led in the total-bases category, with two home runs, a single, and seven RBIs.

Red Sox skipper Joe McCarthy was asked postgame why he took out neither a single position player nor his pitcher at any point during the game, given the ever-inflating lead. "Give the regulars a rest?" he answered. "What for? You never know when a game is won until the last out. . . . Heck, they don't want to come out when they're hitting. Did you ever see any ballplayer that did?"

Extra Innings

- Ted Williams had seven RBIs, a season high for him, but after the game he pooh-poohed the importance of runs batted in. "The way I'm going I'll probably wind up with the highest runs-batted-in total for a season since Lou Gehrig, but runs batted in are still for the birds in my book, and you can quote me." Williams was on a pace to drive in 190, and ended up with 159. "You can have two .330 hitters batting together in the lineup. One will hit in about 65 runs and the other will have about 125 RBIs. There are too many things involved to make RBIs mean whether a guys hits with men on base or not. Give me total bases any time as more important."

- Ellis Kinder was on his way to a 23–6 record in 1949. He admitted he'd coasted the last several innings, and even said that he and Birdie Tebbetts, his batterymate, didn't even bother with signs the last couple of frames. "It's a funny thing, when you don't have to bear down you can control your stuff so much better. . . . A little inside, then a little outside."

- "Boy, I hope they get me 21 tomorrow," mused Mel Parnell, the scheduled starting pitcher for the June 25 game. The final score of that game totted up at 13–2 Red Sox, largely courtesy of a seven-run third inning. This time every player on the Sox had at least one RBI.

- The Sox would have two games in 1950 where they scored 20 runs or more. On June 8, 1950, they would set the new major league record for runs in a game with 29 against St. Louis. Just a few weeks later, on June 29, they set the record for the highest total runs by both teams in a game in a 22–14 slugfest with Philadelphia.

23

October 1 and 2, 1949: Boston at New York

Double Indemnity

In which the Olde Towne Team goes to the wire a second year in a row

After losing 1948's single-game playoff and watching the Boston Braves play the Indians just down the street in the World Series, the Sox regrouped, labored through spring training, played the full season through September, and finally reached first place in the final week.

The Yankees had led all season long, right from Opening Day. At one time, New York held a 12-game lead over the Red Sox. The balance shifted, though, near the end of what proved an 11-game Red Sox winning streak in late September. With a win on September 26, the middle game of three wins against the Yankees, the Sox took over first place. After the games on September 30, the Sox had a 96–56 record. The Yankees were 95–57. Trouble was, there were still two games to play, and American League schedulers had New York hosting the Sox in Yankee Stadium for games on October 1 and 2. It's easier to lose than to win, but the Sox would have to lose both games to lose the hold they had on the pennant; win either game and they would represent the league in the 1949 World Series.

The Yankees had been plagued with illness and injury for much of the season, but the Sox were firing on all cylinders. The *Boston Herald* was brimming with confidence; an eight-column front-page headline blared: "Sox Send Parnell to Clinch Flag Today." In pregame ceremonies for "Joe DiMaggio Day," Joe's Red Sox brother Dominic had to help support the pneumonia-weakened Yankee Clipper. The Sox had their ace, Mel Parnell (25–7, 2.77 ERA), going. It almost didn't seem fair. But Allie Reynolds (17–6, 4.00 ERA) was no slouch as a starter for the Yankees, and Joe D gamely took up his position in center field. The Yankees didn't get this far without being exceptionally skilled competitors. And the 1949 Red Sox did not play well on the road. As they sent up leadoff batter Dom DiMaggio, they were 35–40 on the road (4–5 in New York). DiMaggio singled. Johnny Pesky forced him at second, but then Ted Williams singled. It would likely have been a double, but it hit umpire Cal Hubbard and the Yankees got a break. Reynolds uncorked a wild pitch, and the runners moved up. Pesky scored on a sacrifice fly. Despite another wild pitch, Reynolds was lucky to escape the first, being down just 1–0. In the third inning his control flagged again, walking the bases loaded with one out. Bobby Doerr's single scored one, and New York manager Casey Stengel called on reliever Joe Page, who walked Al Zarilla to force in a run, then walked in Billy Goodman to force in another run. It was 4–0 Sox with the bases loaded and just one out, but Page got hold of himself and got out of the inning with the score still 4–0. It seemed as though the Sox might have had this one sewn up, if only they could hold off New York.

But the Yankees got another break. Joe DiMaggio popped a fluke fly down the line in right; it bounced into the stands for a ground-rule double to lead off the Yankee fourth. When Hank Bauer singled and Johnny Lindell did the same, New York was on the board with two runs of their own. Then the Yanks led off the fifth with three straight singles, resulting in a third run. Parnell was yanked, and Joe Dobson was brought in to stop the bleeding. DiMaggio hit one off the pitcher's glove for a single and the sacks were full, with no one out. A batter later, it became a 4–4 tie, as a run scored on a double-play ball. The Sox were lucky to escape the fifth with it tied.

Over the next few innings, the two contenders managed just one single apiece, and so it stood until there were two out in the bottom of the eighth. Bucky Dent hadn't even been born yet, and Johnny Lindell was one of those players from whom a home run was not expected. He was batting under .240 and had just five round-trippers on the season; he was in the game only because Parnell was a southpaw. He had two hits on the day as he stepped into the box, though, so Stengel let him face the right-handed reliever Dobson. Dobson

OCTOBER 1, 1949: BOSTON AT NEW YORK

Boston Red Sox	AB	R	H	RBI	PO	A
D. DiMaggio cf	5	0	1	0	5	0
Pesky 3b	3	2	0	0	0	2
Williams lf	2	1	1	0	1	0
Stephens ss	4	1	0	1	2	2
Doerr 2b	4	0	2	1	2	1
Zarilla rf	4	0	0	1	0	0
Goodman 1b	3	0	0	1	7	0
Tebbetts c	4	0	0	0	7	0
Parnell p	0	0	0	0	0	2
Dobson p	0	0	0	0	0	1
Totals	29	4	4	4	24	8

New York Yankees	AB	R	H	RBI	PO	A
Rizzuto ss	2	1	1	0	4	5
Henrich 1b	3	1	1	0	8	0
Berra c	4	0	2	1	8	0
J. DiMaggio cf	4	1	2	0	2	0
Johnson 3b	3	0	0	0	1	2
Brown 3b	0	0	0	0	0	0
Bauer rf	3	1	1	1	2	0
Mapes rf	0	0	0	0	0	0
Lindell lf	4	1	3	1	2	0
Coleman 2b	4	0	1	1	0	2
Reynolds p	0	0	0	0	0	1
Page p	4	0	1	0	0	0
Totals	31	5	12	4	27	10

Boston Red Sox	IP	H	R	ER	BB	SO
Parnell	4	8	4	4	2	4
Dobson (L)	4	4	1	1	0	3
Totals	8	12	5	5	2	7

New York Yankees	IP	H	R	ER	BB	SO
Reynolds	2.1	3	4	4	4	2
Page (W)	6.2	1	0	0	3	5
Totals	9	4	4	4	7	7

	1	2	3	4	5	6	7	8	9	R	H	E
BOS A	1	0	3	0	0	0	0	0	0	4	4	0
NY A	0	0	0	2	2	0	0	1	x	5	12	0

OCTOBER 2, 1949: BOSTON AT NEW YORK

Boston Red Sox	AB	R	H	RBI	PO	A
D. DiMaggio cf	4	0	0	0	5	0
Pesky 3b	3	0	0	0	1	0
Williams lf	2	0	0	0	0	0
Stephens ss	4	1	1	0	2	3
Doerr 2b	4	1	2	2	0	6
Zarilla rf	4	0	1	0	1	0
Goodman 1b	3	0	1	1	9	1
Tebbetts c	4	0	0	0	6	0
Kinder p	2	0	0	0	0	2
Wright ph	0	0	0	0	0	0
Parnell p	0	0	0	0	0	0
Hughson p	0	0	0	0	0	0
Totals	30	3	5	3	24	12

New York Yankees	AB	R	H	RBI	PO	A
Rizzuto ss	4	1	2	0	1	7
Henrich 1b	3	1	1	2	10	0
Berra c	4	0	1	0	5	0
J. DiMaggio cf	4	0	1	0	3	0
Woodling lf	0	0	0	0	0	0
Lindell lf	2	0	1	0	1	0
Bauer lf,rf	0	0	0	0	0	0
Johnson 3b	4	1	2	0	0	0
Mapes rf,cf	3	1	0	0	3	0
Coleman 2b	4	0	1	3	3	1
Raschi p	3	0	0	0	1	0
Totals	31	5	9	5	27	8

Boston Red Sox	IP	H	R	ER	BB	SO
Kinder (L)	7	4	1	1	3	5
Parnell	0+	2	1	1	0	0
Hughson	2	3	3	2	1	0
Totals	9	9	5	2	4	5

New York Yankees	IP	H	R	ER	BB	SO
Raschi (W)	9	3	4	4	5	4

	1	2	3	4	5	6	7	8	9	R	H	E
BOS A	0	0	0	0	0	0	0	0	3	3	5	1
NY A	1	0	0	0	0	0	0	4	x	5	9	0

made the pitch he wanted, but—first-pitch-swinging—Lindell powered a 400-foot drive off Dobson deep into the lower deck in left. For the first time in the game, the Yankees had the lead.

Joe Page was a hero, too. He continued to dominate in relief; he threw 6⅔ innings of one-hit baseball. The Sox went down weakly in the ninth, and the game was over. The Yankees had come back from being down 4–0 and won the game 5–4. Both teams had 96 wins. Both teams had 57 losses. The stage was set for an October 2 showdown.

After the October 1 loss, there was certainly still hope in the Boston club-house. All they had to do was win a ball game. But this was now the third time in four years that the Red Sox had faced the possibility of elimination on the last possible day, and if there was more pressure on one team or another, it had to be on the Sox. Vic Raschi (21–10, 3.34 ERA) got the game ball from Stengel; McCarthy had Ellis Kinder (23–6, 3.36 ERA) rested and ready. Either Parnell or Kinder might have pitched in the 1948 playoff game. Just one year later, each got his shot to help clinch a pennant. Parnell had faltered, but Kinder had never lost a game to the Yankees since joining the Red Sox before the 1948 campaign. He took the mound with his teammates' full confidence.

After the Sox failed to capitalize on a walk to Ted Williams, Phil Rizzuto led off for New York, ran the count to 3–2, and then tripled to left off Kinder, the ball getting past Williams, who "played the ball as if he were afraid it would bite him" *(New York Herald Tribune)*. The Scooter scored moments later on Tommy Henrich's grounder to Doerr. Though Joe DiMaggio tripled, too, Kinder got out of the inning down by just the one run.

The 1–0 Yankee lead loomed large. Raschi was masterful; the Red Sox couldn't muster a hit off him until the fourth. After two out, Doerr and Zarilla hit back-to-back singles, but the team couldn't put a run together. Other than those two hits, the only Red Sox base runners were on walks to Pesky in the sixth and pinch hitter Tom Wright in the top of the eighth.

Kinder had been pitching well, too, after the first. Like Raschi, he'd only given up two singles through seven innings. Lifted for pinch hitter Wright, Kinder was replaced by Parnell to throw the bottom of the eighth. As Marvelous Mel took the mound for the second day in a row, the score remained 1–0 in favor of the Yankees. Parnell was greeted by a home run off the bat of Henrich, and Yogi Berra followed with a single. McCarthy exercised a quick hook and hauled in Tex Hughson, who got Joe DiMaggio to ground into a double play. But Johnny Lindell singled, Billy Johnson singled, and Cliff Mapes walked. The bases were loaded for rookie Jerry Coleman. Coleman hit a looping fly—not much more than a dying quail—that dropped safely into short right-center field. Zarilla dove for it, missed by two inches—or, as Arthur Sampson of the *Herald* put it, "the width of a gnat's eye-brow." The ball got by him and was chased down by Doerr. With two out, the Yankee runners had been off on contact. "The boys just stuck their heads down and made like Citation," wrote Arthur Daley in the *New York Times*. Coleman was thrown out at third, trying to get three bases out of it, but he had put the Yankees ahead by a very comfortable 5–0. All they had to do was retire three more Red Sox.

The first one went quietly. Johnny Pesky got his bat on the ball but just popped up to Yogi. The Sox weren't ready to roll over yet, though. Williams walked, and took second when Raschi threw another ball even farther outside the strike zone—a wild pitch. Ted took third when Vern Stephens singled to center, and both Ted and Vern scored when Bobby Doerr hit the first pitch for a triple to center over the head of an exhausted Joe DiMaggio. "At this point the Clipper called time and dramatically took himself out of the game" *(New York Times)*. Still, Stengel stuck with Raschi. Zarilla flied out to Mapes in center field (he'd moved over from right field to take Joe D's spot in center for the ninth, and Bauer took up residence in right field). Center field was where all the action was. Billy Goodman put yet another ball into center, singling and scoring Doerr. It was 5–3 now, with a runner on first base. Two out, but the Sox had the tying run at the plate in the person of their catcher, Birdie Tebbetts. Birdie lifted a pop-up to Henrich foul and just behind the bag at first base, and it was time for the fat lady to warble out a tune. The Yankees had won, and were on their way to the World Series (in New York, against the Dodgers), while the Red Sox had to board the train back to Boston, having lost out once again at the last possible moment.

Some people began to wonder if this ball team was cursed. It was the first time any ball club had ever lost the pennant on the last day of the season for two years in succession. It's never been done since. Johnny Pesky recalled the late 1940s. "I thought we had as good a team as you could put on the field. Something always seemed to happen. We thought there was a black cat on the squad or something."

◄ Extra Innings

- Despite struggling off his sickbed to play in his first game in nearly three weeks, Joe D was 3-for-8 with six total bases in the two games. After the first win, in a bit of postgame Stengelese, the inimitable Casey said that Joe had been "white as a goat" and he hadn't known how long he could stay in the game because "his legs was giving out because he hadda run so much" *(Boston Herald)*. Barely emerging from a three-game hitless slump, Ted Williams might have been better off not playing. He managed just 1-for-5 over the two games. He held the league lead in home runs and runs batted in, but just missed his third Triple Crown when George Kell overtook him for the batting title, with the margin being a slim ten-thousandth of a point: .0001557.

- Joe Page led the league with 27 saves in 1949. Just three years earlier, Boston's Bob Klinger had led the league with nine. The "save" was not recognized as an official statistic until 1969.

• The 3,000 fans lined up outside Fenway's ticket office, waiting for a chance to buy World Series tickets, had to break up and head for home upon hearing the news. Some had been there for more than 48 hours. Over the final four games of the season, the vaunted Red Sox offense had just one batter who'd hit above .200. Eight hitters in the lineup combined for a pathetic .144 average. Williams had gone 1-for-11. The only shining star was Doerr, with a 6-for-15 mark. Loyal fans, though, also numbering 3,000, gave the Red Sox a loud and raucous welcome when the train bearing the defeated team arrived at Boston's Back Bay Station.

24

August 28, 1950: Cleveland at Boston

Against All Odds

In which an 11-run deficit proves surmountable

There is nothing like a great comeback in sports—as any fan of the Red Sox can tell you after the 2004 season. To come back, you have to be down to begin with. On August 27, 1950, the Fenway faithful's spirits were down when the Cleveland Indians scored seven times in the top of the third inning, knocking starter Willard Nixon from the game and then slamming reliever Jim McDonald, literally, when Ray Boone hit a grand slam to cap the scoring. With the score 7–0, a comeback was unlikely. But Bob Feller was on the mound for the Indians, and he was perhaps infected by whatever got Nixon. "Rapid Robert" walked McDonald, then walked Johnny Pesky. After Dom DiMaggio hit into a fielder's choice, Vern Stephens singled to left to score two runs and Walt Dropo belted a three-run job into the screen. Cleveland added a couple more runs in the fifth, and led 9–5, but in the bottom of the seventh, the Red Sox scored twice and had the bases loaded—on three straight infield errors—for the fourth Boston pitcher of the day, Chuck Stobbs. Boston manager Steve O'Neill sent in Clyde Vollmer to pinch-hit against Cleveland's Al Benton. Vollmer drove a grand slam of his own over everything in left. Joe Dobson came in and kept the door shut, not allowing a hit. Boston won 11–9, an amazing comeback, but a mere warm-up for the next day's game, when the hole would be even deeper and dug right in the first inning.

Mickey McDermott started for the Red Sox, and he hit the first batter he faced. A single and another walk followed. A grounder to second brought in the first run, then another walk loaded the bases again. After a shallow fly to center gave the Sox two outs, McDermott walked yet another man—forcing in a second run—before striking out Jim Hegan to end the inning. The Tribe added five more in the second, helped by three more free passes handed out by McDermott, the last of the three coming with the bases loaded. Jim McDonald was brought back in to relieve, and he walked the first batter he faced, too. Then who did McDonald face again but Ray Boone. This time Boone doubled to left, driving in two more runs. For the second day in a row, the Indians led early in the game by a 7–0 score. Their experience the day before had to have impressed upon them that no 7–0 lead was safe at Fenway Park, so they kept at it, adding another three runs in the third, based on two more walks and four hits. Dick Littlefield replaced McDonald and stopped the bleeding. McDermott had hit a batter, walked six and given up one hit. He was responsible for the first six runs. After 2½ innings it was Indians 10, Red Sox 0.

Boston got on the board in the third as DiMaggio hit a two-out triple to score Buddy Rosar, who'd walked. The Indians responded by doubling Boston's lone run, Bobby Avila singling to plate two more for Cleveland in the top of the fourth. The Tribe now led 12–1. All in all, as the *Boston Post's* Jack Malaney wrote, "The Sox had every appearance of a very ordinary bush league team as they went to bat in the fourth." Lou Boudreau took Cleveland's center fielder Larry Doby out of the game to give him some rest.

Bob Lemon had beaten Boston in each of his last four starts facing them. It was late August, and Lemon was already a 20-game winner: 20–7 on the season, sporting the best record in baseball. But in the Boston fourth, the Red Sox finally got to him. Billy Goodman led off with a single. Clyde Vollmer walked. Walt Dropo singled, scoring Goodman. Bobby Doerr walked. Al Zarilla singled to right field, knocking in two more. Buddy Rosar singled home Doerr. Vern Stephens pinch-hit for pitcher Dick Littlefield, but gave the Indians their first out of the inning with a pop fly to Avila at second base. Dominic singled, then Pesky singled to load the bases. Lemon was juiced; the Indians had seen enough of him for the day. Indians manager Lou Boudreau brought in Al Benton to face Goodman, up for the second time in the inning, the same Benton who'd given up a grand slam to Vollmer the day before. This time Goodman doubled off the left-field wall, clearing the bases. All the runs were, of course, charged to Lemon. Benton then struck out Vollmer and got Dropo to ground out to end the inning. The score stood Cleveland 12, Boston 9.

AUGUST 28, 1950: CLEVELAND AT BOSTON

Cleveland Indians	AB	R	H	RBI	BB	SO	PO	A	Boston Red Sox	AB	R	H	RBI	BB	SO	PO	A
Mitchell lf	3	4	2	0	2	0	1	0	DiMaggio cf	5	2	3	3	0	0	5	0
Avila 2b	6	1	3	4	0	1	3	1	Pesky ss	5	2	2	1	0	0	4	4
Doby cf	0	2	0	0	3	0	1	0	Goodman 3b	4	2	3	4	1	0	1	2
Tucker cf	3	0	1	0	0	1	1	0	Vollmer lf	3	1	0	0	2	2	2	1
Easter 1b	5	3	3	2	1	0	8	0	Dropo 1b	5	2	2	2	0	1	3	1
Rosen 3b	4	1	2	2	2	0	1	3	Doerr 2b	4	1	0	0	1	1	4	3
Boone ss	6	0	2	4	0	0	1	2	Zarilla rf	4	2	2	4	1	0	2	1
Kennedy rf	4	0	0	2	1	0	2	0	Rosar c	4	2	2	1	1	0	6	1
Gordon ph	1	0	0	0	0	1	0	0	McDermott p	0	0	0	0	0	0	0	0
Hegan c	5	1	0	0	0	1	5	1	McDonald p	0	0	0	0	0	0	0	0
Lemon p	3	2	2	0	0	1	0	0	Littlefield p	1	0	0	0	0	1	0	1
Benton p	1	0	0	0	0	1	1	0	Stephens ph	1	0	0	0	0	0	0	0
Feller p	0	0	0	0	1	0	0	1	Nixon p	2	1	1	0	1	0	0	0
Gromek p	0	0	0	0	0	0	0	0	Kinder p	0	0	0	0	0	0	0	0
Totals	41	14	15	14	10	5	24	8	Totals	38	15	15	15	7	5	27	14

Cleveland Indians	IP	H	R	ER	BB	SO	Boston Red Sox	IP	H	R	ER	BB	SO
Lemon	3.1	7	9	9	4	1	McDermott	1.1	2	6	6	6	2
Benton	1.2	3	2	0	1		McDonald	1.1	5	4	4	3	0
Feller (L)	2.1	3	3	3	3	3	Littlefield	1.1	4	2	2	0	0
Gromek	0.2	2	1	1	0	0	Nixon (W)	4.1	4	2	1	1	2
Totals	8	15	15	15	7	5	Kinder	0.2	0	0	0	0	1
							Totals	9	15	14	14	10	5

	1	2	3	4	5	6	7	8	9		R	H	E
CLE A	2	5	3	2	0	0	0	1	1		14	15	3
BOS A	0	0	1	8	0	2	0	4	x		15	15	4

Willard Nixon, the Sox starter from the day before, was brought in to pitch and he retired the side in the fifth, sixth, and seventh without a run. "He stopped the bewildered Indians colder than $18 worth of ice," wrote Malaney.

The Red Sox, though, scored twice more in the sixth, pulling to within one run. It was Nixon who kicked it off, singling as leadoff batter. DiMaggio tripled to drive in Nixon, and then scored himself on an error that saw Pesky safe at first. At this point the traumatized Tribe called on Bob Feller to put out the fire. Feller, too, had just started the day before, but he'd been run out in the third inning and so was deemed available. After walking Goodman on four straight pitches and seeing both Pesky and Goodman advance when shortstop Ray Boone couldn't handle Jim Hegan's pickoff throw to second, Feller settled down and struck out Vollmer, Dropo, and Doerr, one after the other. "He was as good as I've ever seen him that inning," said Johnny Pesky, perched on third base and hoping to score the tying run. He didn't. Cleveland 12, Boston 11.

The Indians added an unearned insurance run in the eighth, on a two-base error by Vollmer, a walk to Feller, a force play that moved up the runners, and another error, this time by Pesky. The third out was made when Dale Mitchell was caught trying to steal home. Cleveland 13, Boston 11.

Surely Bob Feller could hold the lead for a couple of innings? Pesky tried to atone for the error by doubling off Feller to lead off Boston's eighth. Goodman doubled in Pesky, and Boston was back within one. After Vollmer lined out to Bob Kennedy at third base, Dropo tripled to the deepest part of center field, scoring Goodman. The 12–1 Cleveland lead had now become a 13–13 tie game, with a runner on third base for Boston and just one out. Steve Gromek came on to face Doerr in relief of the battered Bob Feller. Doerr flied out, and Dropo sprinted home to score. The next batter, Al Zarilla, homered into the right-field stands, and the Red Sox took the lead. Boston 15, Cleveland 13.

The scoring still wasn't over. With one out in the top of the ninth, Nixon gave up a single to Luke Easter and then another to Al Rosen, Easter taking third. Ellis Kinder was called on, as Boston's fifth pitcher of the day, inducing Boone to ground to Pesky at short, while Easter scored from third base. Joe Gordon batted for Bob Kennedy but was called out on strikes, and it was finally all over: Boston 15, Cleveland 14.

Those of the 28,328 who stuck around had seen the greatest Red Sox win overcoming a major deficit; down 12–1, the Sox won the game. In the process, they had beaten the Indians, despite facing future Hall of Famers Bob Lemon and Bob Feller in the same game. The Indians groused that the Red Sox were "lucky." It was a little more than luck; Boston had now won 13 of their last 14 games. They were on a tear. And all without Ted Williams, who had fractured his left elbow during the 1950 All-Star Game.

"Fenway Park is Monte Carlo. Baseball is roulette. And if there are any bodies floating in Muddy River, they should belong to the Cleveland Indians." So ran Harold Kaese's lead in the *Boston Globe* the next morning.

Extra Innings

- The game was in danger of being forfeited in the third inning, when the 1,800 caddies attending the game under the sponsorship of the Massachusetts Golf Association started flinging golf balls onto the field in right.

- Asked about his game-winning homer, and three RBIs on the day, Zarilla humbly mumbled, "Well, if you just keep swinging, you're bound to get one once in a while."

- The Red Sox were near the end of a stretch in which they won 16 of 17 games. Not only was it a joy to read the box scores those two days, it also was a real treat to look at the Red Sox averages printed in the papers. The Red Sox had 14 (!) players with batting averages over .300—two of them pitchers—and this was fairly late in the season, nearly September. Three players already had driven in more than 100 runs apiece. The Sox would finish the season with a team batting average of .302 and amass 1,027 runs scored.

	AB	R	BH	AVG	RBI	HR
Goodman	336	78	124	.369	53	4
McDermott	37	10	13	.351	8	0
Zarilla	388	78	133	.343	43	7
DiMaggio	471	111	158	.333	55	7
Dropo	440	81	142	.323	123	29
Tebbetts	227	31	73	.322	39	8
Williams	268	75	86	.321	86	25
Wright	100	16	33	.320	17	0
Pesky	410	95	131	.320	43	1
Rosar	44	7	14	.318	5	0
Stephens	516	113	157	.304	129	28
Vollmer	152	35	45	.296	32	6
Doerr	470	82	135	.287	103	21

• This 11-run deficit was not the biggest run deficit a team ever had to overcome to win a ball game, though it was close. The record is 12, held by three teams:

The Detroit Tigers beat the Chicago White Sox, 16–15, on June 18, 1911, overcoming a 13–1 deficit and winning it in the bottom of the ninth.

Philadelphia beat Cleveland, 17–15, on June 15, 1925, at Philadelphia. Down 14–2 after 5½ innings, the 13-run bottom of the eighth did the trick.

The Cleveland Indians beat the Seattle Mariners, August 5, 2001, 15–14 in 11 innings. The Mariners were on their way to a record-tying 116-win season, but could not hold a 12–0 lead through three, nor a 14–2 lead from midway through the seventh.

• Three other teams have overcome 11-run deficits, and share the National League record:

The St. Louis Cardinals overcame the New York Giants, on June 15, 1952, first game; 14–12 final. The Cards had been down 11–0 and did not score until the seventh inning.

The Phillies came back against the Chicago Cubs on April 17, 1976, in 10 innings. Final score 18–16. Mike Schmidt hit four home runs. It was both the highest-scoring game for the Phillies of the season, and also the most runs they allowed that season.

The Houston Astros beat the St. Louis Cardinals, July 18, 1994, by a final score of 15–12.

25

May 18, 1955: Cleveland at Boston

Shut Out

In which the Tribe sets a record at Boston's expense

The defending American League champion Cleveland Indians jumped out to an early lead in the 1955 standings, while Boston sputtered along in the middle of the pack. By the time the Indians came to Boston in late May, the Sox were in fifth place, trailing by 7½ games. The Tribe loved visiting; since September 1953 they hadn't lost a game at Fenway Park. (Oddly, they did have back-to-back ties on July 20 and 21, 1954.) On May 17 the Sox finally snapped the streak with a 10–3 win, but on the 18th they were up against a 21-year-old rookie named Herb Score.

Score was Cleveland's $60,000 bonus baby—a huge amount in that era—and by May 18, he had already proved his worth; he could beat major league hitting, and could handle the Red Sox in particular. In six starts, he struck out 57 men in 47 innings, prompting the papers to dub him the "left-handed Bob Feller." Sixteen of those K's had been Red Sox, in a 2–1 Cleveland win on May 1.

Score took the mound at Fenway and breezed through the first eight Red Sox batters he faced, whiffing one after the other. The first man he didn't strike out was the opposing pitcher, Willard Nixon, whom he walked in the bottom of the third.

Nixon had already surrendered one run, as the Tribe's Dave Pope and Dave Philley had knocked singles in the second inning, allowing Pope to score on a ground out. Cleveland notched two more in the fourth. The Sox did not register their first hit until the fifth, when Sammy White doubled off the wall. That one hit looked paltry, though, compared to what Cleveland had done in the top of the inning. The top of the fifth was one of the biggest run-scoring innings in baseball history.

Cleveland's Al Smith started it with a single to center. Bobby Avila and Vic Wertz did the same, though to left and right, respectively, scoring Smith. Next, Nixon hit Larry Doby with a pitch, loading the bases. Pope's fly to center field may have restored hope to the Boston rooters' breasts, but hope was fleeting—Avila scored on the fly, and the next batter, Dave Philley, hit a triple that drove in the two men remaining on base, and he came around to score himself when Billy Goodman botched relaying Jackie Jensen's throw from right. With the bases blissfully empty, Nixon faced Sam Dente. Dente walked to first base, and Nixon to the showers.

MAY 18, 1955: CLEVELAND AT BOSTON																
Cleveland Indians	AB	R	H	RBI	BB	SO	PO	A	Boston Red Sox	AB	R	H	RBI	BB	SO	PO	A
Smith 3b	7	2	4	3	0	0	0	1	Goodman 2b	4	0	1	0	0	1	8	0
Avila 2b	3	2	1	0	1	0	2	0	Joost ss	2	0	0	0	0	1	5	1
Majeski 2b	2	1	1	1	1	0	2	0	Lepcio 3b	2	0	1	0	0	0	2	1
Wertz 1b	5	3	2	5	1	1	1	0	Zauchin 1b	2	0	0	0	2	1	1	1
Doby cf	2	1	1	0	0	1	0	0	Jensen rf	4	0	0	0	0	1	0	0
Kiner ph,lf	3	3	3	1	0	0	2	0	Mele lf	4	0	0	0	0	2	1	0
Pope lf,cf	4	3	2	2	1	0	7	0	White c	4	0	1	0	0	0	5	0
Philley rf	5	1	2	2	1	0	1	0	Klaus 3b,ss	3	0	0	0	0	2	1	2
Dente ss	3	1	1	3	3	0	2	0	Olson cf	3	0	0	0	0	0	2	1
Foiles c	5	1	2	1	1	1	10	0	Nixon p	0	0	0	0	1	0	2	0
Score p	5	1	0	1	0	2	0	0	Kemmerer p	0	0	0	0	0	0	0	1
Totals	44	19	19	19	9	5	27	1	Brodowski p	2	0	0	0	1	0	0	0
									Totals	30	0	3	0	3	9	27	7

Cleveland Indians	IP	H	R	ER	BB	SO	Boston Red Sox	IP	H	R	ER	BB	SO
Score (W)	9	3	0	0	3	9	Nixon (L)	4.1	8	9	8	2	4
							Kemmerer	0.1	3	5	6	3	0
							Brodowski	4.1	8	5	5	4	1
							Totals	9	19	19	19	9	5

	1	2	3	4	5	6	7	8	9	R	H	E
CLE A	0	1	0	2	11	0	5	0	0	19	19	0
BOS A	0	0	0	0	0	0	0	0	0	0	3	1

With one on and one out, reliever Russ Kemmerer entered the game. Before he could record an out, a passed ball allowed Dente to advance to second. Kemmerer walked Herb Foiles, putting two on for pitcher Herb Score. The young lefty bunted—Kemmerer fielded the ball quickly enough to catch Dente at third, while Score reached. With two out but two on, Kemmerer now faced Smith, who singled for the second time in the inning, into right field, scoring Foiles. Kemmerer then issued his third walk of the inning, to Avila, and loaded the bases once again. A grounder, a pop-up, a flyout—any one of them would end the rally, and cap the inning's damage at six runs. But Vic Wertz stepped into the box for the second time, and this time he planted the ball in the center-field bleachers. It was 13–0 Indians, 10 in the inning—and it wasn't over yet. Cleveland manager Al Lopez sent the struggling Ralph Kiner in to hit for Doby. Kiner's average was a paltry .206 on the season, but he slammed a solo shot into the netting in deep center.

That was it for Kemmerer. Dick Brodowski came on and induced Philley to pop up, finally closing the frame. But Brodowski was touched as well in the seventh, when pinch hitter Hank Majeski homered over the Monster in left, sparking a five-run rally. Boston mustered a couple of hits off Score in the eighth, but by that time it hardly mattered.

"He's a smart kid," Lopez said in praise of Score after the game. "He came to me when we got a good lead and said he was going to practice on his curve and his changeup. Naturally, I told him to go ahead."

"The Cleveland Indians could have given the British Regulars a pointer or two on how to conduct a Boston Massacre," wrote Tony Galli in a wire service report for the *Elyria* [Ohio] *Chronicle-Telegram.* When all was said and done, every man in the Cleveland lineup had a hit, except Score himself. Kiner snapped his slump by going 3-for-3, including his fifth-inning pinch homer, The final tally, 19–0, represented not only the most runs ever scored by Cleveland in a shutout, but also the worst shutout loss in the history of the Red Sox. It was the lowest point in a low period of Sox history, an era when owner Tom Yawkey drifted away from the team and a usually explosive offense was never matched with championship-quality pitching. They wouldn't contend again until the year of the Impossible Dream, 1967.

◀ Extra Innings

- Ted Williams missed the pasting at the hands of the Indians, because he had ostensibly retired at the end of 1954. After his divorce was finalized on May 11, however, the Red Sox announced their intentions for him to play again. Williams told newspapers he planned to make his debut in an exhibition game against the Giants the Monday after Cleveland left town. "The slugger, who has been working out daily to get in condition to play, also said he will participate in a pregame home run hitting contest," reported the *Chicago Tribune.*

- Perhaps it was a sign that Boston's luck was finally changing when in 2004, the Indians surpassed their team record of 19, when they racked up 22 runs in a shutout on August 31. The team they shut out? The Yankees. The 22–0 defeat was the worst in Yankee history. The 22–0 score tied the largest shutout score recorded since 1900, when Pittsburgh beat the Cubs on September 16, 1975.

26

September 28, 1960: Baltimore at Boston

Exclamation Point

In which the Splendid Splinter puts the final mark of punctuation on his career

Ted Williams broke in with Boston in 1939, setting a rookie record for runs batted in (145) that has never been topped. He is the last player to have hit .400, he won six batting titles, and he led the league 12 times in on-base percentage. Indeed, he has the highest lifetime on-base percentage of anyone who ever played major league baseball. Come September 1960, though, and Teddy Ballgame was ready to call it a day.

The last home game of a dispiriting season saw the Red Sox entrenched in seventh place, with a record of 64–86 heading into the September 28 game. Top of the heap—who else? The Yankees. During 1960, though, Ted Williams had reached a number of personal milestones—his 500th home run and his 1,800th RBI. Pitchers who feared him had granted him his 2,000th walk. He'd even stolen a base, becoming the first major league ballplayer to have a stolen base in four decades.

The greatest player in Red Sox history might have gone out with a whimper; suffering a pinched nerve in his neck for most of the 1959 season, he'd hit a dismal .254—so bad that when he signed for one final round in 1960, he demanded a 30% pay cut from Red Sox owner Tom Yawkey. Clearly, these were the days before the Players' Association. Ted had wanted one last shot, and he hit a very respectable .316 (the 1960 batting champion was teammate Pete Runnels, who posted a .320 mark).

Ted Williams

SEPTEMBER 28, 1960: BALTIMORE AT BOSTON																
Baltimore Orioles	AB	R	H	RBI	BB	SO	PO	A	**Boston Red Sox**	AB	R	H	RBI	BB	SO	PO	A
Brandt cf	5	0	0	0	0	1	3	0	Green ss	3	0	0	0	2	0	1	3
Pilarcik rf	4	0	1	0	0	0	1	0	Tasby cf	4	1	0	1	1	0	1	0
Robinson 3b	4	1	1	0	0	1	1	1	Williams lf	3	2	1	1	1	0	3	0
Gentile 1b	3	1	1	1	0	1	7	0	Hardy lf	0	0	0	0	0	0	0	0
Triandos c	4	1	2	2	0	0	6	0	Pagliaroni c	3	0	2	0	0	0	8	0
Hansen ss	4	1	2	0	0	1	3	4	Malzone 3b	3	0	0	0	1	0	2	5
Stephens lf	4	0	2	0	0	0	4	0	Clinton rf	3	0	0	1	0	2	2	0
Breeding 2b	2	0	0	0	0	0	0	1	Gile 1b	4	0	0	0	1	7	2
Woodling ph	1	0	0	1	0	0	0	0	Coughtry 2b	3	1	2	0	1	0	2	1
Pearson pr	0	0	0	0	0	0	0	0	Muffett p	2	0	0	0	0	2	1	1
Klaus 2b	1	0	0	0	0	0	1	2	Nixon ph	1	0	0	0	0	0	0	0
Barber p	0	0	0	0	0	0	0	0	Fornieles p	0	0	0	0	0	0	0	1
Fisher p	4	0	0	0	0	2	0	0	Wertz ph	1	0	1	0	0	0	0	0
Totals	36	4	9	4	0	6	26	8	Brewer pr	0	1	0	0	0	0	0	0
									Totals	30	5	6	3	6	5	27	13

Baltimore Orioles	IP	H	R	ER	BB	SO	HR	**Boston Red Sox**	IP	H	R	ER	BB	SO	HR
Barber	0.1	0	2	2	3	0	0	Muffett	7	9	4	4	0	4	1
Fisher (L)	8.1	6	3	2	3	5	1	Fornieles (W)	2	0	0	0	0	2	0
Totals	8.2	6	5	4	6	5	1	**Totals**	9	9	4	4	0	6	1

	1	2	3	4	5	6	7	8	9	R	H	E
BAL A	0	2	0	0	1	1	0	0	0	4	9	1
BOS A	2	0	0	0	0	0	0	1	2	5	6	1

September 28 was Ted's final day, however. The team was going on to New York for a final series against the Yankees, but Ted told both Tom Yawkey and Sox broadcaster Curt Gowdy that he wasn't going to travel to the Big Apple with the ball club. Surely, a ticket to Ted's last game at Fenway must have been the hottest ticket in town. Hundreds of thousands of fans claim to have attended the game. Many more wish they had. Does that not constitute one of the greatest games in Red Sox history? Sadly, and confoundingly, only 10,454 fans actually did turn out.

The matchup was Boston's Billy Muffett (6–4) against Baltimore southpaw Steve Barber (10–7). The game meant nothing to the Red Sox. They couldn't reach sixth place, and they couldn't sink to the cellar. The Orioles were defending second place, worried they might fall to third. Before the game, Williams was honored at home plate with a number of speeches, and Ted accepted a check on behalf of the charity he chaired, the Jimmy Fund. Ted took a potshot at the "knights of the keyboard" but called Yawkey the "best owner in the business" and the Boston fans "the greatest fans in America."

His first time up, the aging Kid was greeted with more applause, but boos showered down on Steve Barber when he couldn't find the plate and walked Williams on four pitches. Ted advanced around the bases and scored on a sacrifice fly, sliding into home. The Sox staked out a 2–0 lead, though the Orioles came right back to tie it up in the top of the second. When Williams came up to bat again in the third inning, he was facing relief pitcher Jack Fisher, and another hearty round of applause accompanied Ted as he strode from the on-deck circle to the batter's box. Ten thousand hopes soared when Ted hit one deep to center, but Jackie Brandt camped under it and hauled it in. "Another day, it might have gone, but the air was just too heavy," Williams recalled in his autobiography, *My Turn at Bat*.

The O's scored a run in the top of the fifth, and Ted came up with a chance to tie it in the bottom of the inning. The applause was heavy, but so was the air—heavy and thick with fog, so overcast that the lights were turned on for the sixth. He hit another offering from Fisher, much farther. High and deep, but again it died in the damp air. Right fielder Al Pilarcik backed up to the far end of the Baltimore bullpen—about 380 feet from home plate—and made the catch. Ted said, "I remember saying to Vic Wertz in the dugout, 'If that one didn't go out, none of them will today.'"

Baltimore built a 4–2 lead with another run in the sixth, so the Sox were down by two when Williams came up in the bottom of the eighth. Jack Fisher was still on the mound, pitching a whale of a ball game. The crowd really rocked the park with their cheers as Ted stepped in, with one out and nobody on base. Ted said he felt the chills on his spine as he'd waited on-deck, wanting so much to hit one out. He knew the odds were against it. The tension built during several minutes of a standing ovation while Fisher and Williams fidgeted and waited.

Fisher's first pitch was a ball. Ted could tell from Fisher's motion that he was going to try to blow the next one right by him. He geared up, and sure enough, it was a fastball—"a ball I should have hit a mile, and I missed the son of a gun. I don't miss, completely miss, very often and I don't know yet how I missed that ball."

For the next pitch, Ted expected another fastball, and he got it. This time he was a little quicker, and this time he got the bat on the ball and drove it deep into right-center field, where it sailed out of the field and bounced off the roof of the Red Sox bullpen for a 420-foot home run. The crowd erupted. Ed Rumill wrote in the *Christian Science Monitor* that "the second standing ovation they gave the big fellow did justice to a full park."

Ted Williams had hit a home run in his last at-bat in the major leagues. You couldn't ask for a better ending for a career. "His greatness as a hitter demanded no less," editorialized the *Boston Herald* the next day. "A triple off the top of the fence would have been sheer anticlimax. This final home run was also demanded by Williams' impeccable dramatic instinct. . . . Ted Williams has been incapable of the mediocre." And no matter how much he might have liked to tip his cap to the fans who demanded it, "I couldn't. It just wouldn't have been me."

To top it off, the Red Sox won the game as well, coming from behind for a couple of runs in the bottom of the ninth to eke out a 5–4 win that defined anticlimax. Ted trotted out to left field in the top of the ninth, sent out by manager Mike Higgins, only to be replaced by Carroll Hardy—and receive another few minutes of cheering as he ran back into the dugout.

Later that night, there was no monster celebration in Ted's honor. "Ted's day wasn't over yet," wrote Christine Paul in a Jimmy Fund newsletter. "A public appearance for the Jimmy Fund awaited him in Rhode Island. Although running behind schedule, Ted had no compunction about throwing a curveball into his travel plans: he insisted on visiting a young cancer patient. The thrilled youngster buckled a belt he had made for Ted around his hero's waist. Ted had come just in time. A few days later, the boy died."

Ted Williams had gone out in style. In his final curtain call, he'd cemented the legend with home run 521.

◄ Extra Innings

- Williams actually hit a home run in his last major league at-bat another time as well. On April 30, 1952, it was Ted Williams Day at Fenway Park. The next day, he was due to report for duty in the Marine Corps, called back to service at age 33. It was his first start since Opening Day. He singled sharply in the first inning, and as the game progressed, he found himself up again in the seventh inning. The score was tied, 3–3, with two out and Dizzy Trout on the mound. Dom DiMaggio was on first base. Ted was off to war, scheduled for a 17-month stretch in the Marines, and he didn't think he'd be coming back to baseball. It was his last time up. He hit Trout's pitch into Fenway's right-field grandstand, putting the Red Sox ahead, 5–3.

  For Williams, Ed Rumill wrote, "the great ovation and turnout for Ted's farewell yesterday may have influenced him to try a comeback when he returns" (*Christian Science Monitor*).

- Ted was the only player to have stolen a base in four different decades until the year 2000, when Rickey Henderson did it. Tim Raines joined that exclusive club in 2001.

◆27

Long Shot

In which a player goes 2-for-11 in a doubleheader but ties one game and wins another

June 18 was a busy day in Boston, beginning with the annual Fathers/Sons game before the scheduled doubleheader. Though not featured in any record books, the Red Sox sons (and now daughters) have never lost one of these games yet, even more than forty years later.

When the Senators and the Red Sox squared off, it was Stubby Mathias against Ike Delock. Neither team scored for the first three innings, but Washington drew first blood with a single run in the top of the fourth. Boston came back with two in the bottom of the frame, only to see the Senators double that with four runs in the fifth. Boston scored once more, making it 5–3. The Senators added another two to their total in the sixth, and, responding once again, the Sox matched that. Both teams took the seventh and eighth innings off. So it stood Senators 7, Sox 5—until the top of the ninth, when the Senators went for the kill with five runs, capped by Willie Tasby's grand slam off Ted Wills. With a seven-run, 12–5 lead, the Senators seemed set. Fans filed out of the stands, some discouraged and ready to call it a day, others to get food and refreshment for the second game of the doubleheader. And the first Red Sox hitter stepped into the batter's box.

That was Vic Wertz, and he made the first out, grounding to first baseman Dale Long, who threw to the pitcher, Mathias, covering first. Then Don Buddin singled to right. Billy Harrell batted for the pitcher, Wills, and struck out. Two out, a man on first. Some of the Senators may have even left the bench to get first crack at the between-games spread.

Chuck Schilling singled to center. Carroll Hardy singled to right-center, scoring Buddin and sending Schilling to third. The score stood at 12–6. Gary Geiger walked, loading the bases. Dave Sisler replaced Mathias on the mound for Washington, hoping to get the final out, but he walked Jackie Jensen, forcing in Schilling. Then he walked Malzone, forcing in Hardy. Now, the Fenway faithful realized, a grand slam could tie the score. Miraculously, that's just what happened. Sox catcher Jim Pagliaroni got his first hit of the day, driving one deep into the left-field net for a grand slam, and the score was knotted at 12 runs apiece. The atmosphere was electrified. Those still in the food lines scurried back to their seats.

Vic Wertz was up for the second time in the inning; this time he earned himself a walk. Senators manager Mickey Vernon called on Marty Kutyna to take over from Sisler. Buddin singled—again—this time to left field. Pete Runnels was sent in to run for Wertz, and Russ Nixon was sent up to pinch-hit for Harrell—a rare instance of a pinch hitter pinch-hitting for a pinch hitter. Nixon singled, a "hard bouncer" (Associated Press) just a couple of inches over the outstretched hand of the second baseman. Runnels scored, and the Red Sox won, 13–12.

They had been down by seven runs, with two out in the ninth inning, and yet they had rallied to win the game. Ted Wills had given up a single, a walk, and a grand slam, walked another batter, then finally retired two batters, was lifted for a pinch hitter, and got the win. And some fans missed it, waiting for a hot dog.

And that was just the first game. The second game that day was also a treat for Sox fans. They had Gene Conley going against Pete Burnside. Boston led 3–0 after three and 5–2 after five, but Washington got two more in the seventh, and Willie Tasby's solo homer into the center-field seats tied it in the eighth. As the game ran into extra innings, relievers Tom Sturdivant

JUNE 18, 1961: WASHINGTON AT BOSTON																
Washington Senators	AB	R	H	RBI	BB	SO	PO	A	Boston Red Sox	AB	R	H	RBI	BB	SO	PO	A
Veal ss	4	0	0	0	1	1	0		Schilling 2b	5	1	1	0	0	0	1	1
Klaus 3b	5	1	1	0	0	0	2	4	Hardy lf	4	2	2	1	1	0	1	0
Woodling lf	4	2	2	2	1	0	4	0	Geiger cf	3	1	0	1	1	2	4	0
Hinton pr,lf	0	1	0	0	0	0	0	0	Jensen rf	4	2	1	1	1	0	3	0
Long 1b	4	2	2	2	1	0	9	1	Malzone 3b	4	2	1	1	1	0	0	2
Tasby cf	5	1	2	5	0	1	3	0	Pagliaroni c	5	1	1	4	0	1	4	1
King rf	3	1	1	0	2	1	0	0	Wertz 1b	4	0	1	1	1	0	10	3
Cottier 2b	5	0	1	0	0	0	1	1	Runnels pr	0	1	0	0	0	0	0	0
Daley c	5	2	3	2	0	0	5	1	Buddin ss	4	3	3	1	1	0	2	3
Mathias p	4	2	1	0	0	0	1	1	Delock p	1	0	0	0	0	0	1	2
Sisler p	0	0	0	0	0	0	0	0	Repulski ph	1	0	0	0	0	0	0	0
Kutyna p	0	0	0	0	0	0	0	0	Muffett p	1	0	0	0	0	1	1	0
Totals	39	12	13	11	4	3	26	8	Wills p	0	0	0	0	0	0	0	0
									Harrell ph	1	0	0	0	0	1	0	0
									Nixon ph	1	0	1	1	0	0	0	0
									Totals	38	13	11	11	6	5	27	12

Washington Senators	IP	H	R	ER	BB	SO	HR	Boston Red Sox	IP	H	R	ER	BB	SO	HR
Mathias	8.2	8	9	7	3	5	1	Delock	5	6	5	1	2	2	1
Sisler (L)	0	1	4	4	3	0	1	Muffett	3.1	5	4	4	0	1	1
Kutyna	0	2	0	0	0	0	0	Wills (W)	0.2	2	3	3	2	0	1
Totals	8.2	11	13	11	6	5	2	Totals	9	13	12	8	4	3	3

	1	2	3	4	5	6	7	8	9	R	H	E
WAS A	0	0	0	1	4	2	0	0	5	12	13	1
BOS A	0	0	0	2	1	2	0	0	8	13	11	1

for Washington and Mike Fornieles for Boston were locked in a relief pitchers' duel—Sturdivant throwing six innings of no-hit ball after coming in to start the seventh, and Fornieles allowing just two hits in his six innings of work.

The first batter in the bottom of the 13th inning was game one hero Jim Pagliaroni. Pags, at this point, was 1-for-10 on the day—his only hit was the game-tying grand slam in the first game (whether he played in the Father/Son game was not recorded). Running the count to 3–2, he finally got the pitch he was waiting for and came through once more, a game-winning solo home run.

"You had a rough day at the plate today," a newspaperman said to the Red Sox catcher. "You were only 2 for 11."

"Gee, that's right," said the weary but pleased Pagliaroni after his 22 innings behind the plate. "My batting average is going to blazes."

Extra Innings

- Another great comeback that comes to mind occurred on Boston's home opener in 1998. Randy Johnson spun a two-hitter through eight innings, and Seattle had a 7–2 lead. It seemed safe to turn it over to the bullpen, but the ball went to Heathcliff Slocumb. He was the first of four Seattle relievers, and not one of them could manage to record even one out. The Sox scored seven times, the final four on the grand slam gopher ball Mike Timlin served up to Mo Vaughn. Boston 9, Seattle 7.

28

August 1, 1962: Boston at Chicago

Sweet Taste

In which a native son finds his groove at last

Massachusetts native Bill Monbouquette was signed as an amateur free agent by the Red Sox in 1955 and came up through the Sox farm system. The pride of Medford debuted with the big league club in mid-July 1958 and established himself from the start.

The 5'11" right-hander had a good fastball, with a slider as a change of speed and sometimes a curve. The Red Sox were not a strong team in the early sixties, and Monbo, as he was known, was the ace of the staff, winning 14 games in 1960 and again in 1961. He was picked to start the All-Star Game in 1960, and represented the Red Sox in the midsummer classic every year through 1964. On May 12, 1961, facing the Senators, he struck out 17 men in a nine-inning game, just one shy of the major league record at the time.

Despite these bright moments, these were times of struggle for both Monbo and the Bosox. In particular in 1962, the pitcher had trouble with consistency, not winning back-to-back starts until June, and struggling mightily in July after the All-Star break. The Sox won his first start after the break, but the score was 11–10, a no-decision, and he proceeded to lose the next three in a row, giving up 17 runs in 10⅔ innings pitched in the losses. The team as a whole went 6–12 in that stretch. On August 1 the *Boston Herald* ran a piece previewing their matchup in Chicago for a two-game set. "Monbo and Schwall Keys to Sox Turnaround," blared the headline. Manager Mike Higgins told the paper, "We have spent two days going over every player in our organization and have come to the conclusion that there is no way we can improve the personnel at the moment. We have the best pitchers we own on our roster at present. It appears our best chance of displaying improvement depends on the players we now have delivering closer to their capabilities."

Monbouquette wanted nothing more than that. He had been working with pitching coach Sal Maglie to try to discover what, if anything, was wrong with his mechanics. At times he seemed surprisingly easy to hit, as though his pitches had been robbed of their power.

After disappointing starts in New York and Washington, neither Maglie nor

AUGUST 1, 1962: BOSTON AT CHICAGO

Boston Red Sox	AB	R	H	RBI	BB	SO	PO	A	Chicago White Sox	AB	R	H	RBI	BB	SO	PO	A
Gardner 2b	5	0	1	0	0	1	1	1	Aparicio ss	4	0	0	0	0	1	2	1
Geiger cf	2	0	0	0	1	0	2	0	Sadowski 2b	3	0	0	0	0	2	4	3
Yastrzemski lf	3	0	0	0	1	2	2	0	Cunningham 1b	3	0	0	0	0	0	6	0
Pagliaroni c	4	1	1	0	0	0	8	0	Robinson rf	3	0	0	0	0	0	2	0
Runnels 1b	4	0	2	0	0	1	8	0	Maxwell lf	3	0	0	0	0	0	3	0
Clinton rf	4	0	3	1	0	0	3	0	Smith 3b	2	0	0	0	1	1	1	1
Malzone 3b	3	0	0	0	1	0	1	2	Landis cf	3	0	0	0	0	2	3	0
Bressoud ss	4	0	0	0	0	0	2	3	Lollar c	3	0	0	0	0	1	6	1
Monbouquette p	3	0	1	0	1	1	0	1	Wynn p	2	0	0	0	0	0	0	4
Totals	32	1	8	1	4	5	27	7	Fox ph	1	0	0	0	0	0	0	0
									Totals	27	0	0	0	1	7	27	10

Boston Red Sox	IP	H	R	ER	BB	SO	HR	Chicago White Sox	IP	H	R	ER	BB	SO	HR
Monbouquette (W)	9	0	0	0	1	7	0	Wynn (L)	9	8	1	1	4	5	0

	1	2	3	4	5	6	7	8	9	R	H	E
BOS A	0	0	0	0	0	0	0	1	0	1	8	0
CHI A	0	0	0	0	0	0	0	0	0	0	0	0

Monbo himself could unlock the secret of why some pitches had zip and some did not. Monbo knew it was mechanical but couldn't quite pin it down. On the plane flight to Chicago, he opened up to a young stewardess named Jan Gibbs. "I'm not having much of a year," he told her glumly. Jan would have none of it. "Tonight you're going to pitch a whale of a game," she told him. Higgins was optimistic, too, because of the weather. "Cool weather like tonight should help him," the manager told reporters. "The thing that hurts him in hot weather is that he has to stop to wipe the sweat from his face and this breaks up his pitching rhythm."

But even in the bullpen, while warming up, Monbouquette told catcher Jim Pagliaroni he still didn't have a handle on the problem. The opposing pitcher, Early Wynn, was suffering no such crisis of confidence. At age 42 he was trying to notch his 298th career win, and he dispatched the Red Sox easily in the top of the first. Monbo took the mound wondering whether another beating lay in store for him or whether this time he would figure it out. The leadoff man, Luis Aparicio, grounded a ball to third, out. Next Monbo struck out Bob Sadowski. And then Joe Cunningham popped a ball foul, catchable for third baseman Frank Malzone, and the inning was painlessly over.

The Sox tried to ignite a two-out rally in the second on a single and a walk, but it fizzled when Eddie Bressoud grounded out. Monbo went back to work. Other than a two-out walk to Al Smith, on which "he started to chase a 3–2 curve and then held up," according to Monbouquette, the inning was much the same as the first, one strikeout and the other two men hitting the ball, but for outs. Once, when he had been pitching in the minors, his coach Chet Paglucci told him going nine would be good for him, regardless of the outcome. That day he got knocked around, 25 hits good for 24 runs. Every start in the past month had felt like that one, it seemed.

Not this one. In the third, Monbouquette got all three batters, two on grounders and one on an easy fly. "I kept thinking about what that girl said," Monbo later told the *Boston Herald.* "And it was about the third inning, I think, I said to myself, 'Dammit, she's right.' I knew I had it, and I started to think about a no-hitter that early." The difference was in his pivot. "I was locking myself when I pivoted," he explained. "I was hurrying as I pivoted, sort of jerky-like, [so] when I threw the ball, it didn't have anything on it." He hadn't realized he was doing it, and he almost didn't realize when he stopped doing it. "[Once] I got the first few batters out, I realized I was doing it correctly, and then I forgot all about it."

Monbo may have forgotten all about it, but his pitching was unforgettable.

He sat down a stream of White Sox batters, one after the other. The Red Sox, meanwhile, had men on in just about every inning, and yet after seven, the score remained 0–0. Curt Gowdy, calling the game for WHDH radio, coolly mentioned to the listening audience that a no-hitter was in the making. That audience, back in Boston, included Bill's three teenage siblings and his father, Frederick, who kept a scorecard. "It didn't bother me that Curt said it," the elder Monbouquette told Bill Kipouras of the *Herald*. "I guess I'm not that kind with a hoo-doo feeling about those things." He was also under doctor's orders not to do anything that would raise his blood pressure, so he forced himself to stay calm.

So did Frederick's son as he went into the late innings. Neither team had put a run on the board. In the top of the eighth it looked as if yet another Boston rally were on the verge of being snuffed out. Gary Geiger had led off with a walk, but Carl Yastrzemski struck out and Geiger was caught stealing when Pagliaroni swung and missed at a 2–1 pitch. But Pags, Pete Runnels, and Lou Clinton hit successive singles to bring a run across for the Red Sox before Frank Malzone flew out.

The one run would be all they would need if Monbo could keep pitching like he was. The curve that had been good at the beginning was no longer as good, but the slider that had been shaky early on was now as good as it had ever been. He sat Chicago down in the bottom half, but it was Early Wynn who worried him. More specifically, it was Wynn's spot in the batting order that Bill had an eye on. Wynn would be due up in the bottom of the ninth, and surely Nellie Fox would pinch-hit for the pitcher. "Nobody had to tell me," Monbo would later say. "I knew all the way I had a no-hitter. The only guy I was concerned about was Fox—he always manages to get a piece of the ball." He told *The Sporting News*, "He murders me; he always has."

Monbouquette struck out Sherm Lollar on three pitches to open the final frame, and then, as he had predicted, he faced Fox. And Fox did get his bat on the ball, but he hit a "tricky grounder" to Malzone, who threw to Runnels for the out. That left only Luis Aparicio and the game would be on ice. He got two quick strikes on Aparicio with fastballs, then reared back and threw another one. Aparicio started to swing and then checked himself at the last moment as the ball tailed out of the strike zone. Umpire Bill McKinley ruled no swing, and the Chicago crowd booed him. Aparicio could neither hold up for the next nor catch up to it, and he swung and missed. He was out, Boston had won 1–0, and Bill Monbouquette had earned himself a place in Red Sox lore.

He leaped in place on the mound. Within seconds, Pagliaroni barreled into him. And first to reach the quickly forming scrum from the bullpen was pitcher Earl Wilson, who had thrown a no-hitter himself just a few weeks earlier, on June 26. "I know how he feels," Wilson declared with authority. "It's a great thrill, something he'll never forget."

"It was the sweet taste of perfection after four disastrous games," wrote Ted Smits for the Associated Press. Monbo had indeed found the key. He would go 6–3 the rest of the way, pitch three shutouts, and give up more than three runs in a start only twice the rest of the season. He finished the season with 15 wins and a 3.33 ERA.

Extra Innings

- Monbo would never forget his homecoming, in which crowds greeted him at the airport. "The majority of those in attendance were teenage girls, armed with autograph books," according to the *Herald*. There Medford's mayor McGlynn presented the native son with a ceremonial gavel and named him honorary mayor for the month of August. A state police cruiser then carried him to the fire engine waiting for him. Perched atop the fire engine and wearing a fire chief's hat, Monbouquette presided over a "joyously honking cavalcade of 50 cars on an eight mile [trip] to Medford" *(Boston Herald)*.

- Monbouquette had previously pitched a one-hitter, a 5–0, May 7, 1960, victory against the Tigers. In September 1964 he would again give up only one hit, while facing the Twins. Unfortunately, the one hit was a two-run homer to Zoilo Versalles, and Monbo lost that game 2–1.

- Monbo was involved in another pitching feat on August 25, 1963. In a doubleheader, he and Bob Heffner combined for 23 strikeouts, and the bullpen added four more, to give the Cleveland Indians 27 whiffs on the day in 24 innings. The Sox would strike out 17 times over the course of the day, as well, making a record-setting total of 44 for both teams.

- With Monbo and Earl Wilson both pitching no-hitters, it was the first time since 1917 that American League teammates had thrown no-hitters in the same season. Ernie Koob and Bob Groom did it— on back-to-back days no less, May 5 and May 6, 1917—for the St. Louis Browns. In the National League the Milwaukee Braves' Lew Burdette and Warren Spahn had turned the trick just a year before, on August 18 and September 16, 1960.

Boston Glee Party

In which a future dentist and the son of a Long Island potato farmer bring the magic back to the Athens of America

For eight seasons, the Red Sox had lost more games than they had won. Not since 1958 had they had a winning team, and in 1966 the only reason Boston didn't finish dead last is that the Yankees were even worse. At least that offered some slight solace.

There were some wonderful individual performers (Tony Conigliaro and Dick Radatz among them), but owner Tom Yawkey had distanced himself from the club, spending most of his time in South Carolina, and the team was in the doldrums, readily reflected in poor attendance figures.

In 1967, everything changed. Dick O'Connell had been general manager for a couple of years and begun to make his mark. He brought in 38-year-old Dick Williams as field manager. Williams helped steer the team away from Yawkey's "country club" mentality and push the Red Sox to more of a hard-nosed, dirty-uniform attitude. He put the team through rigorous fundamental drills in the spring, and when he felt the pitchers were doing too much standing around shagging flies, he set them to playing volleyball. Ted Williams, who was roving the camp as a batting instructor, marched off in disgust after clashing with the manager over these methods.

Dick Williams couldn't have asked for a clearer signal that the old ways were gone. The team took on a younger look as well, as O'Connell signed and Williams encouraged a number of younger players. Carl Yastrzemski and Jose Tartabull were the only true veterans, and they were just 27 and 28 years old, respectively. Of course, attitude alone could not transform the Sox; they needed talent, too, and they got it in great pitching from Jim Lonborg, some good hitting from sophomore George Scott, and great relief pitching from John Wyatt. With the Sox contending for the first time in years, they added talent in midseason as well, picking up an established right-handed starter in Gary Bell, a veteran catcher in Elston Howard, and supersub Jerry Adair.

The Red Sox played .500 ball through the first three months of the year, but in July the team launched a 10-game winning streak that culminated with six road wins and unexpectedly inspired a teeming throng of 15,000 fans to pour out and greet their returning heroes at Logan International Airport. The Red Sox record was still only 52–40—not exactly setting the world afire, but clearly the fan base was thirsting for something to draw on, a team they could get behind.

The Red Sox were not even in first place, but hope, and attendance, surged at Fenway Park. "I felt the franchise was practically reborn," wrote Dick Williams in his 1990 autobiography *No More Mr. Nice Guy*. Heartthrob Tony Conigliaro had shaken off his early-season slump, and he and Yaz topped the club in most offensive categories. They were playing pretty well, but there were several other teams very much in the race, too.

Carl Yastrzemski

On August 18, the California Angels came to town. In the fourth inning, when Scott was called out trying to stretch a single into a double, some radical in the stands expressed his or her displeasure with the umpire by tossing a smoke bomb on the field. There was a 10-minute delay clearing the field, and the smoke still clouded the air when play resumed. Reggie Smith flew out, bringing Tony C to the plate. Tony already had 20 homers and 67 RBIs. But he crowded the plate; it was the way he played, and he'd already suffered a couple of broken bones as a result. Angels pitcher Jack Hamilton may have stiffened up a bit standing around during the delay. He tried to pitch Conigliaro inside, but the pitch sailed, striking the batter in the eye socket. Tony C went down, his cheekbone fractured, his jaw dislocated, and his eye badly damaged.

The Red Sox could not let the gruesome injury deter them from their drive for the pennant. They pulled together and swept the Angels, then added Ken Harrelson to the lineup after he went up for grabs in a free-agent bidding war spurred by his outright release by A's owner Charles O. Finley. Yawkey's interest in the club, like most of New England's, had been rekindled by now, and he opened his wallet to ensure that the slugger would land with Boston and not a competitor.

The Red Sox were fielding a contending team. The idea of winning the pennant remained an "Impossible Dream," but for the first time in more than a decade, it was possible to entertain such a dream. Entering September, Chicago, Minnesota, Detroit, and Boston were all neck and neck.

Then Yaz went on a tear. Over the final two weeks of the season he hit .523, with five homers, driving in 16 runs, and scoring 14 times himself. Were the spark Yaz provided, the great pitching of Lonborg and Jose Santiago, and the new team chemistry all in vain? With just four games to play, Boston dropped the first two to Cleveland and all seemed sunk—except that the Twins had done the same in Kansas City. There were two games left on the schedule, and as Fate would have it, those Twins would be facing those Red Sox at Fenway Park.

The Twins had a slight edge; they only needed a split to win the flag, while Boston would need to win both games. Boston did win the first of the pair, thanks to a three-run homer from the bat of Carl Yastrzemski in the bottom of the seventh inning, giving Jose Santiago a 6–2 lead. Williams used Bell in relief, and Harmon Killebrew hit a two-run homer to bring the Twins to within two, but the Sox squelched any further rally and won the game, 6–4.

At his locker, Yaz stared at the clubhouse door. "I want the feeling of coming through that door with the pennant won," he told Arthur Daley of the *New York Times*. The win set up the final confrontation for Sunday, October 1.

The October 1 game was, in effect, a playoff game. Whichever team won at least secured a tie for the pennant. The Sox sent out their ace, "Gentleman Jim" Lonborg. He had been the team's best pitcher all year, but there seemed to be one shortcoming he'd had: Minnesota had beaten him three times already. In fact, Lonborg had never notched a win against the Twins in his career. As motivation, he wrote "$10,000" inside his glove, the amount being the prevailing estimate of a World Series share.

Not only did the Twins represent a stumbling block, but also Lonborg had something of a jinx at Fenway. His record at home was a mediocre 7–5. Wanting to get every advantage he could, he decided to sleep in a hotel the night before rather than in his own home. "Maybe I was being superstitious," he told the Associated Press. "I figured I'd . . . pretend I was on the road."

He'd be facing a formidable lineup. Harmon Killebrew was neck and neck with Yaz for the home run crown, and the Twins had three players who had more hits than Killebrew: Rod Carew, Tony Oliva, and Cesar Tovar.

With the pennant on the line, things started out rough for the "straw-haired, 24-year-old stringbean" (UPI). The first two outs came quickly enough, but Lonborg was too careful with Killebrew and walked him. Oliva doubled past a leaping Yaz, and Killebrew came in to score when Scott, taking the relay from Yaz, threw the ball beyond the reach of catcher Russ Gibson. The run was unearned, but the score was nonetheless 1–0.

The Twins got another unearned run off Lonborg in the third, again following a two-out walk, this time to Tovar. Killebrew followed with a single to left, and Yaz tried to scoop the ball quickly to hold the runners, but the ball skipped through him for an error, and Tovar scored. After three innings it was 2–0 Twins.

Minnesota had the aptly named Dean Chance on the hill, already a 20-game winner, leading the Twins with a 2.62 ERA. Yaz singled in the first, and Rico Petrocelli singled in the second, but that was all they could muster. Lonborg himself singled in the third but was erased in a double play. Yaz doubled to lead off the fourth, but ended up getting doubled off when Chance snared a George Scott liner headed up the middle. They simply could not get a rally going against Chance.

Until the sixth. Lonborg led the charge himself, opening the inning with a startling bunt single. "The bunt was my own idea," he told the Associated Press. "It was the first thing I thought about when I went to the plate." Adair singled, and then Dalton Jones showed bunt, but swung the bat and singled, too. The bases were loaded for the magnificent Yaz. "I kept telling myself, don't go for the home run, go for the base hit," Yaz told reporters later. Yaz got his third hit of the game, lining the fourth single of the frame, scoring Lonborg and Adair. Ken Harrelson hit an infield chopper, and shortstop Zoilo Versalles fired home to cut down the run, but Jones slid in—safe! And Harrelson stood at first on the fielder's choice. The Red Sox took the lead, 3–2. Williams sent Jose Tartabull in to run for Harrelson. Twins manager Cal Ermer countered with a bolder move. He replaced Chance on the mound with Al Worthington.

Nerves? The packed Fenway crowd screamed for blood. In some 90 innings of work that year, Worthington had thrown only three wild pitches; on entering this game, he uncorked two. The first sent Yaz to third and Tartabull to second, and the second brought Yaz home with another run. Worthington struck out Scott for the first out of the inning, but walked Petrocelli. Reggie Smith came to bat with runners on the corners. He grounded to first, but Killebrew matched Yaz's earlier error with one of his own, and Tartabull scored. Norm Siebern batted for catcher Gibson but grounded out. Lonborg, up for the second time in the inning, was retired by the second baseman. The rally was over, but the score stood 5–2 in favor of Boston.

Lonborg hadn't given up a run since the unearned one in the third. The Twins put up a couple of pinch hitters, but to no avail.

In the seventh, the Sox had a chance to blow the game wide open. Three successive singles from Jones, Adair, and Yaz loaded the bases. But Mudcat

Grant came on to pitch and induced Tartabull to hit into a 3-2-3 double play, and Scott struck out to end the inning.

Red Sox fans know that a three-run lead is never safe at Fenway. There were still six outs remaining. Ermer sent pinch hitter Rich Reese in to lead off the eighth, and he singled. Boston quickly erased him in a double play. That brought up the Killer. Harmon Killebrew stepped in and singled. Tony Oliva then singled, sending Killebrew to third, and sending up the blood pressure of the Fenway Faithful. A home run would tie it, and Bob Allison was up. He had 24 homers for the season, second only to Killebrew on the Twins. Allison lined the ball hard to left field, driving in Killebrew with the third run and sending Oliva to third, but Allison thought he had a double and maybe underestimated Yaz—who gunned him out sliding into second base. Rally over.

Lonborg stayed in the game, and the Twins tried to mount a last-ditch rally in the ninth. Ted Uhlaender singled to start things off, but Rod Carew grounded into a 4–3 double play. That left just Rich Rollins to retire.

The crowd roared, scenting victory. Rollins was so unnerved, he took one of Versalles's bats by accident. He swung at the first pitch, popped it up, and Petrocelli just had to drift back a bit and snag it. He did, leaping up and running toward the mound in jubilation. But most of the Fenway Faithful, it

OCTOBER 1, 1967: MINNESOTA AT BOSTON

Minnesota Twins	AB	R	H	RBI	BB	SO	PO	A	Boston Red Sox	AB	R	H	RBI	BB	SO	PO	A
Versalles ss	3	0	0	0	0	0	1	2	Adair 2b	4	1	2	0	0	0	1	2
Reese ph,lf	1	0	1	0	0	0	0	0	Andrews 2b	0	0	0	0	0	0	2	1
Tovar 3b	3	1	0	0	1	0	1	1	Jones 3b	4	1	2	0	0	0	0	1
Killebrew 1b	2	2	2	0	2	0	8	1	Yastrzemski lf	4	1	4	2	0	0	4	1
Oliva rf	3	0	2	0	1	1	2	0	Harrelson rf	3	0	0	1	0	0	1	0
Allison lf	4	0	1	1	0	2	0	0	Tartabull pr,rf	1	1	0	0	0	0	1	0
Hernandez ss	0	0	0	0	0	0	0	1	Scott 1b	4	0	0	0	0	2	9	1
Uhlaender cf	4	0	1	0	0	0	1	0	Petrocelli ss	3	0	1	0	1	0	2	5
Carew 2b	4	0	0	0	0	0	4	4	Smith cf	4	0	0	1	0	1	1	0
Zimmerman c	2	0	0	0	0	0	3	0	Gibson c	2	0	0	0	0	1	5	0
Nixon ph,c	1	0	0	0	0	0	2	1	Siebern ph	1	0	0	0	0	0	0	0
Rollins ph	1	0	0	0	0	0	0	0	Howard c	1	0	1	0	0	0	0	0
Chance p	2	0	0	0	0	2	1	1	Lonborg p	4	1	2	0	0	0	1	0
Worthington p	0	0	0	0	0	0	0	0	Totals	35	5	12	4	1	4	27	11
Kostro ph	1	0	0	0	0	0	0	0									
Roland p	0	0	0	0	0	0	0	0									
Grant p	0	0	0	0	0	0	1	0									
Totals	31	3	7	1	4	5	24	11									

Minnesota Twins	IP	H	R	ER	BB	SO	HR	Boston Red Sox	IP	H	R	ER	BB	SO	HR
Chance (L)	5	8	5	5	0	2	0	Lonborg (W)	9	7	3	1	4	5	0
Worthington	1	0	0	0	1	1	0								
Roland	0	3	0	0	0	0	0								
Grant	2	1	0	0	1	0	0								
Totals	8	12	5	5	1	4	0								

	1	2	3	4	5	6	7	8	9		R	H	E
MIN A	1	0	1	0	0	0	0	1	0		3	7	1
BOS A	0	0	0	0	0	5	0	0	x		5	12	2

seemed, had beat him there. Enveloping Lonborg in a swirling mass of celebration, the celebrants lifted Gentleman Jim on their shoulders, even tearing a few pieces of his uniform off him. In photos, Lonborg doesn't look the least perturbed. He looks ecstatic. "It was sheer mania," he told the Associated Press.

Boston police rescued him from the delirious mob, some of whom were climbing the screen behind home plate to visit the press box. For all the celebration, the Red Sox gathered in the clubhouse, knowing that if the Tigers won the nightcap of their doubleheader in Detroit (they'd beaten the Angels in the first game), there would be a single-game playoff between Boston and Detroit.

There would be no playoff. A few suspenseful hours later, all New England knew it. The Tigers lost to the Angels, 8–5, and renewed celebration gripped Boston. Firecrackers were set off as thousands blocked traffic in Kenmore Square and gathered on the steps of the State House. Lonborg's victory was his 22nd, tying him for the league lead, and Yaz's remarkable surge (7-for-8 in the final two games) not only sewed up the pennant, it also gave him the Triple Crown for his .326 average, 121 RBIs, and 44 home runs. The Impossible Dream had come true.

Extra Innings

- Talk about "impossible": In an era when the Yankees were awful and having trouble drawing fans, they held "Carl Yastrzemski Night" at Yankee Stadium, attracting throngs of Red Sox fans for a game against Boston late in the season. Yaz, who had grown up on Long Island, had almost become a Yankee, but his father held out for a better deal and got it: from the Red Sox. "The Yankees gave Yaz a Chrysler with Massachusetts plates that read 'Yaz-8' and fans contributed $10,000 in his name to the Jimmy Fund," wrote Glenn Stout and Richard Johnson in *Red Sox Century*. The Red Sox even won the game (though Yaz went hitless).

- Yaz shared the home run crown with Harmon Killebrew; both sluggers had 44 home runs. The figures Yaz posted still stand as the last time any major league player has won baseball's Triple Crown. Carl would eventually come to hold another record, for most games played in the American League, at 3,308. Only Pete Rose has played in more major league games (3,562).

- Lonborg, who had studied medicine at Stanford before going into baseball, would go on to study dentistry at Tufts University and settle in the Boston area. He is a dentist to this day, and both Jim and his wife, Rosemary, are actively involved with the Jimmy Fund.

30

October 9, 1967: Boston at St. Louis

Jim Dandy

In which a gentleman proves himself the master of the hill once again

Here it was, the "summer of love," and the Red Sox had rekindled New England's love for the team. They were in their first World Series in 21 years, only the second under the Yawkey ownership, and playing the St. Louis Cardinals offered Boston a chance to redeem their loss to St. Louis in the 1946 Series.

The Cardinals had breezed to the National League pennant. Their offense was sparked by the hitting of Curt Flood and the speed of Lou Brock, and powered by the bats of Orlando Cepeda and Roger Maris. The pitching was so good that even though ace Bob Gibson broke his leg and missed two months, they hardly missed him. Gibson returned in time to tune up for October, well rested and as dangerous as ever.

The Cardinals won the first game 2–1 at Fenway. Righty Jose Santiago was given the ball because Boston's ace, Lonborg, had thrown a complete game against the Twins on the final day of the season, helping bring home the pennant. Santiago matched Gibson pitch for pitch but came up short. Lonborg was ready for Game Two, and he simply slammed the door on the Cardinals. He had a no-hitter through two outs in the eighth inning before Julian Javier doubled, but Jim won the game—a 5–0 Sox shutout. When the scene shifted to St. Louis, though, the Cardinal bats bounced back, beating both Gary Bell (5–2) and Santiago (6–0), taking a 3–1 lead in the Series. One more loss, and the Impossible Dream would wake to the reality of a World Series loss.

Who else could take the ball for Game Five but Jim Lonborg? Opposing him for St. Louis was future Hall of Famer Steve Carlton. Carlton was a young left-handed strikeout artist who won 14 games for the Cards, but in the eyes of Boston rooters he couldn't possibly match the now tried and tested Gentleman Jim. Lonborg had watched an episode of *Mission Impossible* on television to unwind the night before the game, and everyone understood from his performance against the Twins for the pennant and from the one-hitter in Game Two that he could be impossible to beat. The game started slowly; like heavyweights circling and feinting, neither side struck, and after two innings there was no action of consequence.

OCTOBER 9, 1967: BOSTON AT ST. LOUIS

Boston Red Sox	AB	R	H	RBI	BB	SO	PO	A	St. Louis Cardinals	AB	R	H	RBI	BB	SO	PO	A
Foy 3b	5	1	1	0	0	3	2	4	Brock lf	4	0	0	0	0	1	0	0
Andrews 2b	3	0	1	0	0	0	1	2	Flood cf	4	0	0	0	0	0	2	0
Yastrzemski lf	3	0	1	0	1	1	2	0	Maris rf	4	1	2	1	0	0	3	0
Harrelson rf	3	0	1	1	1	0	1	0	Cepeda 1b	4	0	0	0	0	1	5	0
Tartabull rf	0	0	0	0	0	0	0	0	McCarver c	3	0	0	0	0	0	9	1
Scott 1b	3	1	0	0	1	1	14	0	Shannon 3b	3	0	0	0	0	1	1	3
Smith cf	4	1	1	0	0	1	0	0	Javier 2b	3	0	0	0	0	0	4	3
Petrocelli ss	3	0	0	0	1	1	1	2	Maxvill ss	2	0	1	0	0	0	3	4
Howard c	4	0	1	1	0	0	5	0	Ricketts ph	1	0	0	0	0	0	0	0
Lonborg p	4	0	0	0	0	3	0	2	Willis p	0	0	0	0	0	0	0	0
Totals	**32**	**3**	**6**	**2**	**4**	**9**	**27**	**10**	Lamabe p	0	0	0	0	0	0	0	1
									Carlton p	1	0	0	0	0	0	0	0
									Tolan ph	1	0	0	0	0	1	0	0
									Washburn p	0	0	0	0	0	0	0	1
									Gagliano ph	1	0	0	0	0	0	0	0
									Bressoud ss	0	0	0	0	0	0	0	0
									Totals	**31**	**1**	**3**	**1**	**0**	**4**	**27**	**13**

Boston Red Sox	IP	H	R	ER	BB	SO	HR	St. Louis Cardinals	IP	H	R	ER	BB	SO	HR
Lonborg (W)	9	3	1	1	1	0	4	1	Carlton (L)	6	3	1	0	2	5	0
									Washburn	2	1	0	0	0	2	0
									Willis	0	1	2	1	2	0	0
									Lamabe	1	1	0	0	2	0	0
									Totals	**9**	**6**	**3**	**1**	**4**	**9**	**0**

	1	2	3	4	5	6	7	8	9	R	H	E
BOS A	0	0	1	0	0	0	0	0	2	3	6	1
STL N	0	0	0	0	0	0	0	0	1	1	3	2

But after Lonborg struck out to start the third, Boston third baseman Joe Foy singled off Carlton. Mike Andrews bunted to advance the runner with a sacrifice, but third baseman Mike Shannon juggled the ball and both men were safe. And up came Yaz. Carlton got Captain Carl to look at strike three, putting the inning in the hands of "Hawk" Harrelson. Harrelson, acquired to replace the injured Tony Conigliaro late in the season, had actually been somewhat of a disappointment at the plate in Boston. But not this time. He singled to left, bringing home Foy. Carlton retired Scott, but the Sox had a slim 1–0 lead.

Lonborg protected that lead with the determination of a mother lion. "I [started out] with more of the fastball today," he told reporters. "I was hitting spots, the outside corners. When they started getting a good rip at the pitch away, then I went to the breaking ball." Dal Maxvill had a single in the third, Roger Maris had another in the fourth, but after those meaningless hits, Lonborg retired the next 14 men in a row, bringing the game right to the ninth inning with the Sox still holding that slim one-run lead. "I felt a little tired mentally about the seventh inning," Lonborg admitted, but the Cardinals never threatened.

Steve Carlton had long ago been lifted for a pinch hitter, and the Red Sox faced Ron Willis in the top of the ninth. George Scott walked to start the action, and Reggie Smith doubled down the left-field line, sending Scott to third. They had a very good chance for the all-important insurance run.

Catcher Tim McCarver held out four fingers, then his glove, as they intentionally walked Rico Petrocelli to get to Elston Howard. At age 38, Howard was a prime double-play candidate, but after Willis threw him ball one, manager Red Schoendienst replaced his pitcher with Jack Lamabe. Howard greeted the new pitcher with a soft single into right, driving in Scott. Maris picked up the ball and unleashed a throw to the plate, high, but the swift Smith scored as well. The Sox were now up 3–0, with Petrocelli on third and no one out. Lonborg came to the plate and attempted in vain to lay down a bunt—he eventually bunted foul for strike three—and then Foy struck out swinging, while Rico got himself trapped off third in a rundown. It took five tosses back and forth but the Cardinal infield finally tagged him, and the inning ended, but the 3–0 lead seemed like more than enough for Lonborg to finish the job.

He make it look easy at first, inducing both Brock and Flood to ground out. Maris then slammed a homer to right, but it was too little, too late. Lonborg challenged Orlando Cepeda to try the same, but Cepeda grounded to third.

Jim Lonborg

"Never since Cy Young threw history's first world series [*sic*] delivery in 1903 has any pitcher been as nearly perfect through 18 consecutive innings as Lonborg," wrote Red Smith. The Sox would live to play another day thanks to Lonborg's mastery.

◀ Extra Innings

- Boston pitcher Darrell Brandon had given a good-luck charm to Lonborg before his previous start, a golden paper horseshoe from a fan that Lonborg had kept in his back pocket. Lonborg had thrown it away after the win, but then decided it might still have some luck in it. Brandon retrieved the charm, and Lonborg kept it in an envelope in his pocket throughout Game Five. After securing the win, Lonborg returned the envelope to Brandon for safekeeping in case the Sox could win Game Six and force a deciding Game Seven.

31

October 12, 1967: St. Louis at Boston

Heartbreak Hill

In which we come to love the impossible

Everything seemed possible in the magical summer of '67. Here was a team— the Red Sox—that had finished just half a game out of last place the year before, but this October, they owned the American League pennant. They had also forced a seventh game in the World Series and had a chance to win their first world championship in 49 long years.

A day earlier, the situation had looked familiar to the Boston Red Sox and their fans: win two games in a row against a tough opponent. At Fenway Park. They had done just that to the Minnesota Twins to secure that pennant, and now they had to do the same to the St. Louis Cardinals to bring home the trophy. Jim Lonborg had staved off elimination in St. Louis by winning Game Five, and the Sox stormed back in Game Six. The Sox took a one-run lead in the second, lost it when St. Louis scored twice in the top of the third, but then scored three runs in the fourth on three home runs: one each by Yaz, Reggie Smith, and Rico Petrocelli (his second of the game).

Lou Brock homered off John Wyatt to tie it for the Cards in the top of the seventh, but the Red Sox responded immediately, and forcefully, with a flurry of six hits off four different St. Louis relievers, leading to four more runs in the bottom of the seventh. Boston won the game, 8–4. St. Louis had used eight pitchers in the game, tying a World Series record.

Now if they could win just one last game, they'd have won it all. Was this the team of destiny?

Thus the stage was set for the final showdown at Fenway Park. St. Louis had Bob Gibson (2–0) rested and ready for the start. Boston had a 2–0 winner, too, Jim Lonborg, who had now pitched three straight gems, clinching the pennant and winning Games Two and Five of the World Series, all within a nine-day span. He was ready but he wasn't as rested. "I feel awfully tired," Lonborg told reporters after his Game Five masterpiece. "But I can go in Game Seven." Gibson, too, felt the strain. "Tired?" he said to reporters before the contest. "It gets to you all over. Lonborg is younger than I am but he has had one day less rest than I've had. It should get him before it gets me."

The two aces were set to go head-to-head for the first time.

Things started out well for Gentleman Jim that cool, gray day. Lou Brock and Curt Flood both flew out easily. Roger Maris, the only Cardinal who seemed to have any punch against Lonborg, singled off Lonborg's glove, but was stranded when Orlando Cepeda grounded out. In the second, Julian Javier singled with two out, but was caught stealing to end the inning. But in the third, perhaps fatigue finally began to catch up to Lonborg. Dal Maxvill opened the inning with a triple. Lonborg got the next two outs without allowing the man to score, getting Gibson to line to third baseman Joe Foy, and Brock to pop up to Petrocelli at short. Flood singled to center, though, scoring Maxvill, and then came Maris, whose single sent the speedy Flood all the way to third. Facing Cepeda, Lonborg uncorked a wild pitch, allowing Flood to score. Cepeda grounded out to prevent further damage, but the Cardinals had a lead against Lonborg for the first time in the World Series, 2–0. "It was an improbable hour for the coach to turn back into a pumpkin," ran a story in United Press International. "But . . . the Cinderella Boston Red Sox found themselves back in the world of reality after 11 days of riding in a fairy tale chariot."

Two runs loomed large because of the way Gibson was pitching. Through four innings, the Sox still hadn't made even one hit, and in the top of the fifth, the hole got deeper. Though Lonborg had set the Cards down easily in the fourth, and got Maxvill to ground out to open the fifth, Bob Gibson himself got hold of a fastball and homered into deep center field, hitting the wall above the corner of the bleachers. Before Lonborg could recover from the shock, Lou Brock singled—his first hit off Lonborg in 11 tries—then stole second. He

OCTOBER 12, 1967: ST. LOUIS AT BOSTON

St. Louis Cardinals	AB	R	H	RBI	BB	SO	PO	A	Boston Red Sox	AB	R	H	RBI	BB	SO	PO	A
Brock lf	4	1	2	0	1	0	1	0	Foy 3b	3	0	0	0	1	1	2	3
Flood cf	3	1	1	2	1	0	0	0	Morehead p	0	0	0	0	0	0	0	0
Maris rf	3	0	2	1	1	0	1	0	Osinski p	0	0	0	0	0	0	0	0
Cepeda 1b	5	0	0	0	0	1	6	2	Brett p	0	0	0	0	0	0	0	0
McCarver c	5	1	1	0	0	0	12	0	Andrews 2b	3	0	0	0	0	1	1	2
Shannon 3b	4	1	0	0	0	1	0	0	Yastrzemski lf	3	0	1	0	1	0	2	0
Javier 2b	4	1	2	3	0	1	4	4	Harrelson rf	4	0	0	0	0	2	3	0
Maxvill ss	4	1	1	0	0	0	3	3	Scott 1b	4	1	1	0	0	2	9	0
Gibson p	4	1	1	1	0	1	0	1	Smith cf	3	0	0	0	0	0	2	0
Totals	**36**	**7**	**10**	**6**	**4**	**5**	**27**	**10**	Petrocelli ss	3	1	1	0	0	2	3	2
									Howard c	2	0	0	0	0	0	4	1
									Jones ph,3b	0	0	0	0	1	0	0	0
									Lonborg p	1	0	0	0	0	1	0	0
									Tartabull ph	1	0	0	0	0	1	0	0
									Santiago p	0	0	0	0	0	0	0	0
									Siebern ph	1	0	0	1	0	0	0	0
									Gibson c	0	0	0	0	0	0	1	0
									Totals	**28**	**2**	**3**	**1**	**3**	**10**	**27**	**8**

St. Louis Cardinals	IP	H	R	ER	BB	SO	HR	Boston Red Sox	IP	H	R	ER	BB	SO	HR
Gibson (W)	9	3	2	2	3	10	0	Lonborg (L)	6	10	7	6	1	3	2
								Santiago	2	0	0	0	0	1	0
								Morehead	0.1	0	0	0	3	1	0
								Osinski	0.1	0	0	0	0	0	0
								Brett	0.1	0	0	0	0	0	0
								Totals	**9**	**10**	**7**	**6**	**4**	**5**	**2**

	1	2	3	4	5	6	7	8	9	R	H	E
STL N	0	0	2	0	2	3	0	0	0	7	10	1
BOS A	0	0	0	0	1	0	0	1	0	2	3	1

stole third as Lonborg delivered ball four to Curt Flood. The steal tied the record for stolen bases by a player in a single World Series at six.

And here was Maris again. There was just the one out, so this time he didn't even need to get a hit to contribute. He flew deep enough to right, and Brock tagged and scored on the sacrifice fly. Cepeda flew to left to end things again (he would bat only .103 for the Series). It was the midpoint of the game and the Cardinals were leading 4–0—time for the Red Sox bats to wake up, if ever they would. Was Gibson unhittable? Could they get at least one run back to restore a measure of hope? George Scott did just that, booming out a triple to lead off the bottom of the fifth and scoring on the same play when Julian Javier's relay throw went into the dugout.

But that was all the Sox would get, and in the next half inning, the top of the sixth, the Cardinals would put Lonborg, the game, and the Series on ice. McCarver opened the inning with a double. Mike Shannon tapped a ball in the infield, which Foy muffed, allowing Shannon to reach. Manager Dick Williams visited the mound. "I wanted to take him out," he told reporters after the game, explaining that he knew Lonborg was tired and didn't have his good stuff. "But he wanted to stay in the game. He thought Javier might be bunting and he could get him." Javier was not bunting. He hit a three-run homer into the screen above the Green Monster. Lonborg finished the inning, but he was finished for the season. "Utter weariness bowed his shoulders as he shuffled from the mound," wrote Arthur Daley in the *New York Times*. "His arm couldn't quite match his indomitable spirit." Williams lifted him for a pinch hitter the next inning, to no avail; Jose Tartabull struck out.

Boston would get one more run back in the eighth off Gibson, when Rico doubled and then took third on a wild pitch. Dalton Jones walked, and the next batter, pinch hitter Norm Siebern, grounded into a force play, scoring Petrocelli. Neither Foy nor Mike Andrews could get the ball out of the infield, and the one run was all they could muster. Gibson was simply too good, on his way to being rightly named Series MVP.

With the score 7–2 in St. Louis's favor, Yaz singled to open the ninth, making one last stab at an impossible comeback. But the very next batter, Hawk Harrelson, hit into a double play and erased even that thin threat and hope. Gibson finished it off, striking out George Scott and putting an end to the Sox' magical but ultimately heartbreaking year. Columnist Shirley Povich summed it up this way: "The tumult and the shouting have faded, but not New England's memories of these Red Sox who weren't supposed to win anything . . . yet took the Cardinals all the way to seven games in the World Series." New England had fallen in love all over again, and learned to live with heartbreak again, too. Povich was wrong; the shouting went on at Fenway Park long after the game was over. "All the people of New England are proud [of you]," Williams told his players at their lockers. "Listen to 'em! You can hear 'em still yelling outside." A new generation of fans would carry the torch for the Sox for decades to come.

Extra Innings

- Brock stole one more bag in the ninth, setting the new record for steals in a World Series at seven. The previous record of six had been shared by Honus Wagner, who did it in 1909 with Pittsburgh, and Jim Slagle of the Chicago Cubs, who did it in 1907.

- Jim Lonborg went skiing that winter and on Christmas Eve hurt his knee badly. The 1967 Cy Young Award winner, 22–9 in '67, fell to just 6–10 in 1968. The Sox slipped to 17 games out and just a fourth-place finish, and were even a bit worse in the three years after that. It wasn't until 1972 that they came close again to another pennant.

- For Tony Conigliaro, it was a long comeback from his August 1967 beaning, and he missed the entire season of '68. On April 8, 1969, he made his first start for the Red Sox in almost two years and hit a dramatic home run in the top of the 10th inning to give the Sox a lead against the Orioles. When Baltimore retied the score, Tony C came up again, in the 12th, worked out a walk, and came around to score what proved to be the winning run. He hit 56 homers in two seasons for the Sox, but was never quite the same player he had been. He suffered a heart attack in 1982 and fell into a coma. He never fully recovered and passed away in 1990 at the relatively young age of 45.

32

October 15, 1975: Boston at Cincinnati

Marathon Man

In which El Tiante records a titanic victory to even the Series

After years of sputtering, bad trades, and clubhouse unrest—and missing a pennant by seven games in 1974—the 1975 Red Sox put the talent together to make another run of it. Newcomers Jim Rice and Fred Lynn tore up the league, catcher Carlton Fisk hit .331, and the pitching of Luis Tiant, Bill Lee, and Rick Wise kept them ahead of a strong Baltimore team. The Sox led by 4½ games at the All-Star break, by six on Labor Day. Though Yaz had fallen into disfavor with some fickle fans, Luis Tiant received love from all sides. Every time he pitched, Fenway Park became a festival. Tiant had mastery of four or five different pitches, and he could change arm angles, and further confuse hitters with his twisting, back-to-the-plate windup.

The Cuban-born pitcher had come to Boston after being released by a minor league club where he had been trying to rehab from a collarbone fracture. His father, Luis Tiant Sr., had been one of Cuba's top pitchers and had spent some time in the Negro Leagues. Fans adopted the potbellied, balding, cigar-loving Tiant as their favorite. His teammates did as well, for his terrific clubhouse presence and even more for his mound presence. "He was an outstanding competitor on the mound, a master of game situations," recalled rotationmate Rick Wise. "Starting pitchers can't dictate whether they win or lose; but they can dictate whether the team has a chance to win late in the game. Whether he won or not, he always gave the team a great chance to win. Luis was tremendous in that way."

El Tiante felt he owed it to his fans and to his teammates to always give his best. "When the people are on your side, when they are pulling for you, and chanting your name, it makes you feel good, and it makes you work harder. You don't want to let them down," he said. "Your teammates are going to respect you for what you do on the mound. You can joke all you want outside, you can be the clown, but when you go on the mound, if you are chicken, your teammates won't like you, I guarantee you." Chicken is one thing Luis never was, whether in facing the league's best hitters or in sending a message if the opposing pitcher had hit one of his "guys." "If you do that, if you always give your best and you stick up for them, nobody is going to say anything bad about you. Every time they put the

Luis Tiant

uniform behind you, they are going to play hard. Because you know what? They'll say we have to protect him, we have to do whatever we have to do to win the game for him."

With Tiant on the mound, Red Sox Nation rejoiced. But even as the club cruised into the postseason, there were concerns. Jim Rice was lost to injury on September 21, and although the Sox dispatched the Oakland A's with three straight, their National League opponent didn't look to be any pushover. The so-called Big Red Machine of Cincinnati had won their division by 20 games and polished off Pittsburgh in three straight, as well. Vegas odds had the Sox as the underdog.

Tiant smothered the Reds in Game One, though, a neat five-hit shutout that Boston won 6–0. The next night Bill Lee took the mound and took a 2–1 lead into the ninth, but the Reds offense finally broke through. Dick Drago couldn't hold the lead, and Boston ended up losing, 3–2. Game Three pitted Rick Wise against Gary Nolan. Wise had led the Sox staff with 19 wins and seemed perfect to pitch the pivotal first game in Cincinnati, since he had come from the National League and had had success against Cincy in the past. "I had my greatest game ever against the Reds, when I pitched a no-hitter and hit two home runs against that club," Wise recalled. "But there had been player turnovers and the like and I was a couple years removed from having seen them. I didn't pitch particularly well." Dwight Evans tied the game at 5–5 in the ninth with a dramatic two-run home run, but in the 10th inning a controversial umpire's call led the Reds to the winning run. As Fisk had tried to field

Ed Armbrister's bunt attempt, Armbrister inadvertently made contact with him, and Fisk's throw to second sailed into center. Boston was livid; the call should have been interference (intent was irrelevant), but umpire Larry Barnett didn't see it that way and the Reds capitalized to eke out a 6–5 victory.

"The Series is a pitcher's stage and who can dominate it better this year than Luis Tiant?" wrote Leigh Montville in the *Boston Globe*'s pre-Series predictions. With the Reds up 2–1 in the Series, Tiant took the mound in Cincinnati to try to even things again. "My arm feels all right," Tiant told the *Globe*'s Clif Keane before the game, "but I think that I will need some runs in this game. It won't be as easy as it was at Fenway Park."

Riverfront Stadium was a concrete cavern, an alien landscape compared to Fenway. "It was terrible," recalled Rick Miller. "You played on a carpet, and there was so much rain they had to use a Zamboni to suck the water off the surface. Then you'd go out in the outfield, and it would be loose and folded over in right center. If you rubbed your fingers against the grain it would almost burn you." The Reds sported a lineup crammed with top-caliber hitters such as Pete Rose, Johnny Bench, Ken Griffey, and Tony Perez. "The hitters are always learning," Tiant explained. "The good hitters, they will figure you out. But I don't want to change my way of pitching because these guys can hit the ball 500 feet or 10,000 miles. They have to have a weakness. One spot, somewhere in their swing, they have to have a weak spot, where you can get them

OCTOBER 15, 1975: BOSTON AT CINCINNATI

Boston Red Sox	AB	R	H	RBI	BB	SO	PO	A	Cincinnati Reds	AB	R	H	RBI	BB	SO	PO	A
Beniquez lf	4	0	1	1	0	0	3	0	Rose 3b	3	1	1	0	2	0	1	3
Miller lf	1	0	0	0	0	1	0		Griffey rf	5	0	1	1	0	0	0	0
Doyle 2b	5	0	1	0	0	0	2	3	Morgan 2b	3	1	0	0	2	0	2	7
Yastrzemski 1b	4	0	2	1	1	0	8	0	Perez 1b	4	0	0	0	0	1	12	1
Fisk c	5	1	1	0	0	1	4	0	Bench c	4	0	1	1	0	1	4	0
Lynn cf	4	1	1	0	0	1	4	1	Foster lf	4	1	2	0	0	0	0	0
Petrocelli 3b	4	0	1	0	0	1	1	0	Concepcion ss	4	1	1	1	0	0	3	4
Evans rf	4	1	2	2	0	0	4	2	Geronimo cf	4	0	3	1	0	0	4	0
Burleson ss	4	1	1	1	0	0	0	2	Norman p	1	0	0	0	0	0	0	0
Tiant p	3	1	1	0	1	1	0	2	Borbon p	0	0	0	0	0	0	0	0
Totals	38	5	11	5	2	4	27	10	Crowley ph	1	0	0	0	0	1	0	0
									Carroll p	0	0	0	0	0	0	1	0
									Chaney ph	1	0	0	0	0	1	0	0
									Eastwick p	0	0	0	0	0	0	0	0
									Armbrister ph	0	0	0	0	0	0	0	0
									Totals	34	4	9	4	4	4	27	15

Boston Red Sox	IP	H	R	ER	BB	SO	HR	Cincinnati Reds	IP	H	R	ER	BB	SO	HR
Tiant (W)	9	9	4	4	4	4	0	Norman (L)	3.1	7	4	4	1	2	0
								Borbon	0.2	2	1	0	0	0	0
								Carroll	2	2	0	0	0	2	0
								Eastwick	3	0	0	0	1	0	0
								Totals	9	11	5	4	2	4	0

	1	2	3	4	5	6	7	8	9		R	H	E
BOS A	0	0	0	5	0	0	0	0	0		5	11	1
CIN N	2	0	0	2	0	0	0	0	0		4	9	1

out." In his first start, Tiant had always found that spot. This time, though, whether the Reds made adjustments to him, or his stuff was just not as good, Cincinnati jumped out to an early lead.

Pete Rose opened the action with a single up the middle. Griffey batted second that night and followed with a double into the gap in left-center, and Rose hustled all the way home. Griffey got greedy, though, and tried to take third. Burleson relayed Lynn's throw to Petrocelli and they nabbed him. Good thing, too, since after Joe Morgan drew a walk, Tony Perez grounded to short. Morgan moved to second, and if Griffey had been at third, he would have scored. Johnny Bench then doubled, bringing Morgan home. Tiant escaped the inning down 2–0, but it could have been worse.

Boston could not get any offensive traction until the fourth inning. Sharp back-to-back singles by Fisk and Lynn opened the inning, and the Reds started warming up in the bullpen. Petrocelli popped to short, but both runners advanced on Fred Norman's first pitch to Dwight Evans, which went back to the screen. "Dewey" Evans, the third homegrown star in Boston's outfield, was a good hitter with a cannon for an arm. Although he didn't display a ton of power early in his career, on this night he came through with a triple that cleared the bases and pulled Boston all even, 2–2.

Rick Burleson cashed Evans in promptly with a looping double into left that might have been only a single had the Reds played it a bit more alertly. That was it for Norman, and Pedro Borbon came on in relief to face El Tiante himself. The first use of the designated hitter in the World Series was not until the following year, 1976. Luis hit a single up the middle, and Burleson advanced to third. Tiant went halfway to second, then retreated, and Bench could have picked him off first, except that no one was there to receive the throw. Borbon did get Juan Beniquez to hit a dribbler on the infield, but Perez couldn't get a handle on it; Burleson crossed the plate, Tiant went to second, and there were two on for Denny Doyle. Doyle popped up for the second out, but that brought Yaz to the plate. Yastrzemski was not quite the Triple Crown–winning force he had been in 1967, but he was still a dangerous hitter. He singled to right, Tiant came around to score, and Boston had put up five runs in the inning and batted around. It was 5–2 Red Sox when Fisk came up for the second time. He flied to center, ending the inning, but the question now became: Would a three-run lead be sufficient?

Tiant took the hill in the bottom of the fourth, wanting to put up another zero. He got Perez on strikes, and Bench on a fly to left. On what should have been the third out, George Foster grounded slowly to second and busted out of the box. Doyle rushed his throw and overthrew Yaz, allowing Foster to take second. Tiant then went to work on Dave Concepcion, but Concepcion put bat on ball and just blooped a hit into short left-center. He got a double and an RBI out of it, and the lead was now trimmed to 5–3 Red Sox. Now came Cesar Geronimo, who sent a ball into the right-field corner. By the time the ball was thrown back into the infield, Concepcion had scored and Geronimo stood on third. The pitcher's slot was next, and Borbon was lifted for Terry Crowley. Tiant bore down, and Crowley struck out, but the three-run lead was whittled down to just one: 5–4, Red Sox.

The game became Tiant against the odds. Reds relief pitchers Clay Carroll and Rawly Eastwick kept the Red Sox off the base paths for the most part, so if Tiant was going to win this one for Boston, he would have to shut down the Big Red Machine for five more innings.

In the fifth, Rose walked to lead off, and Griffey swung for the fences but only managed a long out to deep right. Morgan walked, but Perez grounded out, and Bench flew out to left to end that threat.

Tiant gutted it out through the sixth, seventh, and eighth, allowing only a Geronimo bloop and a Foster hit up the middle, both coming on two outs.

Tiant took it right to the bottom of the ninth. All the Reds needed was one run to get back in the game. Geronimo led off the final inning with his third hit of the night. Ed Armbrister pinch-hit for Eastwick and bunted Geronimo to second. No interference this time as Tiant fielded the ball and threw him out, but the tying run was now in scoring position, and Pete Rose was at the plate. Rose had hit .317 in the regular season, and led the league with 47 doubles. He'd hit safely 210 times, the seventh season he'd hit safely more than 200 times. He was a 13-year veteran who already had 2,547 hits and was already dubbed "Charlie Hustle." He'd singled off Tiant back in the first and was 1-for-3 in the game, with one walk.

Tiant was cautious and walked Rose, prompting a visit from manager Darrell Johnson. Tiant told his manager he wanted to stay in the game, and Johnson let him. There were two men on base and Ken Griffey at the plate. Griffey had hit .305 in '75, and was 2-for-7 in the World Series against Tiant. Both hits had been doubles, one in the first game and once earlier in this Game Four. Now he hit the ball squarely, a line shot into left, deep, but the miserable wetness and the turf actually helped. "It was a wet field and [so] I was playing about 15 feet deeper," Lynn later explained. He ran straight back and caught the ball over his shoulder as he neared the 404-foot marker on the wall, a game-saving play.

That left one out to get. On Tiant's 163rd pitch of the night, Morgan popped to Yaz at first, who squeezed the ball in his glove and then ran over to squeeze Tiant on the mound. "It was the best pitch I had all day," Morgan moaned to reporters. "The balding battler . . . taunted the Reds with his tantalizing assortment of slow, slow, and slower stuff," wrote Norm Clarke for the AP wire. Decades later, Peter Gammons would still describe the game as "the guttiest I've ever seen." The wily Cuban had hung on to win it, 5–4, and guarantee that the Series would return to Boston.

◀ Extra Innings

- Rick Miller: "It was a weird Series because it rained so much so we never really worked out. The fields were covered, there was no batting practice. So it was just sitting in the clubhouse waiting for the game. It rained in Boston and in Cincinnati. And the Reds conveniently forgot to get us hotel rooms, so we stayed in [suburban] Ohio in some Ramada Inn and it was terrible. We didn't go anywhere, didn't do anything."

33

October 21, 1975: Cincinnati at Boston

All's Fair

In which an immortal moment in time is granted to a native son

The Cincinnati Reds held a 3–2 lead in the 1975 World Series as the games moved back to Boston. Rainy weather forced the postponement of Game Six three days in a row, allowing the man who earned both of Boston's prior wins to return to the mound. El Tiante—Luis Tiant—would get the ball for Boston (to the chagrin of Bill Lee, who would have been given the ball if not for the delay).

By now the foe was familiar, since he had faced them twice already. The Big Red Machine of Rose and Bench and Morgan. Luis toed the rubber, his familiar turf, in the city where he was adored and where he pitched with all his heart. Pete Rose, "Charlie Hustle," stepped into the box. The Reds were frustrated, feeling that they should have put the Sox away as easily as they had the entire National League. But tonight they could close the deal if they could just solve the mystery of Luis Tiant. In his first start they had managed only five hits and been shut out. In the next, they managed four runs on nine hits. This time they hoped their offensive juggernaut would roll over Tiant, as they had Reggie Cleveland in Game Five.

Carlton Fisk

Rose tagged a pitch from Tiant, and the ball lofted into left, where it looked as if it might drop, except Yaz was there, sliding, and making the catch. Tiant then went to a full count on Ken Griffey. Full counts had been common with Luis, as he and the batters carefully dueled. Griffey walked, but Tiant was unfazed. Morgan popped up at the plate for Fisk, and then Tiant twirled strike three past Johnny Bench to bring the Red Sox to the plate.

Cecil Cooper led off. He had gotten one hit in 13 at-bats in the first three games of the Series and found himself benched for the next two. Now he faced Gary Nolan, who had lasted only four innings in Game Three. Granted, Reds manager Sparky Anderson had earned the nickname "Captain Hook" for pulling pitchers so often, and in fact in Game Three he used five pitchers, including Nolan; each one surrendered one run. Cooper struck the ball well but flew out to center. Denny Doyle followed with a grounder to first. That brought up Mr. Clutch, Carl Yastrzemski. He lined a single to right. Carlton Fisk followed with a single to left. Now Nolan had to get out Fred Lynn to end the inning. Lynn, although he would win both Rookie of the Year and MVP honors for his regular-season play, had been scuffling a bit at the plate in the

Series, or so he felt. He was 5-for-19 (.263) with only one extra-base hit. Make that two—he took Nolan deep, a home run into the bleachers in right, a three-run blast that handed El Tiante a lead. Petrocelli followed with a deep shot of his own, but it was caught by Cesar Geronimo in left-center.

Tiant went back to work. He retired the next three in a row, and opened the third by striking out Geronimo. Anderson sent Darrell Chaney in to pinch-hit for the pitcher, and he hit a fly to deep left-center, but Yaz was there to catch it. Tiant just couldn't keep Rose down; he singled, and that brought up Griffey. Griffey grounded the ball to the right and it deflected off Tiant's glove, but it rebounded to Doyle, who nipped Griffey at first.

The Reds had a new pitcher, Fred Norman, to pitch the third. Cooper continued his weak hitting, popping up to third, but Doyle doubled down the right-field line. Norman got Yaz to pop up, too, but then intentionally walked Fisk and went to a full count on Lynn before losing him to a walk and loading the bases. "Captain Hook" yanked him for Jack Billingham. The move worked: Billingham struck out Petrocelli and the Sox got nothing.

In the top of the fourth, the Reds tried to grab the momentum, now that the Boston attack had been turned back. Tiant, still wily, got the first two outs on a grounder and a called third strike, but Perez lined a base hit to right. George Foster then hit a shot to Rick Burleson at short, but Rooster threw wildly and Cincy ended up with men on the corners. Tiant did not let it bother him. He induced Dave Concepcion to foul out to first, and the Reds' rally was stifled.

Boston would try to tack on another run or two, when Dwight Evans started the inning with a ground-rule double and Billingham walked Rooster on four pitches. Two on and nobody out, and Tiant coming to the plate. Luis did his job, executing a perfect sacrifice, sending both runners into scoring position. It was now in the hands of Cecil Cooper. A fly ball would get a run in, a base hit, maybe two . . . but Cooper grounded directly to Perez at first base, and both runners had to hold. Doyle followed suit, a grounder to second, and the score remained 3–0 Sox.

So to the fifth. With one out, Ed Armbrister pinch-hit for the pitcher and walked. Pete Rose got a pitch he liked enough to hit into center for a single, and Armbrister went to third. Griffey, who had gotten a hit in each of Tiant's previous starts, saw something he liked as well, and drove a ball to the wall. Lynn leaped to try to make the play, but he bounced off the unpadded wall hard, and Griffey ended up with a triple. Lynn lay on the grass in silence but eventually regained his feet, and stayed in the game. It was now 3–2 Sox, with the tying run at third and just one out. Tiant got Joe Morgan to pop up, and if he could retire Bench, he would escape with the lead. But Bench's ball bounced off the wall as well, a single, scoring Griffey. Tiant then struck out Perez, but the score was 3–3 and there was a lot of baseball left to play.

They got to Luis again in the seventh, Griffey and Morgan opening the inning with back-to-back singles. Tiant retired the next two, but then Foster doubled and both runners scored; 5–3 Cincinnati. When Cesar Geronimo hit a home run around the Pesky Pole to lead off the eighth, that was it. The Big Red Machine had finally driven El Tiante from the mound. Roger Moret came on to pitch and got them one-two-three, but hope was at a low ebb. The Reds now had a three-run lead and were six outs from winning the World Series.

The Sox were not about to go too quietly in the bottom of the eighth. Facing the fifth Reds' pitcher of the night, Pedro Borbon, Lynn hit a ball that struck Borbon on the leg as it shot through the box; Lynn was at first with a single. Borbon walked Petrocelli. That was enough for Anderson, who pulled Borbon in favor of Rawly Eastwick. Eastwick, a mustachioed sinkerballer, struck out Evans and got Burleson on a line-out to left. With Moret due next, Darrell Johnson called on Bernie Carbo to bat. After Jim Rice had been lost to injury, the free-spirited Carbo had griped about Johnson's choice to start Juan Beniquez instead of him on days when Yaz played first. Beniquez had exactly one hit in the Series so far, a meaningless single. Carbo felt he could do better, and in his previous turn as a pinch hitter in Game Three, he had hit a home run.

No one expected him to do it again. The mood was morose. Four more outs and the Series would be over, with Cincinnati jubilant on Fenway's field, and the Red Sox left to lick their wounds over the long winter to come. Well, Carbo did do it again. Even though he seemed to be barely catching up to Eastwick's pitches, fouling them off, he hit a home run to the deepest part of the park, into the bleachers in straightaway center field. The homer was good for three runs, knotting the score at six runs apiece. The Red Sox were alive and kicking. "Bernie Carbo has never been given the credit for that homer," said pitcher Rick Wise. "After fighting off pitches and barely staying alive there, [he] put us in the position to win." The miserable Cooper struck out to end the inning, but it was a new game now, and whatever occurred, the Sox would have last licks.

Dick Drago set the Reds down in order in the ninth, and the Red Sox knew if they could scratch one run in the ninth, they would extend the Series to a final Game Seven. Things started off well, as Doyle walked. Then they got better: Yaz singled to right and Doyle went to third. The winning run was 90 feet from home with no one out. A team could hardly hope for a better opportunity.

Captain Hook did his thing, though, and Will McEnaney became the seventh pitcher for the Reds on the night. His first duty was to load the bases by intentionally walking Carlton Fisk. Freddie Lynn came up knowing that a hit, or even many flavors of an out, could make him the game-winner, a fitting cap for his MVP season. Lynn lifted a ball into left, but Foster got under it, perhaps 80 feet behind third. Third-base coach Don Zimmer shouted "No! No!" to hold Doyle, but Doyle heard "Go! Go!" and streaked for the plate. The Reds' left fielder unleashed a throw to Bench, and Doyle was cut down at the plate. Just like that, the Sox went from bases loaded no one out, to two on, two out. Petrocelli came up still looking for his first hit since Game Four. He didn't find it. The game moved to extra innings.

The 10th was relatively quiet, but Drago opened the 11th by hitting Rose with a pitch. Griffey tried to bunt him over, but Fisk snatched the ball and fired accurately to second, erasing the lead runner. Joe Morgan had probably his best swing of the Series as he drove a ball into deep right field, a ball so well

OCTOBER 21, 1975: CINCINNATI AT BOSTON

Cincinnati Reds	AB	R	H	RBI	BB	SO	PO	A	Boston Red Sox	AB	R	H	RBI	BB	SO	PO	A
Rose 3b	5	1	2	0	0	0	0	2	Cooper 1b	5	0	0	0	0	1	8	0
Griffey rf	5	2	2	2	1	0	0	0	Drago p	0	0	0	0	0	0	0	0
Morgan 2b	6	1	1	0	0	0	4	4	Miller ph	1	0	0	0	0	0	0	0
Bench c	6	0	1	1	0	2	8	0	Wise p	0	0	0	0	0	0	0	0
Perez 1b	6	0	2	0	0	2	11	2	Doyle 2b	5	0	1	0	1	0	1	2
Foster lf	6	0	2	2	0	0	4	1	Yastrzemski lf,1b	6	1	3	0	0	0	7	1
Concepcion ss	6	0	1	0	0	0	3	4	Fisk c	4	2	2	1	2	0	9	1
Geronimo cf	6	1	2	1	0	3	2	0	Lynn cf	4	2	2	3	1	0	2	0
Nolan p	0	0	0	0	0	0	1	0	Petrocelli 3b	4	1	0	0	1	1	1	1
Chaney ph	1	0	0	0	0	0	0	0	Evans rf	5	0	1	0	0	2	5	1
Norman p	0	0	0	0	0	0	0	0	Burleson ss	3	0	0	0	2	0	2	2
Billingham p	0	0	0	0	0	0	0	0	Tiant p	2	0	0	0	0	2	0	2
Armbrister ph	0	1	0	0	1	0	0	0	Moret p	0	0	0	0	0	0	0	0
Carroll p	0	0	0	0	0	0	0	0	Carbo ph,lf	2	1	1	3	0	1	1	0
Crowley ph	1	0	1	0	0	0	0	0	Totals	41	7	10	7	7	7	36	11
Borbon p	1	0	0	0	0	0	0	0									
Eastwick p	0	0	0	0	0	0	0	0									
McEnaney p	0	0	0	0	0	0	0	0									
Driessen ph	1	0	0	0	0	0	0	0									
Darcy p	0	0	0	0	0	0	0	1									
Totals	50	6	14	6	2	7	33	14									

Cincinnati Reds	IP	H	HR	R	ER	BB	SO	Boston Red Sox	IP	H	HR	R	ER	BB	SO
Nolan	2	3	1	3	3	0	2	Tiant	7	11	1	6	6	2	5
Norman	0.2	1	0	0	0	2	0	Moret	1	0	0	0	0	0	0
Billingham	1.1	1	0	0	0	1	1	Drago	3	1	0	0	0	0	1
Carroll	1	1	0	0	0	0	0	Wise (W)	1	2	0	0	0	0	1
Borbon	2	1	0	2	2	2	1	Totals	12	14	1	6	6	2	7
Eastwick	1	2	1	1	1	1	2								
McEnaney	1	0	0	0	0	1	0								
Darcy (L)	2	1	1	1	1	0	1								
Totals	11	10	3	7	7	7	7								

	1	2	3	4	5	6	7	8	9	10	11	12	R	H	E
CIN N	0	0	0	0	3	0	2	1	0	0	0	0	6	14	0
BOS A	3	0	0	0	0	0	0	3	0	0	0	1	7	10	1

hit that it looked as if it was going to clear the low three-foot wall. Except Dewey Evans lunged across the warning track and snared the ball in its flight toward the bullpen gate, robbing Morgan of a homer, and then winging the ball back to the infield (Yaz gathered it in well foul but Rick Burleson covered first) to double off Griffey, who was already almost at third and doubling back, incredulous.

Morgan's ball had been caught only by extreme effort, and Johnson was not going to send Drago out again if Boston failed to score in the bottom of the inning. They didn't score. Rick Miller pinch-hit for Drago and flew out. Grounders by Doyle and Yaz ended the 11th. Right-handed starter Rick Wise got up in the Boston bullpen. "I really wanted to get another chance to pitch, since I didn't do so well in Game Three," Wise said. "I knew it would have to be in a relief capacity. But every able arm was in the bullpen that night, so the whole staff was down there. Who knew how long that game was going to go?" Wise recalled. "I was rested, and as a starter I was used to pitching longer. They figured I'd have at least three or four good innings in me." When he got the call, he immediately began to throw, and think about the hitters he would be facing.

Wise faced Bench to start things off in the 12th, and got a foul pop off Bench's bat. Fisk ran after it, and made the catch leaning into the crowd. But Perez hit a single up the middle, and a bloop from Foster put two men on. "Like any other game, you try to get the first man out and go from there. But it didn't happen that way, there were two bloop hits and all of a sudden I had to make some good pitches," Wise said. He bore down. Concepcion hit a harmless fly to right. And then there was Cesar Geronimo. The count ran full, and Wise knew how he wanted to pitch him, and he followed his plan to perfection. "It was an inside fastball. Yep, that was the one I wanted. That was what was called for, that was what I agreed to, and that's what he took for a third strike."

And so, the bottom of the 12th. The first man to bat would be Carlton Fisk. If Tiant was Boston's adopted son, Fisk was New England's own. Born in Vermont and raised in New Hampshire, he was a first-round pick by the Sox in the amateur draft. The Sox had picked fourth that year, and reports had it that the only reason one of the first three teams didn't pick him was that they knew the Sox were the only team he would sign with. In 1972 Pudge Fisk had won the Rookie of the Year Award and a Gold Glove.

And this was his moment. The game was exactly four hours old as he stepped into the batter's box at 12:34 a.m. The first pitch went by for a ball. The second one was a sinker down and in; Fisk put a big hooking swing on it, and the ball flew high toward the left-field corner. "And all of a sudden the ball was there, like the Mystic River Bridge, suspended out in the black of the morning," wrote Peter Gammons in the *Globe*. Fisk leaped in the air, waving both his arms, trying to will the ball to stay fair. In the Red Sox dugout, his teammates were doing the same. It did stay fair. It struck the mesh of the left-field foul pole where it protrudes above the Monster, for a walk-off home run. Fisk's wild body English transformed into a home-run trot and then a running back's shuffle as he made his way around the bases through the fans mobbing the field. Organist John Kiley broke out a rendition of the "Hallelujah Chorus." Up in Charlestown, NH, where Fisk was raised, they rang the bells at the Episcopal church.

Jubilation reigned throughout New England. Not only had the three-day rain-out wait for the executioner's ax to fall ended, but also Carbo and Fisk combined to bring both a reprieve and new hope. The *Boston Globe* proclaimed in a headline, "The best game ever!" Ray Fitzgerald wrote, "How can there be a topper for what went on last night and early this morning in a ballyard gone mad, madder and maddest while watching, well, the most exciting game of baseball I have ever seen." At four hours and one minute, it was also the longest World Series game on record. The underdog Red Sox had done what no expert had thought they would do: push Cincinnati's powerhouse to a winner-take-all Game Seven.

Though the Sox, behind Bill Lee, took a three-run lead into the sixth inning of that final game, the Reds prevailed. And perhaps baseball prevailed, too. More than 70 million people nationwide had been captivated by the Red Sox drama, and more than 75 million tuned in for Game Seven, rekindling interest that had been on the wane for the national pastime. Sox fans, and baseball fans everywhere, would eagerly await next year.

Extra Innings

- The extension of the World Series by three extra days due to rain brought in an estimated $450,000 in extra revenue to Boston's hotels.

- Carlton Fisk's first choice of sports was basketball, and he had aspirations to be a Boston Celtic. But as Fisk would say, "I didn't grow into a power forward." The nickname "Pudge" followed him from childhood, when he had been less svelte.

- Waiting till next year didn't bear fruit for the Red Sox. In 1976 the Yankees won another pennant (though they were swept by the Big Red Machine in the World Series). In 1977 the Sox finished just 2½ games behind, as New York repeated.

- Fisk played five more years for the Red Sox, and then an office snafu resulted in his being awarded free agency. Fisk signed with the other Sox and played 13 more seasons, for Chicago. Catchers tend to have shorter careers than other position players, but Fisk played a record 24 seasons, finishing his career one game short of 2,500 games. He caught in 2,226 of those games, 990 of them for the Red Sox. In the year 2000 he was elected to the National Baseball Hall of Fame in Cooperstown.

- In 2005 the Red Sox held a ceremony officially designating the left-field foul pole the "Fisk Pole," though, of course, fans had been informally using the name for decades.

34

October 2, 1978: New York at Boston

Tie Breaker

In which the Sox become the first team in American League history to force a one-game contest for the second time

This was it! This was the year that Red Sox fans had been thirsting for. In 1967, the Impossible Dream team took it to Game Seven of the Series. In 1975, it was déjà vu. But the 1978 season saw a far stronger team than either of those entries. The key players from 1975 were back, but more mature as players—the Sox had the great outfield of Jim Rice, Fred Lynn, and Dwight Evans. Yaz was at first and Fisk behind the plate. On the mound they had Tiant, Mike Torrez, Dennis Eckersley, and Bill Lee.

They broke out of the box, winning nine of the first 12 games, and kept up a steady pace; they were 45–19 in mid-June and 57–26 at the All-Star break. Even more important, they were way ahead of the competition, particularly the archrival Yankees. A week after the break, the Yankees were a full 14 games behind the league-leading Red Sox. Sportswriters were already working on the Yankees' obituaries—when the New Yorkers caught fire. It wasn't just a late July doldrums for the Red Sox; beginning on July 20, they lost nine of 10 at almost the exact moment the Yankees were winning eight of nine games. By Labor Day the two teams were only five games apart. The Red Sox were very definitely looking over their shoulders at the surging Yanks.

A week and a half later, the Yankees paid a visit to Fenway Park for a four-game set, trailing the Red Sox by just four games. The Sox were battered before

OCTOBER 2, 1978: NEW YORK AT BOSTON

New York Yankees	AB	R	H	RBI	BB	SO	PO	A	Boston Red Sox	AB	R	H	RBI	BB	SO	PO	A
Rivers cf	2	1	1	0	2	0	2	0	Burleson ss	4	1	1	0	1	1	4	2
Blair ph,cf	1	0	1	0	0	0	0	0	Remy 2b	4	1	2	0	0	0	2	5
Munson c	5	0	1	1	0	3	7	1	Rice rf	5	0	1	1	0	1	4	0
Piniella rf	4	0	1	0	0	0	4	0	Yastrzemski lf	5	2	2	2	0	1	2	0
Jackson dh	4	1	1	1	0	0	0	0	Fisk c	3	0	1	0	1	0	5	1
Nettles 3b	4	0	0	0	0	1	1	3	Lynn cf	4	0	1	1	0	0	1	0
Chambliss 1b	4	1	1	0	0	0	8	0	Hobson dh	4	0	1	0	0	1	0	0
White lf	3	1	1	0	1	1	4	0	Scott 1b	4	0	2	0	0	2	8	0
Thomasson lf	0	0	0	0	0	0	1	0	Brohamer 3b	1	0	0	0	0	0	1	1
Doyle 2b	2	0	0	0	0	0	0	0	Bailey ph	1	0	0	0	0	1	0	0
Spencer ph	1	0	0	0	0	0	0	0	Duffy 3b	0	0	0	0	0	0	0	0
Stanley 2b	1	0	0	0	0	0	0	0	Evans ph	1	0	0	0	0	0	0	0
Dent ss	4	1	1	3	0	1	0	2	**Totals**	36	4	11	4	2	7	27	9
Totals	35	5	8	5	3	6	27	6									

New York Yankees	IP	H	R	ER	BB	SO	Boston Red Sox	IP	H	R	ER	BB	SO
Guidry (W)	6.1	6	2	2	1	5	Torrez (L)	6.2	5	4	4	3	4
Gossage (S)	2.2	5	2	2	1	2	Stanley	0.1	2	1	1	0	0
Totals	9	11	4	4	2	7	Hassler	1.2	1	0	0	0	2
							Drago	0.1	0	0	0	0	0
							Totals	9	8	5	5	3	6

	1	2	3	4	5	6	7	8	9	R	H	E
NY A	0	0	0	0	0	0	4	1	0	5	8	0
BOS A	0	1	0	0	0	1	0	2	0	4	11	0

the home stand—Evans, Fisk, Jerry Remy, and Yaz were all suffering from injuries. What followed was dubbed "the Boston Massacre"—the Yankees pulverized the Red Sox, winning all four games and pulling into a dead heat, both teams 86–56. New York outscored Boston in the four games by 42 to 9. The Red Sox committed 11 errors. It was humiliating; four days no Boston fan ever wants to remember.

New York kept on rolling, building up a 3½-game lead, but then the Sox broke out of their slumber and began to salvage the season that looked to be getting away from them. It took everything they had, but Boston won the final eight games of the season, allowing just three runs over their last six games. The Yankees closed strongly, too, winning six of their final seven, but it was New York's loss of their last regularly scheduled game that saw the 162-game season end with the two teams in a dead heat. Both had identical 99–63 records, necessitating a one-game playoff. A coin toss determined the venue as Fenway Park, and the Fenway Faithful rushed from their seats after the October 1 win to get in line for tickets for the next day's playoff game. Whichever team won game 100 won the pennant.

This was it—for all the marbles. Ron Guidry, with a spectacular 24–3 record, started for the Yankees on short rest, and Boston countered with the 16–12 Mike Torrez, who'd come to the Sox from the Yankees before the season. Neither team had a hit until Carl Yastrzemski led off the second with a home run down the right-field line. The Sox added a second run in the bottom of the sixth when Rick Burleson doubled to lead off, Remy bunted him to third, and Jim Rice singled him home. Torrez was working on a two-hit shut-out, and the Sox had a 2–0 lead. Folks were happy at Fenway.

Graig Nettles flied out to lead off the seventh. Chris Chambliss singled to left. Then Roy White singled to center, but Chambliss had to hold at second. No big deal, particularly when Jim Spencer pinch-hit for Brian Doyle and flew out to left. Two out, and Bucky Dent at the plate. The light-hitting shortstop didn't hit for either average or power; he was .239 with 11 doubles, one triple, and four home runs. He'd driven in only 37 runs all year long.

The at-bat started out inauspiciously. Dent took the first pitch for a ball, then proceeded to foul the next one off his foot. Sox fans were not tense; this looked almost comedic. Torrez had been nearly untouchable, only beginning to show signs of tiring. There was quite a delay as the Yankees' trainer worked on Dent's foot with ethyl chloride spray. Rather than take a couple of tosses to Fisk, keeping warm, Torrez stood around idle. Mickey Rivers handed the Yan-kees' batboy a bat, and told him to take it to Dent to replace the one he'd been using; to this day, despite a total lack of evidence, many paranoid Sox fans think that Rivers's bat must have been corked.

Ready to go, plate umpire Don Denkinger signaled to Torrez and play resumed. Whatever the reasons might have been—Torrez having fallen out of his rhythm, a corked bat, Dent's determination, a curse haunting the Red Sox, or simply Fate—Bucky Dent got hold of Torrez's next pitch and hit it high to left field. Even then, in the first moment, there didn't seem to be much to worry about. First of all, this was Bucky Dent. Second, there was a pretty good wind coming in from left field. In the very first inning, a Reggie Jackson shot that looked as if it was going out seemed to hit a wind shear and dropped into Yaz's waiting glove. Six innings later, though, the wind had shifted. The ball had just enough on it to go out, and out, and drop into the screen, leaving Yaz backed up against the wall but empty-handed.

Comedy had turned to tragedy. The Yankees had a 3–2 lead. Stunned silence prevailed.

When Torrez walked Rivers, manager Don Zimmer pulled Torrez and subbed Bob Stanley. Rivers stole second off Stanley, then scored on Thurman Munson's double to center field. New York's lead was 4–2, and they added another run in the top of the eighth when Reggie Jackson homered to lead off the inning: 5–2 Yankees.

Give them credit, the Red Sox didn't roll over. Goose Gossage had taken over for Guidry. Remy doubled to lead off the bottom of the eighth, and after Rice flied out, Yaz singled Remy home. Fisk singled, then Fred Lynn singled, scoring Yastrzemski. It was a one-run game now, with two runs in, two men on, and just one out. Butch Hobson flied out to right and George Scott struck out. Inning over.

In the ninth, Andy Hassler and Dick Drago held the Yankees scoreless, on just one hit. Bottom of the ninth, down by one run. Dwight Evans, still a little foggy from a beaning back in late August, pinch-hit but flied out. Rick Burleson worked a walk, though, and Remy got his second hit of the game with a single to right. That was no ordinary hit, either. Lou Piniella saw the ball head his way, but completely lost sight of it. He had the presence of mind to mask his confusion, in hopes of holding the runner, but he had no idea where the ball was. With nothing better to do, he stuck out his glove—and caught it, on one bounce! Had luck favored the Red Sox this day, the ball might well have passed Piniella by and rolled all the way to the bullpen fence. The tying run would surely have scored, and Piniella thought the rapid Remy might well have had an inside-the-park home run. Wouldn't that have been something!

It was not to be. Burleson had no chance of going from first to third, so it was first and second, one away, but Jim Rice was at the plate. Rice had had a triumphant year. His 406 total bases made him the first American League batter to hit the 400 mark since Joe DiMaggio had done it way back in 1937. And Rice wanted to get into the World Series. He'd suffered a broken wrist late in the season in '75 and was forced to sit out the Series; his presence might well have tipped the scales in favor of the Sox. Now he had his chance, but he flied out to right. Burleson tagged and took third on the play. The tying run was 90 feet from home, and Carl Yastrzemski was at the plate. What a moment for grand drama!

It had been a bit of an off year for the veteran left fielder, but Yaz had hit in clutch situations throughout his career, most notably back in 1967. He was captain of the team. He'd singled off Gossage his last time up, and Goose had now given up five hits in 2⅓ innings. It was, as Peter Gammons wrote in *Sports Illustrated,* "one final two-out bottom-of-the-ninth shoot-out between Gossage, the premier fastball pitcher of his time and Yaz, arguably the premier fastball hitter of his."

First pitch: ball one. The second pitch was right over, and Yaz swung from his heels. But baseball can be a game of quarter inches, and he got under it by just about that much. Instead of going out, it went up—high, but not that high, and twisting foul, coming down, and then it was snagged by Graig Nettles over by the third-base coach's box, and the game was over. Just like that.

Wait till next year? This had been next year. This had been *the* year. A 14-game lead after the All-Star break. Every star had been properly aligned. And then it had all fallen apart. The Sox had put the pieces together again, winning those final eight games in succession. The heavens had seemed to smile once more, until the unexpected—the utterly unexpected—had occurred.

Extra Innings

- Bucky Dent actually went on and had a terrific World Series for the Yankees. No home run heroics, but he did bat .417, with more hits than any other Yankee, and seven runs batted in.

- After the game, Yankees owner George Steinbrenner was quoted in the *Washington Post* as saying, "How could any World Series offer more? I just think it's a shame that the two best teams in the world had to end up in the same division. By 1980 I think you'll see interdivisional play between both leagues with wild-card teams." It wasn't until 1994 that the wild card was instituted, and not until 1997 that interleague play began. Thomas Boswell acknowledged the Boss's comments but wrote, "Such a system might be fairer, but it would preclude a great race like the seven-month pitched battle" that the Red Sox and Yankees had ensured. Time has proven Boswell wrong. After the implementation of the wild card, the Yankees and Red Sox have squared off three times in postseason play—in 1999, 2003, and 2004—and the latter two times the battle raged right into the seventh game of the ALCS.

35

April 29, 1986: Seattle at Boston

Whiff of Immortality

In which a Hall of Fame career gets off the launch pad

Roger Clemens made his major league debut in May 1984, but didn't really make his mark until after shoulder surgery cut short his 1985 season. The 23-year-old Texan came into 1986 determined to show he was as good as—or better than—ever, despite the surgery. He won his first three starts of the season, striking out 19 men in 24⅓ innings. Clemens's ability to throw gas opened his teammates' eyes. Before he faced the Seattle Mariners on April 29, his fourth start, first baseman Bill Buckner told pitcher Al Nipper he thought Clemens would strike out 18 men. "The way he's been throwing and the way [the Mariners] have been striking out, 18 seemed like the number," Buckner later told the *Boston Globe*. Buckner's prediction came partly because of Clemens's prowess, and partly because the M's of '86 had proved to be particularly bad at making contact. In the season's first 20 games they had racked up 166 K's, putting them on pace for some 1,400 total, 200 more than the previous worst (the 1968 Mets with 1,203). In the past two games alone the Mariners had whiffed 20 times. The situation seemed primed for an assault on the record book.

On a chilly April night, Clemens took the hill at Fenway Park on six days' rest, thanks to a rainout and an off day. In the first he would face Spike Owen, Phil Bradley, and Ken Phelps. He would retire them on 21 pitches, striking out the side, despite going to a full count on all three men. All three went down swinging. The first man to hit a ball fair was Gorman Thomas, who led off the second, and lined out to left. Then Jim Presley struck out, and Clemens caught Ivan Calderon looking. In the third, the M's could almost believe they were figuring Clemens out, as only Dave Henderson struck out, and leading off the fourth Owen, facing Clemens for the second time on the day, singled, breaking up both the possibility of a perfect game and a no-hitter.

But not the masterpiece. Clemens came back to strike out Bradley, Phelps, and Thomas. Thomas almost popped out, but Don Baylor dropped the ball, allowing Clemens to finish the batter off. Patrons at Fenway Park were already counting K's, and when Baylor fumbled the foul, there was an approving murmur because attentive fans realized this offered Clemens another chance for a strikeout. When he caught Thomas looking at a 3–2 pitch, the Rocket began a string of eight strikeouts in a row, knocking down some records along the way. At seven, Clemens surpassed Buck O'Brien and Ray Culp, two Sox pitchers who shared the team record for consecutive K's at six. When he got veteran catcher Steve Yeager on a 2–2 curveball, he tied Nolan Ryan and Ron Davis as the only American Leaguers to fan eight in a row. Fans began to put up red K signs on the back wall of the bleachers. "Where'd they come from?" Nipper asked in the next day's *Globe*. "Did those guys run out and get the cardboard and paint? Suddenly they were there."

Spike Owen, though, broke the string, ending the sixth with a fly to center—and some Sox fans had been yelling "Drop it!" wanting Roger to retire the side on a strikeout. Red Sox manager John McNamara checked with his ace to see how he was feeling. "I've been doing that every game this year, making sure his arm feels good," McNamara told the *Globe*. Clemens himself was fine, and he knew he was pitching as well as he ever had.

Boston's offense, meanwhile, had yet to come to life, and the game stood at 0–0. Clemens went out to pitch the seventh and struck out Bradley and Phelps again. Clemens then had Gorman Thomas down 1–2, and the crowd screaming for another K. But Thomas was looking for something in the strike zone, and he

APRIL 29, 1986: SEATTLE AT BOSTON																		
Seattle Mariners	AB	R	H	RBI	BB	SO	PO	A	Boston Red Sox	AB	R	H	RBI	BB	SO	PO	A
Owen ss	4	0	1	0	0	2	1	5	Evans rf	4	1	2	3	0	1	0	0
Bradley lf	4	0	0	0	0	4	2	0	Boggs 3b	3	0	0	0	1	0	0	0
Phelps 1b	4	0	0	0	0	3	6	0	Buckner dh	4	0	2	0	0	0	0	0
Thomas dh	3	1	1	1	0	1	0	0	Rice lf	4	0	1	0	0	0	1	0
Presley 3b	3	0	0	0	0	2	1	1	Baylor 1b	3	0	1	0	1	2	1	1
Calderon rf	3	0	0	0	0	3	1	1	Stapleton 1b	0	0	0	0	0	0	1	0
Tartabull 2b	3	0	1	0	0	1	3	1	Gedman c	4	0	1	0	0	0	20	0
Henderson cf	3	0	0	0	0	3	5	0	Barrett 2b	3	0	0	0	1	1	0	1
Yeager c	2	0	0	0	0	1	4	2	Lyons cf	3	1	1	0	0	0	3	0
Cowens ph	1	0	0	0	0	0	0	0	Hoffman ss	2	0	0	0	1	1	0	0
Kearney c	0	0	0	0	0	0	1	0	Romero pr,ss	0	1	0	0	0	0	0	1
Totals	30	1	3	1	0	20	24	10	Clemens p	0	0	0	0	0	0	0	0
									Totals	30	3	8	3	4	5	27	3

Seattle Mariners	IP	H	R	ER	BB	SO	HR	Boston Red Sox	IP	H	R	ER	BB	SO	HR
Moore (L)	7.1	8	3	3	4	4	1	Clemens (W)	9	3	1	1	0	20	1
Young	0.1	0	0	0	0	0	0								
Best	0.1	0	0	0	0	1	0								
Totals		8	8	3	3	4	5	1								

	1	2	3	4	5	6	7	8	9		R	H	E
SEA A	0	0	0	0	0	0	1	0	0		1	3	1
BOS A	0	0	0	0	0	0	3	0	x		3	8	1

connected for a home run into the first row in the deep-center-field bleachers. Clemens retired Presley on a grounder to first, but he was in a 1–0 hole, despite his mastery. McNamara checked with him again. This time Clemens admitted his legs were cramping a bit, but his arm was fine. McNamara had no intention of pulling his pitcher, who already had 16 strikeouts to his credit.

The Sox batters finally got to Mariners starter Mike Moore in the bottom of the seventh. With two out, Steve Lyons singled and Glenn Hoffman walked. Dwight Evans promptly cashed them both in with a three-run shot. Now Clemens had a 3–1 lead, and he went out for the eighth still throwing heat but unaware of the record numbers he was approaching. Two more men struck out in the eighth, bringing Clemens's total to 18. Clemens didn't know exactly how many men he had set down, only that it had been quite a few.

As he took the mound for the ninth inning, Nipper decided to tell him about the possibility that another record might fall. "Nipper told him he needed one to tie and two to set the record," reported Leigh Montville in the *Globe*. In Nipper's words, "Wouldn't it be a shame if a guy had a chance for something like that and didn't try for it? I wanted him to know. He's not the type of guy who would be affected by knowing."

Clemens was unfazed by the knowledge. He faced Spike Owen once more to lead off the inning. Could Owen make contact again? No; he went down swinging, and the record of 19 men in a nine-inning game was tied. Now Bradley, who already had three strikeouts on the day, came up, and went down looking. It was strikeout 20. Fenway's message board flashed the news that the single-game strikeout record had been broken. Wade Boggs came over from third base to shake Clemens's hand for breaking the record. But the game was not quite over. Ken Phelps's ground out was almost an afterthought, as in striking out 20 men Clemens had accomplished something that had never been done in 111 years of baseball.

"When he has that kind of stuff, it's really not difficult to call the game," his catcher, Rich Gedman, told reporters after the game. "He just threw the ball to spots where they couldn't hit it." It took him 138 pitches (97 strikes) to finish the feat. Seattle put only 10 balls in play, only two of them pulled, as Clemens hit 97 on the radar gun repeatedly and did not go to a three-ball count on even one batter after the fourth inning.

"Watching the Mariners try to hit Clemens was like watching a stack of waste paper diving into a shredder," wrote Dan Shaughnessy in the *Globe*. Clemens's domination was, in some ways, superior to a no-hitter, or even a perfect game, because the record was singularly his. "If setting the major-league record for strikeouts in a game is any measure of a career," wrote the Associated Press, "[then] Roger Clemens is heading for the Hall of Fame." In fact, the Hall received Clemens's spikes, cap, and other mementos of the game.

Clemens's domination would continue all year, and he would finish the season at 24–4 and win both the Cy Young Award and the American League MVP Award, while helping Boston reach the World Series for the first time since 1975.

Extra Innings

- Rich Gedman, by virtue of catching all 20 strikeouts in the game, broke an American League record and tied a major league record with 20 putouts by a catcher in a nine-inning game. Jerry Grote had previously been credited with 20 on April 22, 1970, while catching for the Mets, on the day when Tom Seaver struck out 19 Padres, including the final 10 in a row. Grote also had caught a foul pop for an out. The record would later be equaled by Dan Wilson on August 8, 1997, in the AL, and by Sandy Martinez on May 6, 1998, in the NL. Gedman would still hold the record for most putouts by a catcher on two consecutive days, though, with 36 over April 29 and 30, 1986.

- Spike Owen, who actually made contact twice on Clemens during the 20-strikeout game, had been a teammate of Roger's in college. With the University of Texas Longhorns, Clemens and Owen won a College World Series together in 1983. Later in 1986, Owen was traded to Boston and the two became teammates once more.

36

October 12, 1986: Boston at California

Roller Coaster

In which Hendu giveth and Hendu taketh away

The Red Sox clinched the East on September 28, beating second-place Toronto. Their opponent in the best-of-seven American League Championship Series would be the California Angels. The Sox, who had won with pitching, were a bit banged up as Tom Seaver was lost to a knee injury and Roger Clemens, the odds-on Cy Young favorite, got hit by a line drive on the elbow with just a few days left in the regular season.

Clemens then got roughed up in the opening game of the ALCS, and Boston took a beating, losing 8–1. Boston won the second game but dropped game three. They looked as though they would win game four when Clemens left the game in the ninth with a 3–1 lead, but there were two men on. Pitcher Calvin Schiraldi, who had taken over the closer's role from Bob Stanley and excelled late in the season, allowed both inherited runners to score. Jim Rice lost a fly ball, then Schiraldi hit a man. The Angels scored three runs and sent the game into extra innings, when they won it in the 11th with Schiraldi still on the hill.

DAVE HENDERSON

Dave Henderson

With a 3–1 lead in the series, the Angels prepared to advance to the World Series and erase manager Gene Mauch's previous collapses, with the Phillies in 1964 and the Angels' own fold in the 1982 ALCS. The '82 Angels had led, two games to none, only to lose to Milwaukee.

For game five, in Anaheim, Mauch sent Mike Witt to the mound, the man who had beat Clemens in game one with a five-hitter. Witt's best pitch was an over-the-top "hard" curve, and he used it often.

The Red Sox went with Bruce Hurst. Hurst had been the winner of game two, holding the Angels to two runs. The lefty complemented his fastball with a slow curve and a diving fork-ball, and he mixed in an occasional slider.

The pitchers' duel lasted exactly one inning. In the second, the Red Sox opened the action with a Jim Rice single. Witt came back to strike out Don Baylor and Dwight Evans, but Rich Gedman got a pitch he liked and deposited it over the wall for two runs. Bob Boone answered Gedman's homer with one of his own to lead off the fourth, and the score stood at 2–1 Boston, coming into the bottom of the sixth inning. With two out, Doug DeCinces doubled and Hurst faced 37-year-old shortstop Bobby Grich. The veteran Grich was tall for an infielder and in his prime was good for 20 homers a year. He was no longer in his prime, but he was good for one homer here, with an odd assist from Dave Henderson.

Hendu had entered as a replacement for Tony Armas (sprained ankle) and tracked Grich's deep drive. He leaped, got the ball in his glove, then banged into the padded green wall. As his wrist hit the top of the wall, his glove tipped and delivered the ball to the other side. Home run; 3–2 Angels. Hurst shook it off, struck out Reggie Jackson to end the inning, and took his seat in the dugout.

The Sox still could not break through on Witt. Bob Stanley relieved Hurst beginning in the seventh. George Hendrick singled to greet him, and Devon White pinch-ran. Boone bunted him to second, and Stanley walked Gary Pettis. Mauch smelled blood and sent Rob Wilfong in to pinch-hit. The move paid off, a double, good for one run. Stanley intentionally walked Dick Schofield to fill the sacks and hope for the double play. He got a sacrifice fly out of Brian Downing instead, and the Angels led 5–2.

Witt had scattered six hits over eight innings. He took the mound to start the ninth, and Angels fans were smelling pennant. But Bill Buckner singled. Dave Stapleton came in to run for him and play first base, making for better defense. Though Rice struck out, Baylor drilled a home run to bring the Red Sox within one. Witt got one more out, a pop-up by Evans, and Mauch brought in left-hander Gary Lucas. Lucas had great numbers facing Rich Gedman. The police began moving onto the field to hold back the pennant celebration. But Lucas beaned Gedman on his first pitch, the first batter he hit all year. Mauch yanked him and brought on righty Donnie Moore to face Henderson.

Was Henderson thinking about the homer he hand-delivered over the wall? If not for that, the Sox would be ahead 4–3 right now. He stepped into the box, his only shot at redemption. He worked the count to 2–2 as Moore fired fastball after fastball at him. He fouled off two more. The next one also came in hot and hard, a splitter that should dive off the table, that should leave him swinging like a barn door in a gale. But the ball did not make its characteristic dive. Henderson met it with his bat, and the ball soared toward left field and landed ten rows deep. Few Sox fans had hoped for a homer, but Henderson earned his redemption, and he leaped and danced his way around the bases, a huge grin on his face. His two-run shot gave the Sox a 6–5 lead.

Now if only they could close the deal. Stanley would need to get three outs. He got only one, as the Angels singled twice around a sacrifice bunt, manufacturing a game-tying run off him and Joe Sambito. The Angels tied it at 6–6. The Sox still clung to life, and the game went to extra innings. "It was a game for the Valium pouch and psychiatrist's couch," wrote Michael Madden in the *Boston Globe*.

In the 11th, Boston got to Moore again. He opened the inning by hitting big Don Baylor. Evans and Gedman followed with singles to load the bases. And Dave Henderson strode from the on-deck circle. He didn't hit a grand slam; he hit a fly to center field, but it was deep enough to score Baylor. Moore got Ed Romero to hit a shallow fly to left, and Chuck Finley got Wade Boggs to ground out. The lone run was all the Sox would get, but they led the game, 7–6

OCTOBER 12, 1986: BOSTON AT CALIFORNIA

Boston Red Sox	AB	R	H	RBI	BB	SO	PO	A	California Angels	AB	R	H	RBI	BB	SO	PO	A
Boggs 3b	5	0	1	0	1	0	1	2	Burleson 2b	2	0	0	0	0	0	1	3
Barrett 2b	5	0	0	0	0	0	7	4	Wilfong ph,2b	3	0	2	2	0	1	3	3
Buckner 1b	4	0	1	0	0	0	4	0	Schofield ss	5	0	1	0	1	1	3	5
Stapleton pr,1b	1	1	1	0	0	0	2	1	Downing lf	3	0	0	1	2	0	4	0
Rice lf	5	1	1	0	0	2	3	0	DeCinces 3b	5	1	2	0	0	0	1	0
Baylor dh	4	2	1	2	0	1	0	0	Grich 1b	5	1	1	2	0	2	10	2
Evans rf	5	0	1	0	0	1	1	0	Jackson dh	5	0	1	0	0	3	0	0
Gedman c	4	2	4	2	0	0	8	2	Hendrick rf	3	0	1	0	0	0	1	0
Armas cf	2	0	0	0	0	0	2	0	White pr,rf	2	1	1	0	0	1	1	0
Henderson cf	2	1	1	3	0	1	3	0	Boone c	3	1	3	1	0	0	6	0
Owen ss	2	0	0	0	0	0	1	0	Jones pr	0	1	0	0	0	0	0	0
Greenwell ph	1	0	1	0	0	0	0	0	Narron c	0	0	0	0	1	0	0	0
Romero pr,ss	2	0	0	0	0	0	0	0	Pettis cf	3	1	1	0	1	0	1	0
Hurst p	0	0	0	0	0	0	0	2	Witt p	0	0	0	0	0	0	2	3
Stanley p	0	0	0	0	0	0	0	1	Totals	39	6	13	6	5	8	33	16
Crawford p	0	0	0	0	0	0	1	0									
Totals	42	7	12	7	1	5	33	12									

Boston Red Sox	IP	H	R	ER	BB	SO	HR	California Angels	IP	H	R	ER	BB	SO	HR
Hurst	6	7	3	3	1	4	2	Witt	8.2	8	4	4	0	5	2
Stanley	2.1	4	3	3	2	1	0	Lucas	0	0	1	1	0	0	0
Sambito	0	1	0	0	0	0	0	Moore (L)	2	4	2	2	1	0	1
Crawford (W)	1.2	1	0	0	2	1	0	Finley	0.1	0	0	0	0	0	0
Schiraldi (S)	1	0	0	0	0	2	0	Totals	11	12	7	7	1	5	3
Totals	11	13	6	6	5	8	2								

	1	2	3	4	5	6	7	8	9	10	11		R	H	E
BOS A	0	2	0	0	0	0	0	0	4	0	1		7	12	0
CAL A	0	0	1	0	0	2	2	0	1	0	0		6	13	0

John McNamara was forced to go with Schiraldi for the third game in a row; he hadn't pitched three days in a row all season long. The goat of the previous night's 11-inning loss rose to the occasion. He struck out Wilfong and Schofield and then got Downing to pop up—the first 1-2-3 inning for the Angels all night.

The pennant that had been in California's hands had been snatched away. "That was by far the best game out of more than 2,200 in my career," enthused Don Baylor to reporters. "All of a sudden, you felt like a kid again. The emotion in the dugout was unbelievable." As Dan Shaughnessy put it in the paper the next day, "The Red Sox didn't need a plane to fly home last night."

The next two games were at Fenway, and the Angels never recovered their composure. Oil Can Boyd beat them 10–4 in the sixth game, and Roger Clemens sealed the deal with an 8–1 win in game seven. The Sox were going on to the World Series for the first time since 1975, to try once again for their first world championship since 1918.

Extra Innings

- The game set the new record for the longest game in an ALCS, at three hours, 54 minutes. The previous record had been set the night before, at 3:50. The back-to-back ALCS games on October 17 and 18, 2004, both surpassed the mark.

- The Red Sox bullpen had developed a good-luck ritual earlier in the year. When it got to two outs with two strikes on the batter, each man would stand with his "rally cap" at his chest, upside down and open to the sky. If the batter fouled off the pitch, they would put their hats back on and then remove them again. "We were all talking," reliever Joe Sambito told reporters. "'Yeah, he's going to hit a home run.' And he did!" With Donnie Moore on the mound and Dave Henderson at the plate, the charm worked to perfection.

- Donnie Moore stayed with the Angels for two more seasons, but he was nagged by injuries, booed by fans, and rumored by the front office to be malingering when he went on the DL in 1987. He was haunted by the fact that he might be remembered for just one pitch, à la Ralph Branca, but injuries kept Moore from returning to top form. He fell to drinking, and his marriage suffered. Shortly after being released by a minor league team, Moore committed suicide in 1989.

37

October 18, 1986: Boston at New York

Bright Lights, Big City

In which a masterful Mormon gets on his way to becoming "Series MVP"

After 11 years, the Red Sox were back in the World Series, meeting the New York Mets, in New York, for Game One. These were the party-hearty Mets, the fun-loving crew who were the media darlings of New York and made the Yankees seem old, tired, and boring. Vegas odds were on the Mets for their talent and balance of power and speed, as well as their health. The Mets' lineup was powered by Darryl Strawberry and Keith Hernandez (who was among seven players suspended for drug violations before the season but who were allowed to play if they paid hefty fines in the form of donations to drug prevention programs), and their pitching was topped by a strikeout-throwing phenom named Dwight Gooden.

Of the Red Sox regulars, Tony Armas was still hobbled by the ankle sprain he sustained during the ALCS in Anaheim, Wade Boggs had a pulled hamstring, and Bill Buckner had eight cortisone shots over the course of the season to keep his joints working, but his knees and ankles were giving out. They would also be without the bat of Don Baylor, their designated hitter, when they played at Shea Stadium. Nineteen eighty-six was the first year since instituting the DH rule that the World Series would be played under split rules, AL rules in the AL park, NL rules in the NL park.

With the first game coming only three days after their playoff clincher, the Red Sox held ace Roger Clemens for Game Two and started lefty Bruce Hurst in Game One. As Thomas Boswell wrote on the eve of the Series, "And what is the Mets' only weakness? They don't hit crafty, speed-changing lefties." If he was right, that made Hurst the right man to start Games One, Four, and Seven. A Utah Mormon, Hurst had come up in the Red Sox organization after being drafted in 1976 and making his major league debut in 1981. In 1983 he spent the full year in the rotation and for the next three years pitched right around .500. In 1986 he cut his ERA by a full run and a half, from 4.51 to 2.99, and he went 13–8. He surrendered fewer hits, fewer home runs, and struck out more batters. In short, '86 was the best year of his career, and his record would have been even better if Boston had scored more than nine total runs in his eight losses. In the ALCS, Hurst had pitched twice, struck out eight, and had an ERA of 2.40. What changed? Hurst-watchers attributed it to the fact that he had lost his fear of pitching inside, boosting his overall confidence.

In the World Series, he would be even better. The man he would face, Ron Darling, was the Mets' number three pitcher, a 25-year-old righty with a 2.81 ERA. The Sox and the Angels had played a seven-game series, but the Sox gained energy and momentum by winning the final three games. The Mets, meanwhile, fought a knock-down, drag-out series with the Astros; though it ran only six games, they seemed drained, and neither Gooden nor Bobby Ojeda was ready to go again. So the draw went to Darling, a right-hander whose out pitch was his forkball. Red Sox scout Sam Mele advised the Red Sox batters to be aggressive early in the count, when Darling would be throwing his fastball and curve, and not let him drop that forkball on them with two strikes.

And so the Sox were aggressive. Instead of working the count as usual, lead-off man Wade Boggs bounced the ball to third for an easy out. The next man, Marty Barrett, hit another bouncer to second, but this one was hit slowly enough that he beat it out. But then came Buckner, who grounded into a double play. Hurst came out of the Boston dugout and knew he would have to be on his game this chilly night.

He was. He struck out Mookie Wilson and Lenny Dykstra, then got Hernandez to fly to center, and the duel was on. Darling sat down the next eight men in a row, the final four by strikeout. Hurst was not fully as effective, giving up a walk and a single in the second, the same in the third, and another walk in the fourth, but he never allowed the Mets to mount a rally, and he never let a Mets base runner cross home plate.

After five innings it was 0–0.

New York mounted their toughest threat yet in the bottom of the sixth. Hernandez walked to lead off the inning, and Gary Carter followed that with a sharp single into left to bring Darryl Strawberry to the plate. Strawberry was 24 years old and had led the team in homers with 27. With one swing he could make the game 3–0. Then again, he had led the team—by a wide margin—in strikeouts, with 141. Three pitches later, Hurst caught him looking, strike three, and then induced Ray Knight to hit into an inning-ending double play.

If ever there was a moment for Boston to grab the momentum, this was it. Jim Rice led off the seventh with a walk, then took second on a wild pitch. This was fortunate, since it took off the chance for a routine double play. When Dwight Evans bounced back to Darling, he had to settle for the out at first. Rich Gedman grounded to second baseman Tim Teufel. He anticipated a high hop, pulling up his body and his glove . . . but the ball never hopped, and it scooted through his legs into the outfield. Rice rounded third and kept on running. The throw was late, Gedman took second on the play, and the Red Sox led 1–0.

That would be all they would get, as Henderson fouled out and Hurst struck out, but Hurst was determined to make that one run stand up. After all, the temperature was in the low forties; perhaps everyone's bats were cold. Although Teufel, trying for redemption, singled to open the bottom of the inning, Hurst got the next three outs without seeming to break a sweat. But things were tense with such a slim lead. In the eighth the Sox faced a new pitcher, Roger McDowell, and had no better luck against him. Hurst answered with a three-up, three-down inning of his own.

The Sox tried to get that always important insurance run in the top of the ninth, when Rice singled back through the box and Evans walked. Gedman tried a sacrifice bunt but bounced it right to McDowell, who wiped out Rice with the force at third. With one out, there were still two men on for the hero of the ALCS, Dave Henderson. On 3–2 Hendu came through again, a single, but Kevin Mitchell's throw from left nailed Evans at the plate. Both runners moved up on the play, so the Mets intentionally walked Spike Owen to set up

OCTOBER 18, 1986: BOSTON AT NEW YORK																
Boston Red Sox	AB	R	H	RBI	BB	SO	PO	A	**New York Mets**	AB	R	H	RBI	BB	SO	PO	A
Boggs 3b	4	0	0	0	0	1	1	2	Wilson lf	4	0	1	0	0	1	1	0
Barrett 2b	4	0	1	0	1	2	2	3	McDowell p	0	0	0	0	0	0	0	2
Buckner 1b	4	0	1	0	0	1	4	0	Dykstra cf	3	0	0	0	1	2	4	0
Stapleton 1b	0	0	0	0	0	0	0	1	Hernandez 1b	3	0	0	0	1	0	7	0
Rice lf	2	1	1	0	2	0	2	0	Carter c	4	0	1	0	0	0	9	0
Evans rf	3	0	0	0	1	0	2	0	Strawberry rf	2	0	0	0	2	2	2	0
Gedman c	4	0	0	0	0	1	9	0	Knight 3b	3	0	0	0	1	0	2	2
Henderson cf	4	0	2	0	0	0	5	0	Teufel 2b	3	0	2	0	0	1	0	1
Owen ss	2	0	0	0	2	1	2	0	Backman pr,2b	1	0	0	0	0	0	0	0
Hurst p	3	0	0	0	0	3	0	2	Santana ss	2	0	0	0	0	0	2	2
Greenwell ph	1	0	0	0	0	0	0	0	Heep ph	1	0	0	0	0	1	0	0
Schiraldi p	0	0	0	0	0	0	0	0	Darling p	2	0	0	0	0	1	0	2
Totals	31	1	5	0	5	8	27	8	Mitchell ph,lf	1	0	0	0	0	1	0	1
									Totals	29	0	4	0	5	9	27	10

Boston Red Sox	IP	H	R	ER	BB	SO	HR	**New York Mets**	IP	H	R	ER	BB	SO	HR
Hurst (W)	8	4	0	0	4	8	0	Darling (L)	7	3	1	0	3	8	0
Schiraldi (S)	1	0	0	0	1	1	0	McDowell	2	2	0	0	2	0	0
Totals	9	4	0	0	5	9	0	Totals	9	5	1	0	5	8	0

	1	2	3	4	5	6	7	8	9		R	H	E
BOS A	0	0	0	0	0	0	1	0	0		1	5	0
NY N	0	0	0	0	0	0	0	0	0		0	4	1

a force at any base. With Hurst due to bat, Boston manager John McNamara tabbed Mike Greenwell to pinch-hit. Greenwell gave the ball a ride, but it was hauled in by Dykstra in center and the Sox were denied.

With Hurst out of the game, McNamara handed the ball to Calvin Schiraldi. After Schiraldi had blown the save and the game in ALCS game four, he had broken down in tears in the dugout. His teammates had formed a wall around him to keep prying cameras out. His confidence returned when he nailed down the wild victory in game five, the turning point that set the Red Sox on their World Series charge. He took the mound in New York in front of the screaming mob at Shea that Don Baylor had called "the lion's den."

Schiraldi walked Darryl Strawberry on five pitches; facing one of the strikeout leaders of the league, with a one-run lead to protect, Schiraldi walked him. He took a deep breath. The next man up was Ray Knight. He dropped down a bunt on the very first pitch. Dave Stapleton, the late-inning defensive replacement for Buckner, gathered it in and got the lead runner at second despite a momentary delay trying to dig the ball out of his glove. Wally Backman hit a short fly to left for the second out. Mets manager Davey Johnson pulled the trigger, taking his last shot, asking left-handed swinger Danny Heep to pinch-hit for shortstop Rafael Santana. Schiraldi twirled and was untouchable. Heep struck out, and Schiraldi clenched his fist. The Red Sox had just won their first World Series game since 1975, a four-hit, 1–0 win, scoring in the top of the seventh only because of an opponent's error. They felt unstoppable.

Extra Innings

- None of the Mets would blame Teufel for the loss. Some on the team and in the media speculated that the field might have been a bit uneven after Mets fans celebrated their game five win against Houston in the NLCS by tearing up the grass. Others quite pragmatically pointed out that if no one scores any runs, then everyone is at fault. "There hasn't been a team yet who got shut out and won a game," said pitcher Ron Darling.

- Eastern Airlines and Pan Am went head to head to compete for Boston and New York fans to fly their air shuttles between the two cities. Eastern even offered a baseball trivia contest (with a trip to Aruba as the prize). Both airlines offered a $39 discount fare (off the regular $65) to anyone with a game ticket stub, and free bus rides to and from the ballparks.

38

October 25, 1986: Boston at New York

Loyal to a Fault

In which a generous impulse leads to a lifelong blot on an excellent career

The Sox had a chance to win it all. It was 68 long years since they had last been champs. They had taken the World Series to Game Seven in 1946, again in '67, again in '75 . . . now, though, they had a chance to put their opponents away in Game Six in '86.

With a 3–2 lead in the Series, the Sox were primed to put the past behind them. They had their ace, Roger Clemens, on the mound, and bore a mantle of destiny after the way they had beaten the Angels for the pennant. The Mets seemed ready to roll over. "Dwight Gooden has failed them, and Darryl Strawberry has failed them. So has their defense, their 108-win mystique and their home field advantage," wrote Richard Justice in the *Washington Post* that day.

"It Hurts to Watch Buckner" read a headline in that same paper. Thomas Boswell wrote, "What's the count on Buckner? Two arms, two legs, no ankles. When it comes to visual memories of the 83rd World Series, Buckner may hold the patent. Buckner crawling after a ground ball on his knees. Buckner diving for a popped-up bunt and giving it a Bobo Brazil head butt." Leigh Montville in the *Boston Globe* was equally prophetic. "Buckner's Story Is Painfully Familiar," read the headline on his column. How did they know?

They didn't, of course, but Bill Buckner's struggle to play, while wearing specially designed high-top shoes to shore up his gimpy ankles, was an obvious source of drama. Boston manager John McNamara responded to his heroic struggle by sending Buckner out there every day even though "he couldn't run any worse if his feet were on backward." *(Washington Post)* If they won it all, Buckner's suffering would be remembered as heroic.

And so would Clemens's pitching, and Wade Boggs's resurgent defense. If they could win it.

They got off to a good start. Boggs singled off Bobby Ojeda's glove to open the game. Ojeda retired both Marty Barrett and Buckner easily enough, but then walked Jim Rice, pushing Boggs to second. Dwight Evans doubled, scoring Boggs, and they might have gotten more, but Rich Gedman flew out to right. They scratched another run in the second, on three singles. Two runs seems like a lot when your starting pitcher is mowing like a John Deere. Clemens struck out six of the first nine batters he faced, and did not allow a hit through four innings. Not even a parachutist carrying a "Let's Go Mets" banner who dropped—uninvited—into Shea Stadium could rattle him.

In the fifth, though, the Mets nicked him for a run. It started with Darryl Strawberry, the young superstar slugger. Straw was patient with Clemens this time, and walked. He quickly stole second, and then came in on a Ray Knight base hit. Boston's lead was cut to 2–1. Mookie Wilson followed with a single that bounced off Dwight Evans's chest, allowing Knight to go to third. The Red Sox played at double-play depth, willing to concede the run to get the outs. That's just the trade-off they made: pinch hitter Danny Heep grounded into the 4-6-3, and the lead was gone. The pitcher, Ojeda, obliged with the third out, a grounder, but was happy to take the hill with the score evened up.

Roger McDowell replaced Ojeda in the seventh, though, as Mets manager Davey Johnson decided a fresh arm might be more effective. McDowell committed the cardinal sin of walking the leadoff man, and Buckner moved Barrett over with a grounder. Then Jim Rice smacked a ball to third that Ray Knight could not handle cleanly, and the Sox had men on the corners with one out. Evans then grounded to short, but Kevin Elster tried to get the force on Rice at second. He was too late, but Wally Backman relayed the throw to first in plenty of time to nip Evans. Barrett scored easily from third on the play. With Rice at second, Rich Gedman stepped to the plate. He singled, and Rice ran, but hesitated a moment at third, as if unsure he was being waved home. Third-base coach Rene Lachemann was waving him in, but Rice swung wide of the bag and was out by plenty. The rally was over, and the Red Sox had scratched only the one run, 3–2.

Clemens sat the Mets down in order again in the seventh, but he had thrown 135 pitches and had developed a bleeding blister. With his spot in the batting order due up, McNamara decided to pinch-hit for his ace, as Boston had a chance to pile on some runs. Dave Henderson, good ol' Hendu who had been the hero so often this October, got them going with a single that bounced off Elster's shoulder. Spike Owen bunted him to second, and here came Clemens's spot. Most game-watchers expected the first man off the bench to be Don Baylor, the Red Sox DH. But McNamara chose rookie lefty Mike Greenwell.

Greenwell struck out on three pitches, leaving many a Sox fan to think, "Gee, Clemens could have done that." Boggs was up, and he was given an intentional pass. Barrett walked, too, but his pass was wholly unintentional. Bases loaded. Johnson pulled McDowell in favor of left-hander Jesse Orosco to face Buckner.

McNamara could have pinch-hit for the ailing Buckner here. He could have used Don Baylor, and either left Don in to play first base, or moved in Dave

Stapleton as defensive replacement. But McNamara stuck with Buckner, perhaps loyal to a fault. And, after all, Buckner was a big RBI man. They'd likely not be in the Series at all if not for his 108 RBIs during the regular season. Buckner hit an easy fly to center, and the inning was over. Boston had nothing to show for it. And now Clemens was out of the game.

On the other hand, Calvin Schiraldi was now in it. In the Angels series, Schiraldi had worn both the goat horns and the savior's halo, though the halo was the more recent accoutrement. It was about to take on a bit of tarnish. Pinch-hitting for Orosco, Lee Mazzilli was a native New Yorker who had been released by the Pirates in late July, and signed by the Mets to a minor league contract. He played well enough to make the World Series roster, and here he singled to right field. Lenny Dykstra tried to bunt him over. Schiraldi scooped up the ball with time to nab the lead runner, but bounced his throw, and both men were safe. Backman bunted them both over on a sacrifice; one out. The Red Sox put Keith Hernandez on to set up the double play. But Schiraldi looked as though he didn't want to throw a strike to Gary Carter, either. The count went to 3–0, and finally Schiraldi was forced to throw one over the plate. Gary Carter lifted the ball into left, a liner right at Rice but deep; Mazzilli tagged and scored. Strawberry flew out, limiting the damage, but the save was officially blown. Red Sox 3, Mets 3.

Nobody got nuthin' in the ninth, and the game moved to the 10th. Rick Aguilera had come on to pitch for the Mets, and there at the plate stood Hendu, ready for another role as the hero. He took a strike, then sent a home run into deep left, where it hit a billboard. Dancing in the streets began in Boston. Of course, this was the way it was fated to happen, that the same man who hit the historic homer against the Angels would rise against the Mets.

And then, even better, an insurance run. Boggs doubled, and Marty Barrett brought him in with an RBI single. That seemed like enough, so when Rice ended the inning with two men on, people were still partying. Down in the Red Sox clubhouse, the postgame TV producers hurried to cover the team lockers with plastic, and the trophy was set up.

Schiraldi was still on the mound. He got the first two outs quickly enough on fly balls. This was looking routine. But suddenly Carter singled, a soft hit up the middle, and pinch hitter Kevin Mitchell followed with a line single to center. Come on, Calvin, get it over with, shouted thousands of Red Sox rooters at their televisions, in bars, beating on the dashboards of their cars. Schiraldi got two strikes on Ray Knight. He was one strike away from being mobbed on the mound, as the Red Sox won their first World Series in 68 years. He tried to finish Knight with a fastball in. Knight broke his bat . . .

OCTOBER 25, 1986: BOSTON AT NEW YORK

Boston Red Sox	AB	R	H	RBI	BB	SO	PO	A	New York Mets	AB	R	H	RBI	BB	SO	PO	A
Boggs 3b	5	2	3	0	1	0	1	0	Dykstra cf	4	0	0	0	0	2	4	0
Barrett 2b	4	1	3	2	2	0	1	4	Backman 2b	4	0	1	0	1	0	4	0
Buckner 1b	5	0	0	0	0	0	5	0	Hernandez 1b	4	0	1	0	1	0	6	1
Rice lf	5	0	0	0	1	2	5	0	Carter c	4	1	1	1	0	1	9	0
Evans rf	4	0	1	2	1	0	1	0	Strawberry rf	2	1	0	0	2	0	5	0
Gedman c	5	0	1	0	0	1	9	0	Aguilera p	0	0	0	0	0	0	0	0
Henderson cf	5	1	2	1	0	0	5	0	Mitchell ph	1	1	1	0	0	0	0	0
Owen ss	4	1	3	0	0	1	2	2	Knight 3b	4	2	2	2	1	1	0	0
Clemens p	3	0	0	0	0	1	0	1	Wilson lf	5	0	1	0	0	1	2	1
Greenwell ph	1	0	0	0	0	1	0	0	Santana ss	1	0	0	0	0	1	0	1
Schiraldi p	1	0	0	0	0	1	0	1	Heep ph	1	0	0	0	0	0	0	0
Stanley p	0	0	0	0	0	0	0	0	Elster ss	1	0	0	0	0	0	3	3
Totals	42	5	13	5	5	7	29	8	Johnson ph,ss	1	0	0	0	0	1	0	0
									Ojeda p	2	0	0	0	0	1	0	0
									McDowell p	0	0	0	0	0	0	0	1
									Orosco p	0	0	0	0	0	0	0	0
									Mazzilli ph,rf	2	1	1	0	0	0	1	0
									Totals	36	6	8	3	4	9	30	11

Boston Red Sox	IP	H	R	ER	BB	SO	HR	New York Mets	IP	H	R	ER	BB	SO	HR
Clemens	7	4	2	1	2	8	0	Ojeda	6	8	2	2	2	3	0
Schiraldi (L)	2.2	4	4	3	2	1	0	McDowell	1.2	2	1	0	3	1	0
Stanley	0	0	0	0	0	0	0	Orosco	0.1	0	0	0	0	0	0
Totals	9.2	8	6	4	4	9	0	Aguilera (W)	2	3	2	2	0	3	1
								Totals	10	13	5	4	5	7	1

	1	2	3	4	5	6	7	8	9	10	R	H	E
BOS A	1	1	0	0	0	0	1	0	0	2	5	13	3
NY N	0	0	0	0	2	0	0	1	0	3	6	8	2

But the ball dropped in shallow center and brought in a run; 5–4 now. The term "heart attack closer" had not been coined yet, but perhaps it should have been. Schiraldi could still close the deal . . . no, he couldn't. McNamara pulled him and put in the man whose job as closer Schiraldi had taken, Bob Stanley. Red Sox Nation waited on tenterhooks through the pitching change.

Just think, Stanley might come on, throw one pitch, and the ball be hit for an out, and it would all be over. He would be forgiven for 1978 and for all his struggles all year. When the count went to 2–2, Stanley knew it was his moment. Again, the Sox were one strike away. Here was that pitch—that strike three or that easy grounder.

Instead, what Stanley threw was a wild pitch. It went off Gedman's glove to the backstop. Some argue that it should have been scored a passed ball. But the score that counted was the run. Carter ran home, crossed the plate, and the tying run scored. The save was officially blown again. Now it became necessary just to get out of the inning and send it to the 11th. Evans, Gedman, and Henderson were due up. But first, Stanley still had to get Mookie Wilson out. With several foul balls mixed in, the count went full, and Stanley threw the 10th pitch of the at-bat. Wilson hit the ball on the ground, right side, right at Buckner. He was playing deep behind the bag, guarding the line. He didn't even have to move those gimpy legs; the ball was coming right to him.

And right through him. Untouched. Ray Knight landed at home plate easily, in an already forming scrum of jubilant Mets. And to think, the Mets hadn't even won the World Series yet. They would have to wait through another rainout and Game Seven for that.

And Bill Buckner, so colorfully painted by all the world's scribes before the game as the suffering soldier, the wounded hero who would finally earn that hard-fought victory on heart and guts alone, became the tragic figure. The washed-up old goat. All the attention on his injuries and McNamara's stubbornness in sticking with him made him stand out in the minds of the fans. Never mind that Schiraldi couldn't hold on to his savior's halo, or that Stanley had kicked it right into the dirt, or that Gedman had let the pitch get away from him, Buckner drew the lightning of the fans' ire like a lone silo on the prairie. There was no Game Seven redemption, and no one believed there would be, and that is perhaps the longest-lasting legacy of 1986. Red Sox Nation would never trust euphoria again. The team had "snatched defeat from the jaws of victory" too many times. Pessimism and negativity bloomed. But so did devotion. A new generation of fans was indoctrinated into the legacy of the Red Sox. It would be only a matter of time before their devotion was rewarded (18 years, in fact), though many more came to doubt that it ever would be.

Extra Innings

- The parachutist who dropped onto the field in the first inning was 37-year-old Michael Sergio of Manhattan. Upon landing to wild cheers from the crowd, he was handcuffed, arrested, and charged with reckless endangerment and criminal trespassing. "The Mets said they weren't getting the kind of fan reaction they wanted, so I gave it to them," explained the unbowed Sergio.

- When the Red Sox took the lead in the 10th, Johnny Rufino, the Mets' assistant clubhouse attendant, received a visitor. A representative from Boston was at his door asking if he could borrow the Mets' champagne. Apparently they had forgotten to bring their own. Rufino sent 20 cases to the Red Sox clubhouse. "And now, they're returning it," he told the *New York Times*.

- Many Red Sox fans are pretty sophisticated. They knew that Buckner never should have been in there at first, that McNamara had routinely replaced him in the late innings with Stapleton for defensive purposes. Billy Bucks was welcomed back by fans in '87, and given a standing ovation on Opening Day 1990, when he had been re-signed to a Red Sox contract and was introduced. What wore Buckner down, in time, was simply the repeated showing of the Wilson grounder, hundreds and hundreds of times on television, as commentator after commentator began to talk about this newly discovered "curse of the Bambino." Asked question after question by inquiring reporters seeking their own moment in the sun by securing a moment with Bill Buckner, he understandably just got sick of the whole thing and took advantage of an opportunity to invest in a business venture in faraway Idaho and live a better life.

39

April 12, 1992: Boston at Cleveland
No-Win Situation

In which a journeyman pitcher succeeds in losing

As the 1990s opened, the Red Sox were once again striving to become an elite team. The Yankees were awful, and in 1990 Boston topped the AL East (only to be brushed aside by the Oakland A's in a four-game sweep). For the 1991 season, they added a few free agents, including Jack Clark as a DH/pinch hitter, and pitchers Danny Darwin and Matt Young. Young was a hard-throwing left-hander with a high leg kick and a rebuilt elbow. He had toiled with the basement-dwelling Seattle Mariners in 1990 to a crummy 8–18 record but a decent 3.51 ERA. He had struck out 176 men in 225 workhorse innings, and notched seven complete games. He was hailed on his arrival in Boston as a big pickup. But by September he was out of the rotation as his record dropped to 3–7 and his ERA ballooned to 5.18, "earning the nicknames 'Sigh Young' and 'Door Matt,'" quipped Dan Shaughnessy in the *Boston Globe*.

Young came out of camp in 1992 ready to put the bad year aside and make something of himself. On April 12 he faced the Indians at Cleveland Municipal Stadium, the "Mistake by the Lake." "It was cold, a little chilly, that day, which is typical for early April," Young recalled in the *Lawrence (MA) Eagle-Tribune*. "But it was a nice clear day. It was my first start of the year." The teams were perhaps a bit weary, since they had played a 19-inning game the day before, topping out at six hours, 30 minutes, the longest game in Cleveland Indians history.

Opposing Young was Charles Nagy, who walked Mike Greenwell but otherwise had no trouble retiring the Red Sox in the first. Young then toed the rubber, hoping to do the same, but leadoff man Kenny Lofton worked out a walk and made an instant pest of himself. He stole second, and then even as Young was recording a strikeout against free-swinging DH Glenallen Hill, the pesky Lofton stole third. Carlos Baerga then grounded to short, scoring Lofton, and to add insult to injury, reached base on Luis Rivera's error. Young had only recorded his first out of the season and already he was losing 1–0. He induced Albert Belle and Mark Whiten to fly out, and went back to the dugout hoping for better results next inning.

The second passed uneventfully, but the base on balls came back to bite Young again in the third. This time he opened the inning walking the number nine hitter, Mark Lewis, and then Lofton for the second time. Lewis moved to third when Hill grounded into a force-out, and then Hill stole second. Baerga again came through in his fashion, grounding out but scoring the runner from third. Young was now down 2–0 despite the fact that he had not yet given up a hit.

It was time for the Sox to pick him up. Ellis Burks led off the fourth with a single, then stole second, Mo Vaughn walked, and Luis Rivera singled to bring Burks in. But one run was the total of the mini-rally, as Nagy escaped without further trouble. The Sox tallied two more hits in the fifth, to no avail.

The fifth must have seemed like déjà vu to Young. He started off well,

APRIL 12, 1992: BOSTON AT CLEVELAND																
Boston Red Sox	AB	R	H	RBI	BB	SO	PO	A	**Cleveland Indians**	AB	R	H	RBI	BB	SO	PO	A
Boggs 3b	5	0	2	0	0	0	0	5	Lofton cf	1	1	0	0	3	0	0	0
Reed 2b	5	0	1	0	0	1	2	2	Hill dh	4	0	0	0	0	2	0	0
Greenwell lf	4	0	0	0	1	2	0	0	Baerga 2b	4	0	0	2	0	0	4	4
Burks cf	3	1	2	0	1	1	1	0	Belle lf	4	0	0	0	0	1	3	0
Plantier rf	4	0	0	0	0	3	2	0	Whiten rf	3	0	0	0	1	1	0	0
Clark dh	3	0	0	0	1	2	0	0	Sorrento 1b	3	0	0	0	1	0	7	0
Winningham pr,dh	0	0	0	0	0	0	0	0	Jacoby 3b	3	0	0	0	0	0	2	2
Vaughn 1b	2	0	1	0	2	1	13	1	Ortiz c	2	0	0	0	1	0	11	1
Rivera ss	4	0	2	1	0	1	0	6	Lewis ss	1	1	0	0	2	1	0	1
Flaherty c	3	0	1	0	0	0	6	0	**Totals**	25	2	0	2	7	6	27	8
Cooper ph	0	0	0	0	0	0	0	0									
Brunansky ph	0	0	0	0	1	0	0	0									
Totals	33	1	9	1	6	11	24	15									

Boston Red Sox	IP	H	R	ER	BB	SO	HR	**Cleveland Indians**	IP	H	R	ER	BB	SO	HR
Young (L)	8	0	2	2	7	6	0	Nagy (W)	7	8	1	1	4	10	0
								Arnsberg	1	0	0	0	1	1	0
								Lilliquist (S)	1	1	0	0	1	0	0
								Totals	9	9	1	1	6	11	0

	1	2	3	4	5	6	7	8	9	R	H	E
BOS A	0	0	0	1	0	0	0	0	0	1	9	1
CLE A	1	0	1	0	0	0	0	0	x	2	0	0

striking out Lewis. But he walked Lofton, who stole second and third as Hill again whiffed. This time Baerga's grounder was the third merciful out.

The Sox offense went back to work, trying to chip away at Nagy. But though they tallied three more singles in the sixth, they could not get a man across the plate. The score remained 2–1 Cleveland.

As Cleveland came up for the seventh, Young, and most other observers, began to catch on to the unique situation. "Under normal circumstances, I would have been out of the game in the seventh inning," Young remembered in the *Lawrence Eagle-Trib.* "But it was a no-hitter. And the game was still close." Although he walked Junior Ortiz and Lewis, Young held it together, waiting for the Sox to break through for him.

In the ninth, the Sox were down to their final three outs. Manager Butch Hobson called for Scott Cooper to pinch-hit for rookie catcher John Flaherty. Flaherty was making his big league debut that day, and had doubled in the second and lined out a few times. Cleveland manager Mike Hargrove responded with a new pitcher, Derek Lilliquist, and Cooper was in turn replaced by Tom Brunansky. He walked. Wade Boggs singled him to second. "I'm thinking, at worst, we're going to tie the game," Young recalled. Jody Reed stood at the plate, and Young thought he might bunt the runners over. In fact, "We had the bunt on with Jody on the first pitch, but it was a ball," Hobson later said. "Then we took it off and let Jody swing the bat." But he flew out to left, bringing Greenwell up. A single could tie the game; a double might give the Red Sox the lead. But Greenwell banged into a 4-4-3 double play and the game was over. The Sox had nine hits off Indians pitching, but only one run. The Indians had no hits off Young, but two runs and a win.

The National Baseball Hall of Fame in Cooperstown recognized the achievement—such as it was—by asking for Young's cap and other memorabilia to display in the museum, but Major League Baseball did not consider the game a no-hitter. The year before, the records committee had determined that only games in which the pitcher goes nine innings would be considered no-hitters. "No-hitters are supposed to be when you strike out the last guy and your catcher comes out and you jump around, not when you go to the dugout," Young said glumly to reporters after the game. "It's like being in purgatory."

The game was emblematic of Young's career with the Red Sox. His high hopes to start 30 games a season and bring a pennant to Boston, as well as those of the fans who looked for him to earn his $9 million salary, were dashed. Young was plagued with minor injuries and control problems, and even developed a complex inhibiting his throwing to first base. He ended his career in Boston with a 3–11 record.

Extra Innings

• Young's game of misfortune was the first game of a doubleheader. In the second game, Roger Clemens pitched a two-hitter and won 3–0. That stands as the fewest number of hits allowed in a doubleheader in major league history. Clemens had originally not been scheduled to pitch, but in the 19-inning game in the series opener, one of the scheduled starters, Mike Gardiner, had been forced into the game. Clemens hopped a plane to Cleveland and volunteered to take the mound.

• There have been two other times when a single pitcher gave up no hits but lost the game. On April 23, 1964, Ken Johnson pitched 9 innings for Houston against Cincinnati but lost 1–0. And on July 1, 1990, Andy Hawkins of the New York Yankees lost 4–0 to the Chicago White Sox. Hawkins's remains the worst margin of defeat ever in a no-hit situation. And nothing could be worse than what happened to Harvey Haddix on May 26, 1959. He pitched 12 innings of perfect ball against the Braves, but the game remained tied at 0–0 into the unlucky 13th inning. In that inning, the leadoff man reached, and after a sacrifice Haddix intentionally walked Hank Aaron, only to give up a three-run homer to Joe Adcock. Even weirder, the final score of the game was officially 1–0 because Adcock passed Aaron while rounding bases.

• Nick Cafardo pointed out in the *Boston Globe* that "In past years, funny things have happened to the Red Sox in Cleveland. Such as the infamous fog game, when Oil Can Boyd said, 'This is what they get for building a ballpark on the ocean.' Or the 24–5 rout of the Indians in 1986 when recently acquired Spike Owen tied Johnny Pesky's team record for runs scored with six."

40

September 2, 1996: Boston at Seattle

Green Monster

In which a Sox lifer accounts for every tally

Mike Greenwell patrolled left field for the Red Sox from 1987—eventually winning the job from Jim Rice—through 1996, when injuries limited his playing time. A lefty whose swing Ted Williams praised, he struck out rarely, contending for the 1987 Rookie of the Year award and the 1988 MVP Award, and making All-Star appearances in 1988 and 1989. As his career moved into the nineties, though, he struggled with various injuries, alternating good-year, bad-year. In 1996, at age 32, Greenwell lost two months of the season to a broken finger, suffered from chronic back pain, and was dropped to the number eight slot in the batting order.

After going 22–9 in August, the Sox blazed into September in the wild card mix, vying with the Orioles, White Sox, and Mariners for the final slot in the playoffs. Sox ownership entertained the notion of trading Greenwell to the Giants for reliever Rod Beck, but the deal fizzled before the Sox headed to Seattle, needing to knock the Mariners back in the race.

But Roger Clemens, weakened by a stomach virus, took the hill at the Kingdome, and by the end of the fourth inning had put the Sox in a 5–0 hole. The M's got four runs in the fourth, courtesy of two throwing errors on Roger's part, on top of his shaky pitching. "I knew I was going to be weak," the Rocket told Tony Massarotti in the *Boston Herald*, adding, "We're kind of happy now that nothing happened in that trade." Because Greenwell came to Roger's rescue in the top of the fifth, belting a two-run homer off Bob Wolcott, and then a grand slam in the seventh off Bobby Ayala, to put the Sox up 6–5.

Reggie Harris came on to pitch the seventh for Clemens, but the slim lead seemed even slimmer when he gave up a double to Joey Cora. Next in the lineup came the man leading the batting race, Alex Rodriguez, with a .375 average. Harris was no match for A-Rod, whose two-run homer not only took back the lead, it made him the third-youngest player (at age 21) to hit 35 homers in a season. After walking Ken Griffey Jr., Harris hit the showers, bringing on Kerry Lacy, who walked the next two men before being pulled in favor of Vaughn Eshelman. Eshelman then walked pinch hitter Brian Hunter to force in a run, and the Sox were down 8–6.

Perhaps it just wasn't a good night for pitchers, as in the very next frame the Sox faced the M's fourth pitcher of the night, Norm Charlton, in the top of the eighth. Charlton, like Wolcott and Ayala before him, had no answer for Greenwell. After putting Mo Vaughn and Tim Naehring on via the base on balls, Charlton faced Greenwell with one out. This time Greenwell launched a double down the opposite-field line, and both the lumbering Vaughn and pinch runner Lee Tinsley scored. Seattle manager Lou Piniella came out to argue that the ball either was foul or should have been considered a ground-rule double, holding Tinsley at third. His arguments swayed no one, and Sweet Lou got tossed for his vehemence. Mike Stanley came on to pinch-hit then, and if he could bring Greenwell home, the Red Sox would take the lead.

But the honor of the game-winning hit could only be Greenwell's on this night that the baseball gods had decreed for him. Greenwell himself presaged what might happen. The *Boston Globe* reported him saying, "I was in the dugout and I said to Tim Naehring, 'Wouldn't it be unbelievable if I came up in the 10th and drove in the winning run?'" With the game tied 8–8 going into the 10th, Mike faced Rafael Carmona. This time Carmona had walked Wil Cordero and Jeff Manto, and Greenwell needed only a single to bring in the go-ahead run. He delivered the single, and Heathcliff Slocumb made it stand up, ending the game by inducing the still-dangerous Alex Rodriguez to hit into a 1-4-3 double play.

"No one in baseball worked harder on Labor Day than Mike Greenwell," reported the Associated Press, calling him a "one-man band." The game had lasted 3 hours, 57 minutes. His four hits accounted for more than half the Sox total output of seven. With nine RBIs on the night, Greenwell set a new record for a single player accounting for all his team's runs, then surpassing the previous total of eight shared between Bob Johnson of the Philadelphia Athletics (1938) and George Kelly of the New York Giants (1924).

SEPTEMBER 2, 1996: BOSTON AT SEATTLE

Boston Red Sox	AB	R	H	RBI	BB	SO	PO	A	Seattle Mariners	AB	R	H	RBI	BB	SO	PO	A
Bragg cf	5	0	2	0	0	1	3	1	Cora 2b	4	1	3	0	2	0	1	0
Frye 2b	5	0	0	0	0	1	3	4	Rodriguez ss	4	1	1	3	1	0	1	3
Valentin ss	5	0	0	0	0	1	2	3	Griffey cf	3	2	1	0	2	0	2	0
Vaughn 1b	4	1	0	0	1	2	8	0	Martinez dh	3	0	0	0	2	1	0	0
Jefferson dh	2	1	1	0	1	1	0	0	Amaral pr,dh	0	0	0	0	0	0	0	0
Cordero ph,dh	1	1	0	0	1	1	0	0	Buhner rf	3	1	0	0	2	1	6	0
O'Leary rf	2	1	0	0	1	0	4	0	Sorrento 1b	3	1	1	1	0	2	5	0
Pemberton ph,rf	2	0	0	0	0	0	0	0	Hunter ph,1b	0	0	0	1	1	0	2	0
Naehring 3b	1	2	0	0	3	0	1	2	Strange ph,3b	1	0	0	0	0	0	0	0
Tinsley pr	0	1	0	0	0	0	0	0	Whiten lf	5	1	1	1	0	1	4	0
Manto 3b	0	0	0	0	1	0	0	0	Wilson c	3	0	0	0	0	0	7	0
Greenwell lf	5	2	4	9	0	0	2	0	Diaz ph	1	0	0	0	0	0	0	0
Haselman c	3	0	0	0	0	1	4	2	Marzano c	0	0	0	0	0	0	1	0
Stanley ph,c	2	0	0	0	0	0	2	0	Jordan ph	1	0	0	0	0	0	0	0
Clemens p	0	0	0	0	0	0	0	0	Hollins 3b,1b	4	1	2	1	0	1	0	2
Harris p	0	0	0	0	0	0	0	0	Wolcott p	0	0	0	0	0	0	0	1
Lacy p	0	0	0	0	0	0	0	0	Ayala p	0	0	0	0	0	0	0	0
Eshelman p	0	0	0	0	0	0	0	0	Meacham p	0	0	0	0	0	0	0	0
Brandenburg p	0	0	0	0	0	0	0	0	Charlton p	0	0	0	0	0	1	0	0
Slocumb p	0	0	0	0	0	0	1	1	Jackson p	0	0	0	0	0	0	0	0
Totals	**37**	**9**	**7**	**9**	**8**	**8**	**30**	**13**	Carmona p	0	0	0	0	0	0	0	0
									Totals	**35**	**8**	**10**	**7**	**10**	**6**	**30**	**6**

Boston Red Sox	IP	H	R	ER	BB	SO	HR	Seattle Mariners	IP	H	R	ER	BB	SO	HR
Clemens	6	5	5	3	3	4	0	Wolcott	5.2	2	2	2	2	4	1
Harris	0.1	2	3	3	1	0	1	Ayala	0.2	3	4	4	2	2	1
Lacy	0	0	0	0	2	0	0	Meacham	0.2	0	0	0	0	0	0
Eshelman	0.2	0	0	0	1	0	0	Charlton	0.2	1	2	2	2	1	0
Brandenburg	0.2	0	0	0	1	1	0	Jackson	1.1	0	0	0	0	1	0
Slocumb (W)	2.1	3	0	0	2	1	0	Carmona (L)	1	1	1	1	2	0	0
Totals	**10**	**10**	**8**	**6**	**10**	**6**	**1**	**Totals**	**10**	**7**	**9**	**9**	**8**	**8**	**2**

	1	2	3	4	5	6	7	8	9	10	R	H	E
BOS A	0	0	0	0	2	0	4	2	0	1	9	7	2
SEA A	0	0	1	4	0	0	3	0	0	0	8	10	1

"It's just nice to be able to come through and contribute," Greenwell told the *Boston Globe*. "Everything just clicked for me. It was an unbelievable night. A storybook night."

With the win, Boston moved to within half a game of Seattle and only 2½ behind Chicago and Baltimore. The Red Sox would end up falling just short of the wild card, though, leading to the firing of manager Kevin Kennedy and the hiring of Jimy Williams. It was Greenwell's final major league season as well, as the following year he found himself with the Hanshin Tigers in Japan. He played only a few games for Hanshin before a broken foot cut his time short, and he retired from baseball for good.

Extra Innings

- Mike Greenwell's first three major league hits were all home runs, and in 1988 he set the American League record for game-winning RBIs in a season, at 23.

- Greenwell's name appeared in the news in early 2005, as he spoke out about former teammate Jose Canseco. Canseco admitted both in a tell-all book and on *60 Minutes* that he had used steroids in 1988, the year he beat out Greenwell for the MVP Award. "Where's my MVP?" Greenwell demanded. "He's an admitted steroid user, I was clean. If they're going to start putting asterisks by things, let's put one by the MVP. I do have a problem with losing the MVP to an admitted steroids user." (Steroids were not banned by Major League Baseball at the time.)

41

September 18, 1996: Boston at Detroit

Retro-Rocket

In which a hurler repeats a singular feat

Roger Clemens came into the 1996 season knowing it could be his last in a Red Sox uniform. At 34 years old he was no longer the hot young Texan who 10 years earlier had won 24 games and earned both the Cy Young Award and the MVP Award. There were those who claimed that because of his age and his sub-.500 record in 1996, he was no longer one of the elite pitchers in the game. But Clemens was not just 10 years older than the young stud who struck out 20 Seattle Mariners one April night in 1986, he had also refined his money pitch, the forkball he nicknamed "Mr. Splittee." He believed he could still compete at the highest level, even if his results didn't appear to show it.

On September 18 he took the mound in Tiger Stadium for what could be the first of his final three starts as a Red Sox. General Manager Dan Duquette expressed optimism in the papers that a new deal might be worked out once the season ended, but Clemens accepted the possibility that the only organization he had known since coming into professional baseball might let him go. "As the last 10 days go by, it's going to be a little emotional," he told the *Boston Herald*.

Sometimes Clemens's emotions could get the better of him, but some nights they fueled the Rocket. Spectators got an inkling of which kind of night it might be when in the first inning he struck out Ruben Sierra and Tony Clark, hitting the mid-nineties on the radar gun. Then, in the second, he struck out the side. The small crowd of 8,997 people in Detroit began to take notice. So did home plate umpire Tim McClelland. "That's as dominating as I've ever seen a pitcher pitch," said McClelland after the game. The veteran umpire could see from the best seat in the house that Clemens's location, movement, and velocity were all superior on that night. "Roger threw a two- and four-seamer, forkball, and a slider. He was just dominating."

After Boston got him three runs to work with in the fourth, the Rocket hit cruise control for the fifth and sixth, striking out all six men. He reached the

SEPTEMBER 18, 1996: BOSTON AT DETROIT

Boston Red Sox	AB	R	H	RBI	BB	SO	PO	A	Detroit Tigers	AB	R	H	RBI	BB	SO	PO	A
Frye 2b	4	0	0	0	1	2	0	4	Higginson lf,cf	4	0	0	0	0	2	2	0
Garciaparra ss	3	0	0	0	2	1	0	1	Trammell 2b	4	0	1	0	0	1	3	2
Vaughn 1b	5	0	1	0	0	0	7	0	Sierra dh	4	0	1	0	0	2	0	0
Canseco dh	5	0	1	0	0	1	0	0	Clark 1b	4	0	0	0	0	3	8	0
Valentin 3b	4	1	1	0	0	0	0	0	Fryman ss	4	0	0	0	0	4	1	4
Greenwell lf	4	1	2	0	0	2	0	0	Nieves rf	3	0	1	0	0	2	2	0
Tinsley cf	0	0	0	0	0	0	0	0	Nevin 3b	3	0	1	0	0	2	1	3
Pemberton rf	4	2	3	1	0	0	0	0	Ausmus c	3	0	1	0	0	1	7	0
Haselman c	4	0	3	2	0	0	19	1	Bartee cf	2	0	0	0	0	2	2	0
Bragg cf,lf	3	0	0	0	1	0	1	0	Hiatt ph,lf	1	0	0	0	0	1	1	0
Clemens p	0	0	0	0	0	0	0	0	Thompson p	0	0	0	0	0	0	0	1
Totals	**36**	**4**	**11**	**3**	**4**	**6**	**27**	**6**	Nitkowski p	0	0	0	0	0	0	0	0
									Sager p	0	0	0	0	0	0	0	0
									Totals	**32**	**0**	**5**	**0**	**0**	**20**	**27**	**10**

Boston Red Sox	IP	H	R	ER	BB	SO	HR	Detroit Tigers	IP	H	R	ER	BB	SO	HR
Clemens (W)	9	5	0	0	0	20	0	Thompson (L)	4	6	3	3	2	3	0
								Nitkowski	2	3	0	0	2	0	0
								Sager	3	2	1	1	0	3	0
								Totals	**9**	**11**	**4**	**4**	**4**	**6**	**0**

	1	2	3	4	5	6	7	8	9	R	H	E
BOS A	0	0	0	3	0	0	0	1	0	4	11	0
DET A	0	0	0	0	0	0	0	0	0	0	5	1

15-strikeout plateau to end the sixth, and was greeted at the dugout steps by Mo Vaughn. Unlike when a pitcher is pitching a no-hitter, there is no superstition about congratulating a man on a strikeout roll.

By the time the ninth inning rolled around, Roger's performance looked remarkably similar to that one from 10 years before. He had allowed three hits and walked none. This time he had racked up 19 in the first eight frames, needing one to tie, two to break his own record. The Detroit crowd was more aware of Clemens's record than he was. "I knew I had it in the upper teens," he told reporters later. "I didn't know I was approaching 20." The fans in the stands clamored for their own team to go down on strikes.

Roger Clemens

But the Tigers wouldn't succumb so easily. Alan Trammell popped up to lead off the inning. Next came Ruben Sierra, a dangerous hitter who put a good swing on a ball—a single. Next came Tony Clark, a switch hitter with a long swing who had fanned three times already on the night. He got his bat on the ball this time, though—a fly out to left. That left only Travis Fryman, another three-time strikeout victim. "It was the best movement I've seen any pitcher have. The location was exceptional," Fryman said in the *Boston Globe*. Fryman went down swinging—and missing—to seal the game and Clemens's repeat performance.

In the end, 15 of Roger's 20 K's were swinging strikeouts. Clemens needed 151 pitches to finish the game, 100 of them strikes, and racked up the 100th complete game of his career in the process. But Duquette's words of praise for Clemens in the off-season were only for past accomplishments, not future ones. Infamously stating that Clemens was in the "twilight of his career," Duquette let Clemens go as a free agent to AL East rival Toronto. Since that time Clemens has captured four more Cy Young Awards (two with the Blue Jays, one with the Yankees, and one with the Astros) and two World Series rings, surpassed the 300-win mark, and moved into second place on the all-time strikeout list. As of this writing, he is still pitching.

Extra Innings

• In earning the win on September 18, Clemens not only matched himself with the single-game strikeout record, he also tied Cy Young for wins in a Boston uniform (at the top of the list with 192) and shutouts (38). "When you're chasing the guy they name the pitching awards after, boy, you don't get tired," Clemens told the Associated Press after the game. "Afterward, you finally let the air out, and your shoulders down a bit. Then the sweetness part starts to come out."

• At the time of Roger's gem, only four pitchers had ever struck out more than 16 batters in a nine-inning game after reaching age 30: Eddie Cicotte, Bob Gibson, Steve Carlton, and Nolan Ryan.

42

September 10, 1999: Boston at New York

Upon This Rock

In which a bantamweight Dominican knocks out the Yankees

The 1999 edition of the Red Sox featured a likable bunch of players, including shortstop Nomar Garciaparra; pitchers such as Rich "El Guapo" Garces; and an ace they got for a steal from the Montreal Expos, Pedro Martinez. Pedro had come to the Sox in 1998, and by the next year was sorely needed to anchor a pitching staff beset with injuries. After closer Tom Gordon was lost to surgery, starters Tim Wakefield and Derek Lowe were converted to the bullpen and did well in their roles, while Jason Varitek (acquired with Lowe from the Mariners for Heathcliff Slocumb) blossomed as one of the league's best young catchers.

Comparisons to Boston's previous fastball-hurling stud, Roger Clemens, were inevitable for Martinez, but Pedro and Clemens were a study in contrasts. Clemens, a big, barrel-chested Texan, depended on an array of fastballs (four-seam, two-seam, and split-finger) to overpower hitters and used his legs to generate power in his pitches. Pedro, by contrast, was a slight Dominican who used his almost preternaturally long fingers to put movement on his more than 94-mile-per-hour fastball, and also drop in a devastating circle change and curveball.

But Pedro, like Clemens, was not without his controversies. Pedro arrived only 30 minutes before a scheduled start in August, and manager Jimy Williams scratched him in punishment. Off the field and on days when he did not pitch, he developed a reputation as a clubhouse clown. But on the days he pitched, he became a model of serious intent.

That intent was on early display when he took the mound in Yankee Stadium on September 10, as he cruised toward the end of one of the most successful and dominating seasons in recent pitching history. That night the pregame ceremonies included a tribute to pitcher Jim "Catfish" Hunter, who had passed away the day before. The Yankees emerged from their dugout wearing black armbands on their uniforms. Little did they know that in short order they would be mourning their lack of offense as well.

Pedro was also propelling the Red Sox toward a potential playoff berth. That night the Sox opened a three-game set 6½ games behind their AL East rivals. "With one good weekend . . . Boston could be at the Yankees' throats," wrote Buster Olney in the *New York Times*. Pedro stuffed it down their throats from his very first pitch, a 97-mile-per-hour fastball to Chuck Knoblauch. His second pitch hit Knoblauch on the arm, but the runner was erased trying to steal. Next came Derek Jeter. Pedro threw three pitches to Jeter, one at 93, one at 95, and one at 97, and that was all it took to send Jeter back to the bench, shaking his head.

And yet, in almost typical Red Sox fashion, they would be quickly behind in the score. With two out in the second inning, Pedro made one mistake, a fastball to DH Chili Davis that caught too much of the plate. Davis slammed it into the bleachers in right-center for one run, one hit, and one RBI, all in one swing. The chances for a no-hitter were now gone, and the Sox were down 1–0, but Pedro shook it off. He closed the second with a curveball to Ricky Ledee and another strikeout.

SEPTEMBER 10, 1999: BOSTON AT NEW YORK

Boston Red Sox	AB	R	H	RBI	BB	SO	PO	A	New York Yankees	AB	R	H	RBI	BB	SO	PO	A
Offerman 2b	4	0	2	1	1	0	1	0	Knoblauch 2b	3	0	0	0	0	1	5	2
Lewis rf	4	0	0	0	0	1	1	0	Jeter ss	3	0	0	0	0	2	2	6
Garciaparra ss	3	1	0	0	2	0	0	0	O'Neill rf	3	0	0	0	0	1	2	0
Stanley 1b	5	1	4	2	0	0	4	0	Williams cf	3	0	0	0	0	2	2	0
Huskey dh	5	0	0	0	0	1	0	0	T. Martinez 1b	3	0	0	0	0	1	9	0
O'Leary lf	4	0	3	0	1	0	1	0	Davis dh	3	1	1	1	0	2	0	0
Buford cf	4	0	0	0	0	2	1	0	Ledee lf	3	0	0	0	0	3	1	0
Varitek c	4	0	1	0	0	0	17	1	Brosius 3b	3	0	0	0	0	2	0	3
Veras 3b	4	1	2	0	0	0	2	1	Girardi c	2	0	0	0	0	2	6	1
Totals	**37**	**3**	**12**	**3**	**4**	**4**	**27**	**2**	Strawberry ph	1	0	0	0	0	1	0	0
									Pettitte p	0	0	0	0	0	0	0	3
									Nelson p	0	0	0	0	0	0	0	1
									Totals	**27**	**1**	**1**	**1**	**0**	**17**	**27**	**16**

Boston Red Sox	IP	H	R	ER	BB	SO	HR	New York Yankees	IP	H	R	ER	BB	SO	HR
P. Martinez (W)	9	1	1	1	0	17	1	Pettitte (L)	6	8	2	2	3	2	1
								Nelson	1.1	0	0	0	0	0	0
								Stanton	0.2	3	1	1	0	1	0
								Grimsley	1	1	0	0	1	1	0
								Totals	**9**	**12**	**3**	**3**	**4**	**4**	**1**

	1	2	3	4	5	6	7	8	9		R	H	E
BOS A	0	0	0	0	0	2	0	0	1		3	12	0
NY A	0	1	0	0	0	0	0	0	0		1	1	0

Scott Brosius and Joe Girardi went down in the third. In the fifth, Pedro faced Chili again, but this time he struck out the side. The performance was so masterful that the cheers for Pedro began to spill from his Dominican supporters at the Stadium to the regular crowd, and some intrepid fans began to post K signs along the face of the upper deck. The signs were soon ripped down, but the support for Pedro in the crowd increased.

But it was not until the sixth inning that the Sox offense supported their starter. Yankee lefthander Andy Pettitte opened the inning with a walk to Nomar Garciaparra and then faced former Yankee Mike Stanley. Stanley, a power-hitting catcher who had been popular with Yankee fans, powered a ball right over the wall for two runs. "My team backed me up by giving me the lead [and] I wasn't going to let that lead go away," Pedro told reporters later.

All he had to do was keep pitching the way he was, and he did. Jeter, in his fourth full year in the league and already the de facto leader of the Yankees, did his best to break through against Martinez in the seventh. He put up a battle, an "epic" nine-pitch at-bat, but in the end stared at a 3–2 curveball as it crossed the plate. Paul O'Neill and Bernie Williams followed suit, closing the inning and bringing Pedro's strikeout total to 12. In the eighth, Davis and Ledee went down again for numbers 13 and 14. The 2–1 lead seemed huge, and after the Sox tallied another in the top of the ninth, on a triple from Wilton Veras and a single from Jose Offerman, 3–1 seemed as insurmountable as Everest.

Still, the Yankees would try. After all, Boston had the bullpen going, just in case. Maybe Pedro was tiring? No, that was only wishful thinking on the Yankees' part. Brosius swung and missed at a curveball to open the bottom of the inning. It wouldn't be long before he went back to the bench, Pedro's number 15. Joe Torre sent Darryl Strawberry in to pinch-hit for Girardi. What did the veteran slugger plan to do against Pedro? "I didn't really have a plan," Strawberry later told the *New York Times*. "I didn't have a clue." It took Pedro only four pitches to send Straw packing, blowing him away with a high fastball. That brought up Knoblauch. On 1–2, Pedro tried to blow the high, hard one by Knoblauch, too, but the pesky second baseman fouled it off. Pedro could have gone to his changeup or even dropped in a curve, but he had confidence that Knoblauch wouldn't catch up to the next one. It came in at 97, and Pedro was right. Knoblauch swung and missed.

Pedro raised his hands to the sky as the cheers rained down. "He was so damn-near perfect that even an antagonistic Yankee Stadium crowd of 55,239 was cheering him by night's end," according to the *Boston Herald*. The win gave him a 21–4 record, and although he didn't know it at the time, he had just set a new record for strikeouts of Yankee batters in a game. "Think about that," wrote Steve Buckley in the *Herald*. "None of the great ones—Bob Feller, Walter Johnson, Lefty Grove, Nolan Ryan—ever struck out 17 Yankees in a game." He had sat down 22 men in a row and he struck out seven of the last eight. He did not walk a man, and struck out every man in the lineup at least once. Only the home run and the hit-by-pitch of Knoblauch kept it from being a perfect game. Dan Shaughnessy called it "the greatest performance ever against baseball's signature franchise" in the *Globe*. "These are the world champion Yankees and Pedro reduced them to putty."

As Paul O'Neill put it: "We didn't get beat by the Red Sox. We got beat by Pedro Martinez."

◀Extra Innings

- Sox GM Dan Duquette acquired Pedro twice, once when he was GM for Montreal, and again for Boston. The first time, Duquette traded Delino DeShields to get the young Martinez. "The second time, when he got Martinez for Pavano and Armas, Yankees and Indians execs nearly cried," wrote Jon Heyman in *The Sporting News*.

- Sweet revenge: The game was the anniversary of the final night of the "Boston Massacre," a four-game set late in the 1978 pennant race when the Yankees swept the Sox at Fenway, outscoring them by a total of 42 to 9.

- The game was Pedro's third one-hitter of his career. In one of them, June 3, 1995 for Montreal, he pitched nine perfect innings in San Diego. The Expos scored one run in the tenth, and Pedro went out to try to finish the frame. He gave up a leadoff double to Bip Roberts, and manager Felipe Alou replaced him with Mel Rojas, who earned the save. Some six weeks later, Pedro's brother Ramon threw a no-hitter against the Marlins.

43

October 16, 1999: New York at Boston

Cy Young versus Cy Old

In which the mantle passes while the Rocket goes down in flames

In 1999, the Red Sox reached the postseason in consecutive years for the first time since 1915–1916, riding the back of workhorse ace Pedro Martinez. Pedro won pitching's Triple Crown that season, with the lowest ERA (2.07), most strikeouts (313), and most wins with his 23–4 record. The small-statured

OCTOBER 16, 1999: NEW YORK AT BOSTON

New York Yankees	AB	R	H	RBI	BB	SO	PO	A
Knoblauch 2b	2	0	0	0	1	0	1	2
Sojo ph,2b	1	0	0	0	0	0	1	1
Jeter ss	3	0	1	0	0	2	2	4
Bellinger ph,ss	1	0	0	0	0	1	0	1
O'Neill rf	3	0	0	0	2	0	0	0
Curtis lf,cf	1	0	0	0	0	0	0	0
Williams cf	3	0	0	0	0	1	3	0
Spencer lf	0	0	0	0	1	0	0	0
T. Martinez 1b	4	0	1	0	0	2	7	0
Davis dh	3	0	0	0	1	2	0	0
Ledee lf,rf	4	0	0	0	0	2	1	0
Brosius 3b	3	1	1	1	0	0	1	0
Girardi c	1	0	0	0	0	1	2	0
Posada c	2	0	0	0	0	0	4	0
Irabu p	0	0	0	0	0	0	2	0
Stanton p	0	0	0	0	0	0	0	1
Totals	**31**	**1**	**3**	**1**	**3**	**13**	**24**	**12**

Boston Red Sox	AB	R	H	RBI	BB	SO	PO	A
Offerman 2b	6	2	3	0	0	1	1	1
Valentin 3b	6	2	3	5	0	1	1	1
Varitek c	4	0	0	0	1	1	13	0
Hatteberg c	0	0	0	0	0	0	0	0
Garciaparra ss	5	1	4	3	0	0	1	0
O'Leary lf	5	2	2	0	0	1	2	0
Stanley 1b	4	1	2	1	1	0	5	0
Daubach dh	4	2	2	2	0	1	0	0
Huskey ph,dh	1	0	0	0	0	0	0	0
Lewis cf,rf	5	1	2	1	0	0	3	0
Nixon rf	4	2	3	0	0	1	1	0
Buford ph,cf	1	0	0	0	0	0	0	0
Gordon p	0	0	0	0	0	0	0	1
Totals	**45**	**13**	**21**	**12**	**2**	**6**	**27**	**3**

New York Yankees	IP	H	R	ER	BB	SO	HR
Clemens (L)	2	6	5	5	2	2	1
Irabu	4.2	13	8	7	0	3	2
Stanton	0.1	0	0	0	0	0	0
Watson	1	2	0	0	0	1	0
Totals	**8**	**21**	**13**	**12**	**2**	**6**	**3**

Boston Red Sox	IP	H	R	ER	BB	SO	HR
P. Martinez (W)	7	2	0	0	2	12	0
Gordon	1	1	1	1	0	1	1
Rapp	1	0	0	0	1	0	0
Totals	**9**	**3**	**1**	**1**	**3**	**13**	**1**

	1	2	3	4	5	6	7	8	9	R	H	E
NY A	0	0	0	0	0	0	1	0		1	3	3
BOS A	2	2	2	0	2	1	4	0	x	13	21	1

Martinez (170 lbs., listed generously at 5'11") had pitched 213 innings, with five complete games. But the wear and tear finally showed in the opening game of the ALDS against the Cleveland Indians. Suffering from back pain, Pedro was forced to leave the game in the fourth, leading 2–0, and the Sox ultimately lost 3–2.

The Sox dropped the next game as well, but then won two in a row, forcing a final game five, in which Pedro made a heroic appearance out of the bullpen, arriving in the fourth inning with the game locked in an 8–8 tie. That night he didn't have his top-shelf stuff and his back was still balky, but his ability to change speeds and deceive batters was more than enough to shut down the Indians. The Indians, after all, were just a stepping-stone to the opponent the Sox most wanted to face: the New York Yankees.

The Yankees' road to the ALCS was easier than that of the Sox, as they swept the Texas Rangers, allowing the powerful Texas offense only a single run in the series. The Yankees were not as dominant against the Sox, but they eked out a 4–3 victory in game one that was helped by a blown umpire's call, and a 3–2 win in game two in which the Sox narrowly missed a few home runs. New England seethed at the losses, but the Yankees had not yet seen their best. With Pedro having pitched in game five of the division series in relief, he was slated to start in game three of the championship series. No one, least of all the

Yankees, had forgotten that a month prior, Pedro had pitched a one-hit gem at Yankee Stadium. Ailing or no, how much better might he be at Fenway Park on a beautiful autumn day?

The pitching matchup only served to propel the pregame hype one more notch. Pedro Martinez would face former Sox ace Roger Clemens in what bumper stickers being sold outside the park touted as "Cy Old vs. Cy Young." Somehow they had never matched up in the regular season. Joe Torre had foreseen the ALCS showdown while watching TV. "We pretty much set our pitching up [already] and I watch Pedro come out of that bullpen I'm going boom, boom, boom," he told *The Sporting News* as he counted off the ALCS games on his fingers. "Yeah, that's what's going to happen." Clemens, like many first-rank free agents who join a New York team, had spent the season trying to adjust to the city—its fans, media, and expectations—with mixed success. Clemens's reputation from his years in Boston was mixed when it came to postseason play. He held a 2–4 record in postseason games, and was so overtaken by his emotions in a 1990 ALCS game that he was ejected by home plate umpire Terry Cooney in the second inning. Sox fans and players alike looked forward to the game. As Sox pitcher Bret Saberhagen told the *New York Times*, "I will remember this game tomorrow for the rest of my life. It is a matchup for all matchups. It is a dream matchup."

Pedro's first inning was not overpowering, but it was effective: two fly balls, a harmless single from Jeter, and a strikeout of Bernie Williams that brought the crowd to its feet. Clemens could not say the same. The first batter he faced, Jose Offerman, tripled on the second pitch he saw, sending the ball rattling past a sun-blinded Paul O'Neill into Fenway's spacious right-field corner, and then third baseman John Valentin hit a home run into the net over the Green Monster. Clemens, like many power pitchers, was known to sometimes give up runs in the first inning but then settle down and become lights out. If he could get the next three men out, perhaps this would be one of those times. But although Jason Varitek grounded out, the next batter, Nomar Garciaparra, reached on second baseman Chuck Knoblauch's habitual throwing error (he had developed throwing yips on the play to first base shortly after coming to New York and they never left him). After Troy O'Leary flew out to center, Mike Stanley worked a walk. Clemens struck out Brian Daubach to escape further damage, but the Sox held a 2–0 lead.

And they had Pedro Martinez on the mound. In the second, Pedro struck out the side. Clemens resumed pitching, but the results were similar to the first inning as he gave up another two runs, this time on three hits and two walks. Martinez struck out two more Yankees in the third, while Clemens opened the inning by allowing a single to Mike Stanley on his first pitch. At that point, Joe Torre had seen enough, and he sent the sputtering Rocket to the showers. On came Hideki Irabu, a Japanese import who had excelled at times and struggled at others. The first batter he faced, Daubach, homered. Now it was 6–0 Red Sox, and as the inning stretched on, Pedro retreated to the clubhouse to have his back treated. He was hurting but did not show it, not so far as the Yankees could tell.

The Sox continued to pile on runs, adding two more in the fifth, another in the sixth, and then exploding for four more runs in the seventh—during which the crowd chanted "Where is Ro-ger?" in jubilation (and others called in response: "In the sho-wer!"). The Yankees managed only three hits the whole game, and only one run, which came on a solo homer off reliever Tom Gordon, who had replaced Pedro in the eighth. Pat Rapp pitched the ninth for Boston, flawlessly, to wrap up the 13–1 victory. Raucous fans stormed a huge cloth banner hanging at Fenway commemorating Clemens's two 20-strikeout performances for the Red Sox. Police intervention saved the banner, but not Clemens's reputation. The day belonged to Pedro in more than one way.

Combining his ALDS and ALCS appearances, Pedro had racked up 17 innings, 31 strikeouts, only five hits, and no runs. And all this with a sore back. Although he was mostly throwing between 88 and 92 miles per hour, Pedro struck out 12, a new Red Sox postseason record. "His repertoire last night included 38 fastballs, 32 changeups, 22 curveballs, and 13 cut-fastballs," wrote Tony Massarotti in a thorough recap in the *Boston Herald*. "Sixty-seven of his 105 pitches were strikes." Not a great ratio, but a baffling combination for the Yankee lineup. "Even though he averaged 90 to 91 [on his fastball], because of all the changeups and curveballs he threw, it probably looked like 95," opined pitching coach Joe Kerrigan. "He's a magician with the ball."

"I haven't had time to rest," Pedro told reporters who asked about his back after the game. "I haven't had time to treat it right. I'm just out there with God in front of me, and my teammates. I'm not hiding anything. I'm hurting. I'm hurting with every pitch I throw. But I manage to do it somehow, and I'm not going to quit doing it until I know I'm not getting anybody out."

Unfortunately, Pedro did not get another start against the Yankees, as the next two games went to New York. The Yankees went on to win their third World Series in four years. Pedro won the Cy Young Award, his second, becoming the third pitcher to win the award in both leagues. It would be a few years before these AL East rivals would meet in the postseason again.

◀ Extra Innings

- Clemens would eventually become the fourth pitcher to win Cy Young Awards in both leagues. After being lured out of a brief, two-month retirement to pitch for his hometown Houston Astros in 2004, Roger went 18–4, passed Steve Carlton to move into second place on the all-time strikeout list, and won the award easily.

44

April 27, 2002: Tampa Bay at Boston

How Lowe

In which a pitcher sinks to new heights

At the trading deadline during the 1997 season, Derek Lowe and Jason Varitek arrived in Boston from Seattle, swapped for Red Sox reliever Heathcliff Slocumb. Sox fans would have traded Slocumb for the proverbial bag of baseballs; he was 0–5 with Boston, with a 5.79 ERA, and it seemed that bringing him on to close a game was like throwing gasoline on a fire.

The move would turn out to be one of the most lopsided in recent baseball history, as Slocumb would flop in Seattle, while the two men who became Red Sox would become integral parts of the team's success over the next several seasons. When asked about the trade a few years later, Varitek would remind people that, in Seattle's opinion, "[Derek] was a one-pitch pitcher and I couldn't catch, hit or throw" *(Boston Herald)*. Seattle was wrong. Varitek soon blossomed into a rare commodity: a switch-hitting, power-hitting catcher with a blend of top-shelf defensive and offensive skills. By 2005, Varitek's demeanor of consistency and hard-nosed play would also earn him the rarely bestowed title of Boston team captain (not to mention a new long-term contract).

Lowe, on the other hand, was never considered a model of consistency. His "one pitch" was a sinking fastball, though in reality he also threw a curve and changeup, all low in the zone. In 1998, his first full season with Boston, he both started and relieved, but in 1999, when closer Tom Gordon was felled by injury, Lowe took over the closer's spot. At first he excelled in relief, as his sinker caused many a batter to ground into an inning-ending double play. But some high-profile meltdowns and the appearance that errors in the field behind him negatively affected him led some to question his mental toughness. He found himself hounded by the Fenway Faithful. "I would get up in the bullpen to go to the restroom and [the fans] would boo me," Lowe recalled. "That sticks with a person, so I would slither along the bullpen wall so they wouldn't see me. You don't forget those things." Jackie MacMullan described Fenway Park in the *Globe* as "Lowe's Little Shop of Horrors, the place that decimated his confidence, his identity, and nearly his sanity."

Lowe himself questioned his assignment to the bullpen. "With his stuff, he was never a high-strikeout guy," Varitek said. Lowe was a ground-ball pitcher, and ground balls sometimes go through. Pitching-coach-cum-manager Joe Kerrigan experimented with using Lowe as a starter in September 2001.

For the 2002 season, Lowe was moved back into the rotation. He added a cut fastball to his repertoire and hoped to start fresh in the eyes of the fans and the American League East. He opened his season exactly the way he wanted to, pitching seven full innings in each of his first three starts, giving up only one hit to the Orioles, only two hits to the vaunted Yankees, and a total of 11 hits over the three games. He had a hiccup against Kansas City on April 21, when he gave up only four hits, but three walks and five earned runs; fortunately, strong run support earned him the 8–7 win. Overall, many observers were ready to declare the "Derek Lowe starter experiment" a success. But the best was yet to come.

APRIL 27, 2002: TAMPA BAY AT BOSTON

Tampa Bay Devil Rays	AB	R	H	RBI	BB	SO	PO	A	Boston Red Sox	AB	R	H	RBI	BB	SO	PO	A
Tyner lf	4	0	0	0	0	2	0	0	Henderson cf	4	3	2	1	1	1	2	0
Winn cf	3	0	0	0	0	2	4	1	Offerman 1b	3	3	2	0	2	0	13	0
Cox 1b	3	0	0	0	0	0	4	0	Garciaparra ss	5	0	2	2	0	0	1	2
Hall c	3	0	0	0	0	0	10	0	Ramirez lf	3	1	1	1	2	0	1	0
Grieve rf	2	0	0	0	0	0	0	0	Daubach dh	4	1	1	0	1	3	0	0
Conti rf	1	0	0	0	0	0	3	0	Hillenbrand 3b	4	1	1	2	0	0	1	3
Vaughn dh	3	0	0	0	0	0	0	0	Varitek c	5	1	1	2	0	2	6	0
Abernathy 2b	2	0	0	0	1	0	3	2	Nixon rf	5	0	2	0	0	2	2	0
Johnson 3b	3	0	0	0	0	1	0	1	Sanchez 2b	4	0	1	2	0	2	1	5
Escalona ss	3	0	0	0	0	1	0	0	Lowe p	0	0	0	0	0	0	0	0
James p	0	0	0	0	0	0	0	0	Totals	37	10	13	10	6	10	27	10
Sosa p	0	0	0	0	0	0	0	0									
Harper p	0	0	0	0	0	0	0	0									
Zambrano p	0	0	0	0	0	0	0	0									
Creek p	0	0	0	0	0	0	0	0									
Totals	27	0	0	0	1	6	24	4									

Tampa Bay Devil Rays	IP	H	R	ER	BB	SO	HR	Boston Red Sox	IP	H	R	ER	BB	SO	HR
James (L)	2.1	5	6	6	2	1	1	Lowe (W)	9	0	0	0	1	6	0
Sosa	1.2	4	2	2	1	1	0								
Harper	2	1	0	0	0	4	0								
Zambrano	1	2	0	0	0	1	0								
Creek	1	1	2	2	3	3	0								
Totals	8	13	10	10	6	10	1								

	1	2	3	4	5	6	7	8	9	R	H	E
TB A	0	0	0	0	0	0	0	0	0	0	0	2
BOS A	1	0	6	1	0	0	0	2	x	10	13	0

The afternoon of April 27 was sunny but brisk, the kind of day that at 55 degrees is just warm enough to make winter-weary New Englanders rush outside to greet the daylight. Lowe took the hill at Fenway Park to face the Tampa Bay Devil Rays. Varitek crouched behind the plate. He knew, as did anyone who reads the papers, that the Devil Rays were at the bottom of the league in many offensive categories. But they had speed, and had surprised the Sox with wacky wins in the past. Although Lowe recorded the first out easily on Jason Tyner, Lowe worried that trouble was brewing when the second batter, Randy Winn, skied a ball to left-center. If the wind had been blowing out, the ball might have carried over the wall, or banged off the Monster for a double. But the wind was blowing in, and the potential hit became a can of corn.

The Rays were not so lucky in the bottom half of the inning. Forty-three-year-old Rickey Henderson led off the game with the 80th leadoff homer of his marathon career. Henderson was making the start at leadoff and playing center because Johnny Damon was recovering from a pulled muscle. On just the second pitch he saw from Delvin James, Henderson smacked the ball out and styled his way around the bases.

Lowe settled down to pitch a 1-2-3 second inning; with one out in the third, though, he walked Brent Abernathy. "All I saw that at-bat were five sinkers, and it was ridiculous how much he had it moving," Abernathy told the *St. Petersburg Times*. Moving too much to hit. Abernathy was stranded, and the Rays began to mutter on their bench. What would it take to get to this guy? Steve Cox came up in the fourth inning, trying to get a ball in the air. He did—a line drive into right—but Trot Nixon was there to grab it at the warning track. The Rays began to toss the term "no-hitter" around in their dugout, Abernathy told the *St. Pete Times*. "You know how the saying is that you don't say anything to a pitcher about a no-hitter? Well, we're in the dugout, 'Somebody tell this guy he's got a no-hitter. Somebody bust up the no-hitter.' We were just trying to mention it as much as possible." Catcher Toby Hall concurred: "We were trying to get the baseball gods working for us, but they weren't listening today."

Indeed, the Rays were not only handed a hot pitcher to handle, they also faced a Sox offensive onslaught. Thanks to a two-run double by Varitek and a two-run single by Rey Sanchez, the Sox rallied for six runs in the third. The lead only increased Lowe's confidence. In the sixth inning he was able to set the Rays down with only 13 pitches.

The Fenway crowd began to sense something special in the air. "Once we got through the sixth inning, we knew we had a chance," Varitek told reporters. Lowe's one-hitter in Baltimore just a few weeks earlier had been broken up by a Tony Batista single in the eighth. Sox pitchers Pedro Martinez and Tim Wakefield had both taken no-hitters into the ninth against this same Tampa Bay club in years past, only to give up a hit. Varitek tamped down the rising anticipation in his chest. "We had to go out by out, hitter by hitter."

On the bench, Lowe's teammates tried to do the same. Utilityman Carlos Baerga was told he had to stay in the clubhouse, rather than come out to the dugout in the late innings, as was his custom. Manager Grady Little tried not to move in his seat. Pitcher Tim Wakefield, antsy and needing to blow off steam, asked if he could warm up. He was told yes, but not while Lowe was pitching.

Lowe cruised through the seventh and eighth. "I think the crowd carried him the last two innings," Varitek said, aware that these were the same fans who had booed Lowe at every opportunity the previous season. "If anything, that adrenaline rush kicked in. This crowd can do that to us. It's a great crowd to have behind you."

The Red Sox tacked on two more runs in a long bottom of the eighth to make the score 10–0, while Lowe jittered in the dugout, knowing he was going back out for the ninth.

He retired Russ Johnson on a soft liner to second. But then, with one out and two to go, Lowe thought it might all be over. Shortstop Felix Escalona lofted a ball into left-center. "He made good contact on that one," Lowe said after the game. "I thought it was going to drop in the gap. I was almost afraid to look." But the ageless Rickey Henderson charged in and to his right, scooping the ball out of the air with a basket catch at his knees while on the run. "I just told it to stay in the glove," Henderson told the *Boston Globe*.

That left one out to go. Jason Tyner was the 28th man to face Lowe that day. "I'm such a huge golf guy, and I [was thinking] of Tiger Woods at the Masters where he says, 'Finish the deal.' You've got to finish it. That's what I kept telling myself," Lowe later said. "You've got eight innings, 8⅔ is good, but no one remembers 8⅔, you know? . . . You've got to be able to finish it." He got Tyner down 0–2, while the crowd cheered breathlessly. Then Tyner laid off two pitches out of the strike zone. Lowe went to his changeup, and Tyner hit the ball on the ground, to second. Rey Sanchez handled the easy chance and that was it. Lowe pumped his fist and quickly disappeared in a mob of relieved teammates. When he emerged from the clump, he waved his hat to the fans as he went to the dugout.

Team management quickly went to work and set up a microphone to allow Lowe to share the afterglow with the fans. "I deserved it," Lowe said of the previous season's boos, while thanking them for the day's cheers. "They're as much a part of this as we are," he said. "Hopefully, they'll remember the day, too."

Extra Innings

- Lowe's was the first no-hitter at Fenway in 37 years. The previous had been pitched by Dave Morehead against Cleveland on September 16, 1965, before just 1,247 fans. Hideo Nomo had pitched a no-no the previous season for the Sox, at Baltimore. Varitek caught that one, too.

- Upon tossing the no-hitter, Lowe became the third pitcher in history to have thrown a no-hitter and to have recorded a 40-save season. The other two are Dennis Eckersley and Dave Righetti.

- Even 3,000 miles away, Sox president Larry Lucchino was infected by the usual baseball superstitions about jinxing a no-hitter. Lucchino planted himself on his couch in San Diego, where he caught the game on satellite TV. "It's very unusual for me to sit and watch a game from start to finish," he said. "Usually I'm walking around, talking business. But I watched every golden moment of this one. And I'm so superstitious, I didn't want to move."

- At least three people are known to have witnessed both the Morehead and Lowe no-hitters: the late Dick Radatz, Lee Thomas, and coauthor Bill Nowlin.

45

July 23, 2002: Tampa Bay at Boston

Birthday Bash

In which the franchise player gives Boston a present

The longer Fenway Park stands, the more of a temple to memory and greatness it becomes, no less so now in the twenty-first century than in the twentieth. It was a fitting setting for the celebration of Ted Williams's life that took place a few weeks after his passing, drawing together teammates and dignitaries and thousands of fans for what the *Boston Herald* called a "grand adios." As Steve Buckley wrote, the festivities "struck the perfect balance between teary-eyed nostalgia and lodge hall merriment, as the old Kenmore Square ballyard was magically transformed into a lyric little social club for thousands of the Splendid Splinter's closest friends." A total of 20,500 turned out on a night when there was no ball game, to honor the man and the franchise he epitomized. "Nights like this are why Boston is a special place to grow up a baseball fan, no matter how many years without a World Series title or how many heartbreaking defeats to the New York Yankees," opined Tony Massarotti. Among the players who participated in the ceremony were former Red Sox greats such as Dom DiMaggio and Carl Yastrzemski. Sitting there among them, the closest of the current players to Ted, was Nomar Garciaparra.

Garciaparra had been carrying the flag as top Sox since his sensational rookie year in 1997, when he was unanimously named Rookie of the Year and made the All-Star team. He had 209 hits on the season, set a new rookie record with a 30-game hitting streak, scored 122 runs, and knocked in 98. Nomar set Red Sox Nation on fire, and Ted Williams took notice. "The first time I remember talking to him was on the phone," Garciaparra recalled for the Fenway crowd during the tribute. "He just kept drilling me to find out how much I knew about hitting. . . . I felt like I was on the hot seat." Ted was impressed with what he heard. "He's as good a young player as anyone I've ever seen come into the big leagues," he would later say. "He's tremendous. One of the very best young hitters I ever saw. He's a smart kid and he knows all about hitting." Garciaparra and Williams bonded in the latter years of Ted's life, over growing up in Southern California and over the subject of hitting, their rapport growing as time went on. When asked what Ted had said to him during Williams's stirring appearance on the field at the 1999 All-Star Game at Fenway Park, Nomar answered, "When he called to me, he said, 'I'm sorry I missed your party last night.' I knew him on that level. He gave me so many compliments that he turned my face red . . . but to be able to say he's my friend means even more."

The next day the Red Sox were due to play a doubleheader against the Tampa Bay Devil Rays to make up for an earlier rainout. It would also be Nomar's 29th birthday, and he would provide his own fireworks. On the mound knuckleballer Tim Wakefield went for the Sox, and hard-throwing Tanyon Sturtze for the Devil Rays. Things got off to a tough start as the Rays jumped on Wakefield for four runs in the first two innings, including a two-run homer by Steve Cox in the first. But the fireworks started in the third inning. First, Johnny Damon led off with a home run to ignite the rally. Lou Merloni then singled, bringing Garciaparra to the plate. Sturtze, who often struggled with his control, took the count to 3–0 and then tried to pump a fastball past the Boston shortstop. Nomar turned on it and sent it over the screen in left to bring the Sox to within one. Manny Ramirez followed with a near-foul home run around the Pesky Pole. Sturtze struggled, walked a few, and then gave up a two-RBI double to Trot Nixon, making the score 6–4 Boston. Brandon Backe came on in relief, but his luck (or skill) was not much better that day, at least when it came to facing Nomar. Batting for the second time in the inning, with one on and two out, Nomar hit a two-run shot. When the inning ended, the Sox had taken a 10–4 lead.

The party continued in the fourth inning, with the crowd serenading him with "Happy Birthday" as he stood in the on-deck circle. This time when Nomar came to the plate, Backe was still laboring through his relief appearance and the bases were loaded. On a 2–2 curveball, Nomar unloaded for a grand slam, three homers in three plate appearances, eight RBIs in the game, and another step in the eventual 22–4 win over the Rays. With the blast, Nomar became only the fourth Red Sox player to have two three-homer games to his credit, joining the ranks of Mo Vaughn, Jim Rice, and—of course—Ted Williams. Nomar also became the first major leaguer ever to hit three homers in two back-to-back innings, as well as the first to hit three homers on his birthday. He also became the first Red Sox player in history with two games of 8 RBIs or more to his credit. "You don't see a day like this coming," Nomar told reporters after the game. He claimed he didn't do anything differently because it was his birthday—easy to believe, since Nomar was notorious for always following the same routine, right down to his particular way of going up the dugout steps. "You don't say, 'I'm feeling good, I'm going to hit three today,'" he said, causing John Powers to conclude in the *Globe* that "Nomar Garciaparra merely did what Ted Williams told everyone to do. Get a good pitch to hit and swing away."

JULY 23, 2002: TAMPA BAY AT BOSTON

Tampa Bay Devil Rays	AB	R	H	RBI	BB	SO	PO	A	Boston Red Sox	AB	R	H	RBI	BB	SO	PO	A
Winn cf	4	0	2	1	0	2	3	0	Damon cf	5	4	4	2	1	0	4	0
Abernathy 2b	3	1	0	0	0	0	2	1	Merloni 2b	4	4	1	0	2	1	0	3
Cox 1b	4	1	1	2	0	0	5	0	Garciaparra ss	5	3	3	8	1	0	2	3
Huff dh	4	0	0	0	0	0	0	0	Ramirez lf	6	2	3	5	0	1	3	0
Hall c	4	0	1	0	0	0	4	0	Hillenbrand 3b	5	0	0	0	1	1	1	2
Conti rf	4	1	2	0	0	1	2	0	Daubach dh	5	1	1	0	1	1	0	0
Gomez ss	3	1	0	0	1	1	3	4	Offerman 1b	5	2	1	0	0	0	8	0
Sandberg 3b	2	0	0	1	0	0	4	0	Nixon rf	5	3	4	3	0	0	5	0
Crawford lf	3	0	1	0	0	0	1	1	Mirabelli c	4	3	2	3	1	0	4	1
Sturtze p	0	0	0	0	0	0	0	0	Wakefield p	0	0	0	0	0	0	0	0
Backe p	0	0	0	0	0	0	0	0	Banks p	0	0	0	0	0	0	0	1
Kent p	0	0	0	0	0	0	0	0	Totals	44	22	19	21	7	4	27	10
Phelps p	0	0	0	0	0	0	0	0									
Totals	31	4	7	4	1	4	24	6									

Tampa Bay Devil Rays	IP	H	R	ER	BB	SO	HR	Boston Red Sox	IP	H	R	ER	BB	SO	HR
Sturtze (L)	2.1	8	9	7	3	1	3	Wakefield (W)	5	5	4	4	1	4	1
Backe	1.1	6	7	7	1	1	2	Banks (S)	4	2	0	0	0	0	0
Kent	2	1	2	0	2	1	0	Totals	9	7	4	4	1	4	1
Phelps	2.1	4	4	4	1	1	2								
Totals	8	19	22	17	7	4	7								

	1	2	3	4	5	6	7	8	9		R	H	E
TB A	2	2	0	0	0	0	0	0	0		4	7	2
BOS A	0	0	10	6	0	2	1	3	x		22	19	0

Circumstance combined with talent created a memorable afternoon at Fenway Park. A year later, Nomar was asked by reporters how he remembered his great day. "To me it's just another number, another day," he said humbly. When asked if he had seen a tape of the game, he replied, "I don't look back on many games. It's not me. I have a memory, that's good enough for me."

◀ Extra Innings

- Perhaps the Ted Williams tribute helped to dispel the cloud hanging on the Sox after two heartbreaking last-at-bat losses to New York in the previous two games—at least briefly. In the nightcap, the Sox took a 4–0 lead into the ninth inning, only to watch the bullpen surrender five runs before recording an out. They got the winning run to the plate in the bottom half of the inning but lost 5–4.

- By hitting two home runs in Sunday's game against the Yankees, Nomar also tied a major league record by hitting five homers in two games. Twenty-five other players have accomplished that feat.

46

June 27, 2003: Florida at Boston

Hook, Line, and Sinker

In which the new-look Red Sox blow the soon-to-be champs out of the water

The 2003 Florida Marlins who arrived at Fenway park for an interleague series were not the same team that had won the 1997 World Series, then the soonest after inception that any expansion team had won it all. Thanks to a fire sale after their stunning win, owner Wayne Huizenga gutted the team of most of its talent, then sold the franchise to a shrewd but soft-spoken businessman named John Henry. John Henry, in time, sold the team so he could acquire a prime franchise: the Boston Red Sox.

In the years after disposal king Huizenga's fire sale, the Marlins had built up a good farm system stocked with pitching talent, but the pitchers could seemingly never stay healthy. The blame for their frequent and lengthy trips to the disabled list was finally laid on manager Jeff Torborg's head, and early in the 2003 season Torborg was canned in favor of 73-year-old Jack McKeon. McKeon had been unceremoniously dumped by Cincinnati not long before, and relished the chance to get back in the game. The turnaround was notice-able, and with the leadership of third baseman Mike Lowell and a new acqui-sition, established catcher Ivan Rodriguez, by midsummer Florida was shaping up to be a decent if unspectacular team. No one could have predicted the events about to befall them at Fenway Park.

With a bunt, a fielder's choice, and a single, the Marlins scored a run in the top of the first off Boston's Byung-Hyun Kim. Then it was time for the Red Sox to bat. Former Sox pitching prospect Carl Pavano took the ball—and faced an onslaught.

The action began with center fielder Johnny Damon. Signed as a free agent from cost-conscious Oakland, Damon put speed at the top of the lineup; he doubled. Second baseman Todd Walker singled to bring Damon home and tie the game. Third up was Nomar Garciaparra, whose double sent Walker to third. Pavano went to work on Manny Ramirez, one of the premier hitters in the league, now in his third season in Boston. Manny went right to work, too, homering over the Monster and bringing the score to 4–1.

If seeing the bases empty helped Pavano, it did not show in the results. The next batter was big DH David Ortiz. Ortiz had played six years with the Twins, mostly riding the bench, before the Sox made him their everyday designated hitter in 2003. He pulled a double into right. Kevin Millar was up next; he had been a Marlin the season before, but in the off-season had been headed to play in Japan before the Sox hauled him in. Millar singled and Ortiz scored, mak-ing the score 5–1 and still nobody out. McKeon gave Pavano the hook and brought in the lefty Miguel Tejera.

Perhaps McKeon hoped that Tejera could do something with Trot Nixon, who was often benched against left-handed pitching. The hope was in vain. Nixon singled, bringing Bill Mueller to the plate. A spry gloveman who had spent his entire career quietly putting up decent offensive numbers in the National League, Mueller was pleased to find he could feast on American League pitching. He walked to load the bases this time, though, for today's number nine hitter, Jason Varitek. Tek singled in two more runs, moving Mueller to second and turning the lineup over.

Damon came up for the second time in the inning now, with two on and still no one out. This time he did one better than the time before, as he tripled to clear the bases and make the score 9–1. One more run and the Sox would set a new record for runs scored before the first out. Walker was the man to do it, and with a quick single, he did just that.

McKeon had tried two pitchers, and neither one had recorded an out. He yanked Tejera and moved on to Allen Levrault, who finished his warm-up

JUNE 27, 2003: FLORIDA AT BOSTON

Florida Marlins	AB	R	H	RBI	BB	SO	PO	A	Boston Red Sox	AB	R	H	RBI	BB	SO	PO	A
Pierre cf	4	2	1	0	1	0	6	1	Damon cf	7	3	5	3	0	1	4	0
Castillo 2b	2	0	0	0	0	0	0	0	Walker 2b	5	3	4	3	1	1	3	4
Mordecai 2b	2	0	0	1	0	1	0	2	Garciaparra ss	4	1	1	0	0	0	0	2
Rodriguez c	2	0	2	1	0	0	2	0	Sanchez ss	3	0	0	1	0	2	0	1
Redmond c	3	1	2	1	0	0	8	0	Ramirez lf	3	2	2	3	0	0	0	0
Lowell 3b	2	0	1	0	0	0	1	0	Mirabelli ph,1b	3	1	1	0	0	1	4	1
Fox 3b	0	2	0	0	2	0	0	0	Ortiz dh	4	4	3	3	1	0	0	0
Encarnacion rf	2	1	1	2	1	0	2	0	Millar 1b,lf	4	3	3	2	1	0	7	0
Banks rf	2	0	0	0	0	1	0	0	Nixon rf	4	4	3	0	2	0	1	0
Lee 1b	5	1	2	3	0	0	2	0	Mueller 3b	5	3	4	6	1	1	1	3
Cabrera lf	4	1	0	0	1	2	1	1	Varitek c	4	1	2	4	1	1	6	0
Gonzalez ss	4	0	0	0	1	1	2	0	Kim p	0	0	0	0	0	0	0	0
Hollandsworth dh	4	0	1	0	0	1	0	0	Rupe p	0	0	0	0	0	0	1	0
Pavano p	0	0	0	0	0	0	0	0	Seanez p	0	0	0	0	0	0	0	0
Tejera p	0	0	0	0	0	0	0	0	Almonte p	0	0	0	0	0	0	0	0
Levrault p	0	0	0	0	0	0	0	0	Shiell p	0	0	0	0	0	0	0	0
Olsen p	0	0	0	0	0	0	0	0	Totals	46	25	28	25	7	7	27	11
Neal p	0	0	0	0	0	0	0	0									
Totals	36	8	10	8	6	6	24	5									

Florida Marlins	IP	H	R	ER	BB	SO	HR	Boston Red Sox	IP	H	R	ER	BB	SO	HR
Pavano (L)	0	6	6	6	0	0	1	Kim (W)	5	7	5	1	2	4	0
Tejera	0	4	5	5	1	0	0	Rupe	1	0	0	0	0	1	0
Levrault	3	6	6	6	5	2	2	Seanez	1	1	0	0	1	1	0
Olsen	3	9	4	4	0	4	0	Almonte	1	1	2	2	3	0	0
Neal	2	3	4	4	1	1	0	Shiell	1	1	1	1	0	0	1
Totals	8	28	25	25	7	7	3	Totals	9	10	8	4	6	6	1

	1	2	3	4	5	6	7	8	9	R	H	E
FLA N	1	0	0	0	4	0	0	1	2	8	10	0
BOS A	14	2	1	2	1	0	1	4	x	25	28	1

pitches and faced Nomar. For a moment, it seemed as if perhaps order had been restored, when Nomar popped to the catcher. But Manny singled and Ortiz walked, and the bases were loaded again. A double play would end the inning.

Millar made an out—just one, the second out—but it was a productive one, as he lofted a fly to center that scored Walker. Levrault then walked Nixon to reload the bases. A ground ball would end it, with a force at any base. But the Sox simply were not done hitting. Mueller doubled, scoring two. Then Varitek walked, and the bases were, yet again, loaded; the lineup had now turned over a second time. Damon had already faced two pitchers in this long first inning, and he'd gone 2-for-2, a double and a triple. For variety's sake, he singled off Levrault, bringing home Nixon, and had Bill Mueller not then been cut down at the plate trying to score as well, the inning might still be going on to this day, with Damon able to bat a fourth time and a shot at the cycle. Third-base coach Mike Cubbage had waved Mueller home from second when Mueller didn't have a chance. One suspects Cubbage might have had mercy in mind. Bottom of the first: Boston 14, Marlins 1. There were 10 consecutive at-bats with a hit, and by game's end the Sox had tied their own club mark of 28 hits in a single game.

Damon alone went 3-for-3 and was three-fourths of the way to the cycle, in just the first inning. As the game wore on, Damon had four more chances to hit the homer that would have given him the cycle. One long foul ball to right had the distance, but he got around on the ball too quickly and it landed well foul. Damon did add a couple of singles, a 5-for-7 evening out.

Pity those fans with tickets who showed up fashionably late after the first inning. "What'd I miss?" they would ask before glancing at the scoreboard. Of course, such fans would have had to arrive more than a little late. The bottom of the first began at 7:16 and went to 8:06, a 50-minute half inning. Marlins pitchers threw 91 pitches. The first out came on the 59th pitch of the frame. "You getting the feeling it might not be the Marlins' night tonight?" Red Sox telecaster Jerry Remy asked partner Sean McDonough after a Manny Ramirez single dropped neatly over the Florida first baseman's head.

Almost every hit was a solid smash—there were no cheap hits and no errors. And the Marlins played error-free ball for the full game, striking out seven Sox. In the end, even though the Marlins did score eight runs, the Sox tallied a 25–8 win. In honor of the amazing inning, the metal plate showing "14" that hung in the first-inning slot in the manual scoreboard at the base of the Green Monster was signed by all the Red Sox players in the game and sent to the National Baseball Hall of Fame and Museum in Cooperstown.

◀Extra Innings

* Damon was not the first Red Sox with three hits in an inning. On June 18, 1953, Gene Stephens performed the feat in a 17-run inning the Sox pasted on the Tigers. Pitcher Ellis Kinder also had two hits in that inning, and the Sox won 23–3. Damon and Stephens are the only two players in modern baseball to have accomplished the feat. Three pre-1900 players did as well, all in the same inning and for the same team, the 1883 Cubs: Fred Pfeffer, Ned Williamson, and Tommy Burns. Damon did become the first player ever to get three different types of hits in one inning.

* In the first inning, when neither Carl Pavano nor Miguel Tejera recorded an out before being pulled, it was the first time since 1973 that the first two pitchers for a team failed to record an out. The previous time the hapless team was the Kansas City Royals, and they were managed by none other than Jack McKeon.

* After the game a cantankerous Jack McKeon griped that Sox manager Grady Little had let the Sox run up the score by tagging up and scoring on short flies, a violation of the unwritten rule of baseball that with a huge lead

the team ahead should not pile on runs. Little apologized to McKeon before the next game, prompting a shocked response from John Henry. "Grady apologized?" he asked of reporters who were trying to get the former Marlins owner's take on the situation. "I disagree with that. That's old school. What about the fan who pays $50 and gives up his Friday night to come out here? Don't we owe it to our fans to play hard all the time?"

The very next night, the Sox were tentative on the base paths. They took a 9–2 lead into the seventh inning, and the Marlins did not hold Johnny Damon on first. Damon could have easily taken second base on defensive indifference. Damon ended up stranded, and the Fish mounted a comeback, scoring four in the eighth and four in the ninth to win the game 10–9.

◦ Inning summary:

Damon doubled.

Walker singled. Damon scored.

Garciaparra doubled.

Ramirez homered. Walker and Garciaparra scored, too.

Ortiz doubled.

Millar singled. Ortiz scored.

Tejera came in to relieve Pavano. Nixon singled.

Mueller walked.

Varitek singled. Millar and Nixon scored.

Damon tripled. Mueller and Varitek scored.

Walker singled. Damon scored.

Levrault came in to relieve Tejera. Garciaparra popped up—one out.

Ramirez singled.

Ortiz walked.

Millar hit a sacrifice fly—two outs. Walker scored.

Nixon walked.

Mueller doubled. Ramirez and Ortiz scored.

Varitek walked.

Damon singled. Nixon scored. Mueller was thrown out trying to score—three outs.

14 runs on 13 hits, with two men left on base.

47

October 6, 2003: Boston at Oakland

A-Ball

In which the Red Sox take another step toward the Big Dance

Four years is a long time when your team is the Red Sox and you have such a perennial wealth of talent on the roster yet you miss the postseason three years in a row. Since losing four out of five to the Yankees in the 1999 American League Championship Series, the Red Sox hadn't booked another playoff berth until October 1, 2003. Thanks to the wild card, they now had another shot.

In successive days at Oakland's Network Associates Coliseum, though, the Red Sox lost the first two games of the 2003 American League Division Series.

The first game was hard fought, Oakland tying the game 4–4 with a run in the bottom of the ninth, and then winning it in the 12th on Ramon Hernandez's two-out, bases-loaded squeeze bunt toward third base. Game two was resolved early, as the A's jumped on Tim Wakefield for five runs in the bottom of the second; Barry Zito held the Sox to one run, and Oakland won, 5–1. The A's were feeling good. For three years in a row they'd been defeated in the division series. They weren't about to allow it to happen a fourth time.

The series moved to Boston, but the Red Sox would have to win three in a row to come out of the best-of-five series alive. Game three was one that the A's almost seemed to give away, if one could say that about a game tied 1–1 after 10 innings of play. An error and an obstruction, both by Eric Chavez in the Red Sox second inning, resulted in their lone run. In the Athletics' sixth, they had a shot at a big inning, but two plays cost them the chance to score. First, Eric Byrnes collided with Jason Varitek in a close play at the plate; after impact, the ball rolled a considerable distance away. Tek had the presence of mind to retrieve the ball, run back, and tag Byrnes, who was hopping around thinking of his ankle rather than being doubly sure he'd touched home plate. Home plate umpire Paul Emmel gave the out sign; Varitek had blocked the plate, and the oblivious Byrnes was tagged out. After an intentional walk to Chavez, Hernandez hit the ball to Nomar Garciaparra, but Nomar muffed it badly, allowing a run to score.

Miguel Tejada looked to be set to score, too, but he simply stopped running a third of the way between third base and home. Had he just run home, and argued about obstruction later, he would have scored. The ruling was that, yes, he'd been obstructed, but it was on his way to third, not after he'd rounded the bag. He was awarded "next base" (third), but then any further progress was at his peril. Varitek's tag of Tejada after he had stopped was ruled a valid out. Trot Nixon's two-run walk-off homer in the bottom of the 11th won it for the Red Sox, 3–1, and the tide had turned.

Game four was a close one, a 5–4 Red Sox win. Oakland held a 4–2 lead after 5½, but Todd Walker hit a solo homer in the bottom of the sixth, and in the bottom of the eighth David Ortiz drove in Nomar and Manny Ramirez with a two-run double to right field to put Boston out in front to stay. Scott Williamson got the win in relief.

Both teams traveled transcontinentally to play the deciding game the very next night. "The ball club [is] looking forward to this flight back out to the West Coast," said manager Grady Little. "Right now we're still playing, and we have a chance." It was a Barry Zito vs. Pedro Martinez matchup, two Cy Young Award winners dueling for the right to advance their team to the league championship series, two pitchers who could not be more different. Zito, the finesse lefty with his surfer looks and nose-to-toes curveball, and Pedro, the diminutive Dominican with the blazing fastball and devastating changeup. Neither team expected to score runs in bunches, and the first three innings passed scoreless.

Then, in the bottom of the fourth, with two out and a man on, Jose Guillen's double drove home Scott Hatteberg. Guillen was thrown out trying to stretch it to a triple and the inning was over, but Oakland had a 1–0 lead.

The score stood 1–0 through five; with Zito pitching for Oakland, there was no guarantee the Sox would ever score. Although Zito's 2003 won-loss record was nowhere as good as Pedro's, Zito's ERA for the year was an excellent 3.30, good enough to rank him seventh in the American League. Boston's bats woke up in the sixth, though. Jason Varitek homered to lead off the inning and tie the score. Before Zito could regain his composure, Johnny Damon walked. Garciaparra popped up to the first baseman, but Zito hit Todd Walker and then served up a gopher ball to Manny Ramirez. "All the time at bat I was looking in and he gave me the fastball and I drove it to left field," Manny later told reporters. "I told Zito he was going to make a mistake and I was going to be waiting." By the time Zito struck out David Ortiz and got Kevin Millar to pop to second, it was 4–1 Red Sox.

In the bottom of the sixth, Oakland got one back as Martinez gave up doubles to Erubiel Durazo and Tejada. In Oakland's seventh, Pedro got the first two men out and then Jermaine Dye hit a looping fly ball to short center field. Johnny Damon ran in to make the catch, but second baseman Damian Jackson—who'd replaced Todd Walker at second—ran back to get it, and the two collided head-to-head. Hard. Damon was knocked unconscious, and remained on the ground for several minutes. An outfield gate was opened and an ambulance drove right across the field. Damon had played center field for Oakland in 2001, and he still had many fans in the Bay Area. No one knew if Damon was dead or alive; it had been that hard a collision, and he'd been motionless for so long. The EMTs lifted the stretcher bearing Damon's prone body, and horrified fans worldwide were relieved to see the Sox center fielder give a sign with his right hand that he was still alive and now conscious again.

Dye had reached first base (the play was ruled a single, not an error), but was thrown out trying to reach second. Despite the shock of seeing two teammates go down so hard, baseball instincts prevailed and Garciaparra had retrieved the ball, while Bill Mueller ran over from third base to cover second. Nomar threw to Mueller, and Dye was dead at second. Inning over. The score remained 4–2 Red Sox, but a bit of a pall hung over the game. Ten minutes after impact, play resumed.

The Red Sox were set down 1-2-3 in the top of the eighth, but Chris Singleton doubled off Pedro to lead off the eighth, and pinch hitter Billy McMillon singled him home. Manager Grady Little called on Alan Embree to take over for Martinez. Embree got two outs, then yielded to Mike Timlin, who secured the third out.

OCTOBER 6, 2003: BOSTON AT OAKLAND

Boston Red Sox	AB	R	H	RBI	BB	SO	PO	A	Oakland Athletics	AB	R	H	RBI	BB	SO	PO	A
Damon cf	2	1	1	0	1	0	1	0	Ellis 2b	3	0	0	0	0	1	2	3
Brown ph,cf	1	0	0	0	0	0	0	0	McMillon ph	1	0	1	1	0	0	0	0
Garciaparra ss	4	0	0	0	0	0	1	9	Menechino pr,2b	0	0	0	0	0	0	0	0
Walker 2b	2	1	0	0	0	1	1	0	Long ph	1	0	0	0	0	1	0	0
Jackson 2b	1	0	0	0	0	0	2	0	Durazo dh	4	1	1	0	0	1	0	0
Ramirez lf	4	1	1	3	0	3	1	0	Chavez 3b	4	0	0	0	0	1	0	0
Ortiz dh	4	0	1	0	0	1	0	0	Tejada ss	4	0	1	1	0	2	0	2
Kapler pr,dh	0	0	0	0	0	0	0	0	Hatteberg 1b	2	1	0	0	2	0	10	0
Millar 1b	4	0	2	0	0	0	10	0	Byrnes pr	0	0	0	0	0	0	0	0
Mueller 3b	3	0	0	0	0	1	0	3	Guillen lf	3	0	2	1	1	0	4	0
Nixon rf	4	0	0	0	0	2	0	1	Hernandez c	2	0	0	0	0	0	6	2
Varitek c	3	1	1	1	0	1	8	0	Dye rf	3	0	1	0	0	0	2	0
Martinez p	0	0	0	0	0	0	0	1	Melhuse ph	1	0	0	0	0	1	0	0
Totals	32	4	6	4	2	8	27	14	Singleton cf	3	1	1	0	1	1	3	1
									Totals	31	3	7	3	4	8	27	8

Boston Red Sox	IP	H	R	ER	BB	SO	HR	Oakland Athletics	IP	H	R	ER	BB	SO	HR
Martinez (W)	7	7	3	3	1	6	0	Zito (L)	6	4	4	4	2	4	2
Embree	0.2	0	0	0	0	0	0	Lilly	2	0	0	0	0	2	0
Timlin	0.1	0	0	0	0	0	0	Bradford	0.1	2	0	0	0	1	0
Williamson	0	0	0	0	2	0	0	Rincon	0.2	0	0	0	0	1	0
Lowe (S)	1	0	0	0	1	2	0	Totals	9	6	4	4	2	8	2
Totals	9	7	3	3	4	8	0								

	1	2	3	4	5	6	7	8	9		R	H	E
BOS A	0	0	0	0	0	4	0	0	0		4	6	0
OAK A	0	0	0	1	0	1	0	1	0		3	7	0

The Sox singled twice in the top of the ninth but didn't score, and it was still 4–3 in their favor with Oakland down to its last at-bats. Scott Williamson was asked to save the game and give the Red Sox the chance to advance to the league championship series against the New York Yankees, who'd won the other division series the day before.

Williamson walked Scott Hatteberg and then walked Guillen. Little beckoned for Derek Lowe to save the game. Lowe had lost game one, in relief. He'd been the game three starter, going seven innings, allowing only one unearned run, but since the game had run 11 innings, he didn't get credit for the win. Now he was called on for the third time in the short series. Lowe had experience in both roles. He'd begun as a starter, but in 1999 the Red Sox had converted him to a reliever. He did a good job in '99 and then led the league with 42 saves in the year 2000. In 2001 he relieved as well, but his ERA jumped a full run, and he lost twice as many games as he won. Back to the starter role in 2002, he performed exceptionally (21–8, 2.58 ERA). He'd won 17 games in 2003, but his ERA had jumped to 4.47, leading Sox fans to wonder which Derek Lowe they would get on this night, the good one or the bad one.

The sinker was working; it was the good Lowe.

He first faced Oakland catcher Ramon Hernandez, who put down a perfect sacrifice bunt, moving both base runners up. The tying run was on second now, with just the one out. Lowe did not let it bother him. He and the Boston bench had picked up the A's strategy against him. "They kind of gave their hand away what they were doing at the plate by continually looking away, away, away," Lowe said in a press conference after the game. "If you [do that] you can't look for a pitch on both sides of the plate, so it opens up the inner half." Lowe ran the sinker in to pinch hitter Adam Melhuse, and it worked to perfection: Melhuse struck out. Then Terrence Long batted for Frank Menechino and Lowe struck him out, too, called out looking at the last pitch, another sinker running in. "It comes down to execution, can you make the pitch or not," Lowe said. "I was able to make two of them."

Sox fans, who had stayed up late on the East Coast to see the outcome of the game, erupted with joy. Now the jubilant fans were looking for a shot at the Yankees in the ALCS. This year looked as if it could be the year.

Extra Innings

- This was the fourth consecutive year that the A's had made the playoffs but failed to make it out of the first round. This was not even the first time they had won the first two games only to lose three in a row. In 2001, the A's took the first two from the Yankees but lost the next three.

- To rest up for his start, Pedro Martinez took over a row of three seats on the team's charter flight to Oakland, and created a tent for himself out of blankets. He was not disturbed.

48

October 16, 2003: Boston at New York

The Hardest Battle

In which two ancient foes go to the very brink

The 2003 postseason for the Red Sox was already a dramatic one after their five-game win over Oakland in the division series, but the drama level could only go up in the next round, when they would meet the Yankees head-to-head.

The Sox won the first game in Yankee Stadium behind the superb knuckleball of Tim Wakefield. New York starter Mike Mussina surrendered three home runs, and the Sox sewed up a neat 5–2 victory with another great outing by their bullpen, who had been terrific against Oakland as well. The next two games did not go so well, though, as Andy Pettitte held the Sox to two runs in game two. As the Yankees cruised to a 6–2 victory, the Bronx crowd chanted "We want Pedro!" In game three, Pedro faced off against Roger Clemens, a rematch of their 1999 postseason face-off. But this time Clemens stayed relatively cool as tempers flared on both benches, eventually erupting in a brawl that saw Don Zimmer, then a Yankee coach, charge Pedro, who gripped his head and deftly pushed him to the ground. Brawling aside, the game had other notable on-field moments, including the return of Johnny Damon from the concussion suffered in Oakland—he had three hits and scored a run—and Derek Jeter's home run off Pedro, the first homer to a right-handed batter Pedro surrendered all year. In the end, the Yankees edged out a 4–3 win. The next day the Sox returned the favor, eking out a 3–2 win, again behind the baffling pitching of Tim Wakefield. "You're better off trying to hit Wakefield when you're in a drunken stupor," Yankees slugger Jason Giambi said. But the Yankees won game five 4–2 as they got three runs off Derek Lowe in the second inning, while the Sox could get only two runs off Yankees starter David Wells, one on a Manny Ramirez solo shot. Overall the Sox had been averaging three runs a game, prompting their general manager, Theo Epstein, to say, "We're just not hitting well as a team right now."

So the series shifted back to the Stadium for game six. Once more, the Sox faced elimination, but their bats finally came to life. Journeyman John Burkett was the starter for the Red Sox, and his teammates treated him to a 4–1 lead after three innings. Two outs into the fourth, he surrendered three runs. Save for a solo homer by Jorge Posada, the Red Sox bullpen then shut down the Yankees through 5⅓ innings, accentuating the mastery the bullpen had shown throughout the postseason. The Sox hitters continued to pile on the runs, though, the last two on Trot Nixon's two-run homer in the top of the ninth. The 9–6 win for the Red Sox evened the series at three games apiece.

The drama couldn't get any higher. Baseball's two biggest rivals facing each other in a final game seven for the first time ever, and each with its ace on the mound in Yankee Stadium: ex-Red Sox Roger Clemens facing Pedro Martinez. Both pitchers had brought their A-game, Pedro changing speeds and Clemens rearing back with high heat. But after the first inning, Pedro seemed to rev it up, while the Rocket began to flame out.

Red Sox hearts soared when Clemens yielded three runs in the top of the sec-ond. For whatever reason, Trot Nixon always had good swings against Clemens, including a number of memorable home runs over the years. After Kevin Mil-lar singled, Nixon took Clemens deep, a two-run shot. Then, with two out, Jason Varitek hit a line-drive double to right. Damon grounded to third, but an error by Enrique Wilson (playing third that day, because of his uncanny ability to hit Pedro) allowed Varitek to come home with the unearned run. Clemens looked even worse in the fourth, when Millar homered to lead off the inning. After Clemens walked Nixon, and Bill Mueller singled, manager Joe Torre looked to his pen and summoned starter Mike Mussina to stem the tide. He did, getting a strikeout and a double play just when the Yankees needed it—but the Sox led 4–0, and it looked as though Destiny was wearing a "Cowboy Up" T-shirt that evening. The ALCS was Boston's to lose, they had Martinez on the mound, and he'd given up only one hit through the first three frames.

Pedro pitched no-hit ball in the fourth and surrendered a solo home run to the pumped-up Jason Giambi in the fifth, but set down New York 1-2-3 in the sixth. Only nine outs stood between Boston and its first World Series appear-ance since 1986. They had a 4–1 lead.

Felix Heredia took over from Mussina in the seventh and got the first two batters; Jeff Nelson struck out Garciaparra for the third out. Pedro went out for the seventh, and after getting the first two outs easily enough, gave up a second home run to Giambi. Pedro seemed a little pooped, even though the pitches he threw to Giambi had registered at 95 miles per hour on the radar gun. Enrique Wilson singled, and then Karim Garcia singled, and Red Sox fans tensed, but Pedro buckled down and struck out the free-swinging Alfonso Soriano. Pedro seemed fortunate to have escaped the seventh without further damage. As he walked his walk from the mound to the dugout, Pedro pointed to the heavens

OCTOBER 16, 2003: BOSTON AT NEW YORK

Boston Red Sox	AB	R	H	RBI	PO	A		New York Yankees	AB	R	H	RBI	PO	A
Damon cf	5	0	0	0	7	0		Soriano 2b	5	0	0	0	1	4
Walker 2b	5	0	1	0	0	3		Johnson 1b	4	0	0	0	14	0
Garciaparra ss	5	0	1	0	3	0		Jeter ss	5	1	1	0	3	4
Ramirez lf	5	0	1	0	3	0		Williams cf	5	1	2	1	1	0
Ortiz dh	5	1	2	1	0	0		Matsui lf	5	1	2	0	1	0
Kapler pr,dh	0	0	0	0	0	0		Posada c	5	0	1	2	9	0
Millar 1b	5	2	2	1	6	1		Giambi dh	5	2	2	2	0	0
Nixon rf	4	1	1	2	1	0		Wilson 3b	3	0	1	0	1	2
Mueller 3b	5	0	1	0	0	1		Sierra ph	0	0	0	0	0	0
Varitek c	4	1	2	0	8	0		Boone pr,3b	1	1	1	1	0	1
Jackson pr	0	0	0	0	0	0		Garcia rf	3	0	1	0	3	0
Mirabelli c	1	0	0	0	1	0		**Totals**	**41**	**6**	**11**	**6**	**33**	**11**
Totals	**44**	**5**	**11**	**4**	**29**	**5**								

Boston Red Sox	IP	H	R	ER	BB	SO	HR		New York Yankees	IP	H	R	ER	BB	SO	HR
Martinez	7.1	10	5	5	1	8	2		Clemens	3	6	4	3	1	1	2
Embree	0.1	0	0	0	0	0	0		Mussina	3	2	0	0	0	3	0
Timlin	1.1	0	0	0	2	1	0		Heredia	0.2	0	0	0	0	1	0
Wakefield (L)	1+	1	1	1	0	0	1		Nelson	0.2	0	0	0	0	1	0
Totals	**10**	**11**	**6**	**6**	**3**	**9**	**3**		Wells	0.2	1	1	1	0	0	1
									Rivera (W)	3	2	0	0	0	3	0
									Totals	**11**	**11**	**5**	**4**	**1**	**9**	**3**

	1	2	3	4	5	6	7	8	9	10	11		R	H	E
BOS A	0	3	0	1	0	0	0	1	0	0	0		5	11	0
NY A	0	0	0	0	1	0	1	3	0	0	1		6	11	1

in his characteristic way, signaling the end of his outing. After he'd come down the dugout steps, he was embraced by David Ortiz and congratulated by the other players. Pedro was done, and everyone knew it. He'd thrown seven innings and surrendered just the two solo home runs to Giambi. He'd done his job, and the Boston bullpen—which had been spectacular for weeks, and was sufficiently rested—had just six more outs to get.

When Ortiz homered off David Wells in the top of the eighth, it was a big insurance run, boosting the lead back to three runs: Boston 5, New York 2.

But then Sox fans worldwide couldn't believe what they saw: rather than Scott Williamson or Mike Timlin taking the trek in from the bullpen to mow down the Yankees in the bottom of the eighth, out from the dugout popped Pedro. He'd escaped the seventh without serious damage, but barely. Psychologically speaking, he'd already left the game, and yet there he was. Grady Little wasn't going to trust a relief staff that was tried and tested; instead, he handed the ball back to his ace. Pedro would not decline; he's too proud a man for that. "Pedro wanted to stay in there," Little told reporters later. "He wanted to get the job done just as he has many times for us all season long, and he's the man we all wanted on the mound." Just who "we all" is remains in question. What Jason Varitek thought has never been revealed, and perhaps never will be. There is no doubt that Pedro Martinez is one of the premier pitchers of all time, but experienced Sox fans (as well as the sabermetricians in the Sox front office) knew his effectiveness tailed off rapidly after 100 pitches and almost dropped off the shelf after another 10. (In this game, his pitch count was exactly 100 through seven innings.) Every bit of statistical evidence at their disposal said this was an unwise move. Grady Little believed in his starter, though, and felt Martinez had more fuel in reserve. "He had enough left in his tank," Little would say after the game.

Martinez got Nick Johnson on a pop-up to short. Five outs to go. He got two strikes on Derek Jeter, but then Jeter doubled. Pedro started with two strikes on Bernie Williams, too, but Bernie singled, scoring Jeter. Pedro's pitch count was 115. Grady stayed put. For the third batter in a row, Pedro got two strikes on Hideki Matsui, but then Matsui hit one down the line for a ground-rule double, Williams holding at third. There was no more margin for error, with a two-run lead and the go-ahead run at the plate. Grady emerged at last from the dugout; next up was the switch-hitting Posada. The bullpen was more than capable; Timlin had thrown 9⅔ innings of one-hit ball in the playoffs. Little stuck with Pedro, again to the incredulity of Red Sox Nation. He lasted another five pitches, going to a 2–2 count, but then Posada doubled, scoring both base runners and tying the game. Grady came out and gave Pedro the hook. This time there was no point at the sky, no hugs in the dugout. The Yankees had tied the game and had a runner on second base with just one out.

Alan Embree was summoned. He got his man, Giambi, on a fly to center. Timlin came in and intentionally walked pinch hitter Ruben Sierra, then unintentionally walked Garcia, but closed out the inning, retiring Soriano on an infield force play. Now it was bullpen versus bullpen, the Sox relievers who had pitched so well in October versus the key to the Yankees' dynastic success: Mariano Rivera.

With Rivera on the mound, Boston didn't score in the top of the ninth. Every time the Yankees came to bat, all it would take was one run and the season was over for the Red Sox. Timlin set them down 1-2-3 in the ninth. Ortiz doubled in the 10th, but that was all. Tim Wakefield replaced Timlin, and the Yanks went down 1-2-3 in the tenth. This was everything a baseball fan could want—extra innings in a game seven between the two biggest rivals in baseball. The winner would take the pennant and earn itself a berth in the 2003 World Series.

Rivera handled the Red Sox easily in the top of the 11th—the first time since becoming the Yankees' closer that he pitched three complete innings—and the game went on. The Yankee bullpen was spent, whereas Wakefield could pitch several more innings if called upon. First up in the bottom of the 11th was Aaron Boone, who'd come into the game after Wilson had been pinch-hit for in the bottom of the eighth and taken Wilson's place at third. If Wakefield got by the .254-hitting Boone, he'd be facing Garcia and then Soriano. The Red Sox would have the top of their order up in the 12th—Johnny Damon, Todd Walker, and Nomar Garciaparra, with Manny Ramirez right behind Nomar.

But there would be only one more batter in the game.

Recent history dubbed it the "Aaron Boone game," and it outranks the "Bucky Dent game" as one of the most consequential, momentous, and painful games in Red Sox history, won by one of the more improbable opponents. Boone swung at the first pitch he saw, and he hit it into the seats down the left-field line, gone. The Yankees had won on a walk-off and the season was over for the Red Sox.

There would be no Buckneresque goat horns for Tim Wakefield, who surely would have been the series MVP had game seven turned out differently. Instead, Red Sox Nation considered it the game Grady Little lost rather than the one Aaron Boone won. Not much time passed before Grady Little was out of a job. And a year passed before the Red Sox would have their shot at redemption.

Extra Innings

- There was no way Grady Little was going to survive as manager of the Boston Red Sox after the way things turned out. He'd been a good manager, with one of the winningest records in team history, but the decision to favor Pedro over a rested, effective bullpen doomed any chance at continuing. As a promotional giveaway, the Brockton Rox independent league baseball team created a Grady Little "bobbing arm" doll, which showed Grady giving the sign to bring in a left-hander. But people were so sore about Grady that after fielding many incensed complaints, the team canceled the giveaway.

49

October 17 and 18, 2004: New York at Boston

Sequel

In which the stakes are higher and the road harder than ever before

After 2003's devastating defeat at the hands of the Evil Empire, could the 2004 Red Sox pick themselves up and start all over again? Could they slog through 162 games just to see if they could get back in the playoffs, and maybe earn another shot at the Yankees, the team they should have beaten the year before? The 2004 season would be the last chance for some of the Sox. Several large contracts were up for renewal: Pedro Martinez, Nomar Garciaparra, Derek Lowe, and Jason Varitek were all superstars, and there was no way the Red Sox could re-sign them all. They did lock up David Ortiz early in the year, and they got off to a decent start. Before long, though, they settled into a prolonged doldrums, playing .500 ball for a couple of months. For a team with that much talent, it was discouraging to see them lose one game for every win. Fans kept hoping they'd make a run for it, maybe put together a long winning streak. New manager Terry Francona preached patience, saying it would all come together.

The team finally gelled in July, in a game at Fenway Park against the hated Yankees, when catcher Jason Varitek and new Yankees' superstar Alex Rodriguez brawled after A-Rod was plunked by Bronson Arroyo. Varitek's intensity seemed to light a fire under the Sox, who beat the Yankees not only that day, on a Bill Mueller walk-off home run off Mariano Rivera, but the next day as well, starting the tear that would land them in contention.

Ultimately, the 2004 team drove in more runs than any team in baseball history. And their pitching was pretty good, too, behind new ace Curt Schilling and Pedro Martinez. The bullpen was, as at the end of 2003, solid, and despite spinning their wheels in the first half of the season, by September it was clear that no team in the West would overtake the Sox for the wild card—that is, if the Sox didn't just win the East outright. They didn't—the Yankees still outpaced them—but the wild card assured them of their second playoff spot in two years. The Red Sox would meet the 2002 world champion Anaheim Angels in the division series. The first two games at Anaheim weren't even close. The Red Sox scored one run off Jarrod Washburn in the top of the first, and then piled on with seven more (on four hits) in the top of the fourth. Curt Schilling gave up three runs (two earned) in 6⅔ innings, but those seven runs sank the Angels: 9–3 Boston. Game two was 8–3 Red Sox. The Angels held a two-run lead for half an inning, but Boston took a lead into the ninth—and then put up four runs to seal Anaheim's fate.

The two teams flew to Boston for game three. The Red Sox took an early lead, but Anaheim evened it up, with five runs in the top of the seventh, as Bronson Arroyo lost his effectiveness, walking the first two batters, and neither Mike Myers nor Mike Timlin could put the brakes on. Vladimir Guerrero's grand slam made Boston's rooters catch their breath as the two teams were tied, 6–6. After Johnny Damon singled to start off the bottom of the 10th, the Angels retired the next two batters, and brought in Washburn to pitch to

David Ortiz. One pitch was all it took. Two-run homer, and the Red Sox had swept the ALDS. Would they face the Twins in the next round, or would they get a crack at the Yankees once again? Fate decreed the rematch.

Next up: the New York Yankees.

Unfortunately, the horse the Sox had ridden all year, Curt Schilling, turned up lame in the opener. Mike Mussina had a perfect game through 6⅓ innings, while Schilling was unable to throw well. He surrendered six runs in the first three innings and limped off the field. He was in evident pain. The Yankees rang up an 8–0 lead before Boston began to score. As soon as Mark Bellhorn doubled to break up Mussina's masterpiece, the Moose faded fast. He couldn't even close the inning, and coughed up four runs. The Sox closed the score to 8–5, but Schilling's injury cast a pall over Sox aspirations. A two-run double by Ortiz made a one-run game of it, but it was short-lived when Manny Ramirez let Bernie Williams's double drift over his head and New York scored their ninth and 10th runs. Final: New York 10, Boston 7.

With Martinez pitching game two, Boston hoped to break even, but even though Pedro was strong, he still gave up three runs in the first six innings. That might not have been so bad but for the pitching of Jon Lieber, who surrendered only three hits. He had a one-hitter through six. Joe Torre had always maintained that starting pitching was the key to postseason success, and Yankee pitching was dominating. In back-to-back starts, Mussina and Lieber had allowed one hit between them in their first 12 innings. Both pens performed well. Final: New York 3, Boston 1.

Game three was, for Red Sox fans, about as bad as it could get. Already down 0–2 in the series, behind two brilliant starts by New York pitchers, they hoped that relocating to Fenway would turn things around. Instead, it got worse—a lot worse. The team had already lost Schilling for the rest of the year, it seemed, with an ankle injury that was untreatable by normal means. Pedro couldn't stop them. Twenty-seven-year-old Bronson Arroyo was cast in the role of stopper, and he couldn't stop the Yankees, either. In two-plus innings he was charged with six earned runs. Curtis Leskanic gave up three, and Tim Wakefield, brought in out of desperation, gave up five more. The hits just kept on coming, and at the halfway point it was 13–6 Yankees. Then they scored four more times. With the score 17–6 Yankees, there were thousands of empty seats. This was playoff baseball, Boston against New York, but the Red Sox were being routed. They'd lost two games, and were losing this one by a monstrous margin. Final: New York 19, Boston 8.

"Everything went wrong leading up to [game four]," recalled Jason Varitek. "If everything had gone right, and we were still down 3–0, we could have scratched our heads. But things didn't go right. We didn't pitch the ball well, and with that lineup that we were facing, you had to pitch the ball well."

All hopes for a reversal of fortune and a chance to overcome the 2003 ALCS loss seemed to have washed down the drain. The game four matchup was Derek Lowe against Orlando Hernandez, and though "El Duque" could be unpredictable, Lowe had one of the worst ERAs of any starter in the league. The Yankees got two quick runs. There was a bit of hope as the Sox scored three times in the bottom of the fifth, but as soon as the Yankees batted, they put two more runs on the board to take the lead back, 4–3. So the score remained until the bottom of the ninth.

The Red Sox were down to their last three outs, losing by a run, and the Yankees naturally had Mariano Rivera on the mound—no less than the most reliable closer in the history of baseball. But Kevin Millar showed patience and worked a walk to lead off the inning. Manager Terry Francona immediately put in midseason pickup Dave Roberts as a pinch runner, and everyone knew what his instructions were: steal second and get in scoring position with no one out. Easier said than done, and Rivera kept a wary eye. Posada was poised, too, to make the throw from behind home plate—but Roberts pulled it off, just barely beating the throw. The steal was the key move on offense in the series.

OCTOBER 17, 2004: NEW YORK AT BOSTON

New York Yankees	AB	R	H	RBI	BB	SO	PO	A	Boston Red Sox	AB	R	H	RBI	BB	SO	PO	A
Jeter ss	4	1	1	0	1	0	2	3	Damon cf	5	1	0	0	1	0	4	0
Rodriguez 3b	5	1	1	2	1	1	0	1	Cabrera ss	6	1	1	0	2	3	2
Sheffield rf	5	0	0	0	1	1	2	0	Ramirez lf	3	1	2	0	3	1	3	0
Matsui lf	5	1	2	0	1	1	4	0	Ortiz dh	5	1	2	4	1	1	0	0
Williams cf	6	0	1	1	0	1	2	0	Varitek c	5	0	0	0	0	3	9	1
Posada c	4	1	2	0	2	0	10	0	Nixon rf	5	0	0	0	0	0	2	0
Sierra dh	6	0	2	0	0	1	0	0	Millar 1b	2	0	1	0	2	0	9	1
Clark 1b	6	0	2	1	0	1	7	2	Roberts pr	0	1	0	0	0	0	0	0
Cairo 2b	4	0	1	0	1	1	5	2	Reese 2b	1	0	0	0	0	1	0	0
Sturtze p	0	0	0	0	0	0	0	0	Mueller 3b	5	1	2	1	0	1	1	4
Rivera p	0	0	0	0	0	0	1	1	Bellhorn 2b	2	0	0	0	1	2	2	4
Totals	45	4	12	4	7	7	33	10	Mientkiewicz ph,1b	1	0	0	0	0	0	2	0
									Lowe p	0	0	0	0	0	0	1	2
									Embree p	0	0	0	0	0	0	0	1
									Leskanic p	0	0	0	0	0	0	0	1
									Totals	40	6	8	6	8	10	36	16

New York Yankees	IP	H	R	ER	BB	SO	HR	Boston Red Sox	IP	H	R	ER	BB	SO	HR
Hernandez	5	3	3	3	5	6	0	Lowe	5.1	6	3	3	0	3	1
Sturtze	2	1	0	0	0	1	0	Timlin	1	3	1	1	3	0	0
Rivera	2	2	1	1	2	2	0	Foulke	2.2	0	0	0	2	3	0
Gordon	2	0	0	1	1	0	0	Embree	1.2	2	0	0	1	0	0
Quantrill (L)	0	2	2	2	0	0	1	Myers	0	0	0	0	1	0	0
Totals	11	8	6	6	8	10	1	Leskanic (W)	1.1	1	0	0	0	1	0
								Totals	12	12	4	4	7	7	1

	1	2	3	4	5	6	7	8	9	10	11	12	R	H	E
NY A	0	0	2	0	0	2	0	0	0	0	0	0	4	12	1
BOS A	0	0	0	0	3	0	0	0	1	0	0	2	6	8	0

OCTOBER 18, 2004: NEW YORK AT BOSTON

New York Yankees	AB	R	H	RBI	BB	SO	PO	A	Boston Red Sox	AB	R	H	RBI	BB	SO	PO	A
Jeter ss	7	0	1	3	0	2	4	4	Damon cf	6	1	1	0	1	2	3	0
Rodriguez 3b	4	0	0	0	2	2	1	2	Cabrera ss	6	1	2	0	1	1	3	1
Sheffield rf	4	0	0	0	3	3	0	0	Ramirez lf	6	0	2	0	1	0	4	0
Matsui lf	7	0	1	0	0	1	2	0	Ortiz dh	6	2	3	3	1	3	0	0
Williams cf	7	1	2	1	0	1	6	0	Millar 1b	2	0	0	0	2	0	4	1
Posada c	6	1	2	0	1	1	13	3	Roberts pr	0	1	0	0	0	0	0	0
Sierra dh	5	1	3	0	2	2	0	0	Mientkiewicz 1b	2	0	1	0	0	1	4	0
Clark 1b	7	0	1	0	0	4	10	1	Nixon rf	4	0	1	0	0	1	4	0
Cairo 2b	6	1	2	0	0	0	4	5	Kapler pr,rf	2	0	0	0	0	0	2	0
Loaiza p	0	0	0	0	0	0	1	0	Varitek c	4	0	0	2	1	1	15	0
Totals	53	4	12	4	8	16	41	15	Mueller 3b	6	0	1	0	0	1	0	1
									Bellhorn 2b	6	0	2	0	0	2	2	4
									Martinez p	0	0	0	0	0	0	1	0
									Timlin p	0	0	0	0	0	0	0	1
									Totals	50	5	13	5	7	12	42	8

New York Yankees	IP	H	R	ER	BB	SO	HR	Boston Red Sox	IP	H	R	ER	BB	SO	HR
Mussina	6	6	2	2	2	7	0	Martinez	6	7	4	4	5	6	1
Sturtze	0.1	0	0	0	1	0	0	Timlin	1.2	2	0	0	1	1	0
Gordon	0.2	2	2	2	1	0	1	Foulke	1.1	1	0	0	1	0	0
Rivera	2	1	0	0	0	1	0	Arroyo	1	0	0	0	0	2	0
Heredia	0.1	1	0	0	0	1	0	Myers	0.1	0	0	0	0	1	0
Quantrill	1	2	0	0	0	0	0	Embree	0.2	1	0	0	0	2	0
Loaiza (L)	3.1	1	1	1	3	3	0	Wakefield (W)	3	1	0	0	1	4	0
Totals	13.2	13	5	5	7	12	1	Totals	14	12	4	4	8	16	1

	1	2	3	4	5	6	7	8	9	10	11	12	13	14	R	H	E
NY A	0	1	0	0	0	3	0	0	0	0	0	0	0	0	4	12	1
BOS A	2	0	0	0	0	0	2	0	0	0	0	0	0	1	5	13	1

Bill Mueller singled next, scoring Roberts to tie the game. With that one little nick on Rivera, that blown save, the tide turned. "We counted on breaks [like that]," Johnny Damon would later say. "You need them in this game to advance in the playoffs. Because any good team can get there, but you need the breaks to help you along the way."

The ninth-inning reprieve bailed out Boston, and their bullpen kept the Yankees scoreless through the 12th. The Yankees brought on Paul Quantrill to take over for Tom Gordon. Gordon and Quantrill had been New York's bullpen workhorses all season, but some feared that they were worn down by overwork. The fears were justified. First up for Boston: Manny Ramirez, who singled to left. The big guy was up next, Big Papi, David Ortiz. And he hit a big home run, winning the game for the Red Sox, 6–4, in the bottom of the 12th. The Yankee sweep, which seemed so sure some six hours before, was gone, and the Red Sox had grabbed the momentum.

But the Sox were still down three games to one, and every commentator and journalist reminded people that never in the history of baseball had any team come all the way back from a 0–3 deficit in a seven-game series. Several had won game four, as the Sox had here. Fewer had won game five, and almost no one had ever come back to even a seven-game series. No one, ever, had won four games in a row after being down 0–3. And yet hope flickered, as rumors of a special shoe being prepared for Schilling and reports of confidence and excitement from the Red Sox clubhouse began to circulate. "We had confidence," Varitek said. "A lot of people in that clubhouse had been on teams before that had come back, so we had that in our corner. We gained confidence once we finally won a game."

Game five started in the late afternoon, and the Red Sox were pleased to score twice in the first off Mussina, but the Yankees got one in the second and three more in the sixth, for a 4–2 lead. Pedro Martinez took it this far, but then had to call it a day after six full innings. The Red Sox rallied to score twice in the bottom of the eighth, when Ortiz homered off Tom Gordon to lead off the inning and then Millar—again—walked. Once more, Dave Roberts came in to run for Millar. There was no steal this time, but Trot Nixon singled and Roberts ran to third. First and third, nobody out. Joe Torre signaled to the Yankees' pen for Rivera once again. Jason Varitek drove the ball, deep enough for a game-tying sacrifice fly. In back-to-back games, an exhausted Rivera had now twice been unable to hold the lead.

Tied 4–4 after eight, the score remained tied into extra innings, all the way through the 13th. The game was running longer than game four, and midnight was approaching. The Red Sox looked to Wakefield to hold down the fort starting in the 10th, but with the season on the line, Francona kept Jason Varitek in to catch him. Wakefield's regular catcher had been Doug Mirabelli, but Varitek's bat was too valuable to lose in such a tight contest. "For some reason he had a nasty knuckleball that night," Varitek remembered. In the 13th inning three knucklers got past Tek to the backstop, and the crowd began a nervous murmur. "At the time, you know, I'm not really worried about what people are saying, I'm worried about catching the doggone thing. I didn't want to be the one that made us lose a game, especially having Wake be the guy that was left on the mound the year before. I did not want that to happen. We probably scared the heck out of the entire Red Sox Nation, but the final result was we got the job done."

Wakefield threw the final three innings, allowing just a single in the 12th. When the Red Sox came up in the 14th, the game had broken the record set in game four: this was now the longest-running game in playoff history.

Demoted to the bullpen for the series, Esteban Loaiza had thrown three innings for New York, and he struck out Bellhorn to lead off the bottom of the 14th. He walked Damon. Orlando Cabrera struck out, too, but Loaiza walked Manny Ramirez, pushing Damon into scoring position. Up came Big Papi again. He already had two walk-off hits to his credit this October, and the Fenway crowd pleaded with him for one more. With two out he fought off pitch after pitch but finally stroked one into shallow center field, scoring Damon from second. It was his second walk-off game-winning hit in a row.

The Sox had come from behind twice—first in game four and now in game five—and tied it up twice late in the game, both times because Mariano Rivera proved less than perfect. Both games ran into extra innings, and Boston won both games in dramatic fashion. Walking a tightrope of possible elimination, the Sox had done the near impossible. By virtue of having ended moments before midnight, both wins occurred on October 18.

Over the next two games, they would do the impossible. A surgically stitched Curt Schilling came back from the dead (or so it seemed) and, with blood seeping through his sock, threw seven innings of four-hit, one-run ball, and the Yankees were beaten 4–2. Whereas Boston's starting pitching had been resurrected, New York's faltered. After the 2003 campaign, the Yankees had lost Roger Clemens, Andy Pettitte, and David Wells, and attempted to fill those very big shoes with Kevin Brown and Javier Vasquez. Brown had not proven effective, and had even punched a cement wall in frustration late in the season, while Vasquez had simply wilted in the second half. The Red Sox demolished both in game seven: first Brown, and then Vasquez, in relief.

Game seven wasn't even close. David Ortiz hit a two-run homer off Kevin Brown in the first, and Johnny Damon hit a grand slam off Javier Vasquez in the second. That was more than enough. The Yankees scored one run in the third, but the Red Sox immediately doubled that with another Damon homer. Final score: Boston 10, New York 3. Perhaps Fate could have it no other way, that for the so-called Curse to be reversed, the Sox would have to do something that had never been done before. The Red Sox had just completed the greatest comeback in baseball history, and they had done it against their archrivals in impossible circumstances. Two nights in a row they had dragged the games into extra innings. A total of 26 innings in not much more than 26 hours were more than enough! Facing elimination, the Red Sox had won game four and then come back and won game five, too. Emboldened, and with the Yankees feeling the pressure now, in the pressure cooker that Yankee Stadium can be, the Sox simply took it all the way.

◀Extra Innings

- Beginning with the 1907 World Series and prior to the 2004 ALCS, there have been 25 times that a team faced a deficit of 0–3 in a seven-game play-off series. In 20 of those 25 times, the team that had already showed dominance simply went on to sweep. The only exceptions were:

the 1910 World Series, where the Cubs won one game, only to lose in five

the 1937 World Series, where the Giants won one game, only to lose in five

the 1970 World Series, where the Reds won one game, only to lose in five

the 1998 NLCS, where the Braves won two games, only to lose in six

the 1999 NLCS, where the Mets won two games, only to lose in six

In short, no team had ever forced a seventh game, and only two of 25 teams had gone so far as to force a sixth game. The Red Sox were not only the first team to force a game seven, they also became the first to win it.

◆50

October 27, 2004: Boston at St. Louis

Hallelujah

In which the Red Sox accomplish something many snakebitten fans still remain skeptical ever occurred

After the Greatest Comeback in Baseball History, and beating the Yankees to pull it off, one could argue that the 2004 World Series was inevitably going to be an anticlimax. Everyone reading this book knows the Red Sox won, and won the Series in four games. Was one among them one of the greatest games in Red Sox history? After all, the Red Sox never trailed at any time in any of the four games. They almost seemed to win it with minimal effort, as though predestined to fly back to Boston with the trophy.

The answer is yes. After waiting 86 years to win a World Series, and after coming so close so many times, always to fall just short, to win a World Series was a very big thing indeed. The final game of the Series must be considered one of the greatest highlights of Red Sox history.

The 2004 World Series pitted an exhausted yet exhilarated Red Sox team against the St. Louis Cardinals, the franchise that had beaten Boston in both the 1946 and 1967 World Series.

Game One was the only one that offered any tension. The Series opened in Boston, and the Fenway Faithful were still keyed up from the league championship series. Everyone was exhausted, wrung out. Yet this was the World Series, back in Boston for the first time since 1986. People turned to each other in their seats before the game, exchanging the same thoughts: "This really is the

World Series!" And then it got under way. Woody Williams pitching for the Cardinals and Tim Wakefield for the Red Sox.

David Ortiz, the MVP of the ALCS, was still red-hot, and he hit a three-run homer in his first World Series at-bat. It was 4–0 after one inning, and 7–2 Sox after three. But St. Louis scored three in the fourth and two in the sixth, and it was all tied up. The Sox got two in the bottom of the seventh; the Cardinals retied it with two of their own in the top of the eighth. In the bottom of the eighth, Mark Bellhorn homered off the Pesky Pole for the go-ahead runs. Boston had never been behind but had seen the Cardinals tie it twice. The Sox won, 11–9.

Game Two pitted Matt Morris against Curt Schilling, his tendon once more surgically sewn into place. Again the Red Sox scored in the first inning, two runs on Varitek's triple to center. St. Louis got a run in the top of the fourth, but Mark Bellhorn doubled in two and increased the lead from two runs to three. Orlando Cabrera knocked in two more in the sixth, and the final was Boston 6, St. Louis 2. Even though the Red Sox committed four errors in each of Games One and Two, they won both. The Series traveled to St. Louis.

Yet again, Boston scored in the first inning, as Manny Ramirez hit a home run off St. Louis starter Jeff Suppan; 1–0. Boston built a 4–0 lead, and Pedro Martinez shut out the Cards through seven. Pedro was on the ropes in the third, but Suppan inadvertently helped him out. If there was any play that signaled that the Series would be Boston's, it was Suppan's sad baserunning in the bottom of the third. The score was still 1–0 Red Sox. Suppan started a rally with a single, and when Edgar Renteria doubled to right field, the Cardinals had men on second and third with nobody out. Larry Walker was up, one of the few Cardinals who'd shown some power in the Series. This time, though, he grounded to second base. The ball wasn't hit that hard, and Suppan should have scored on a hit to the right side of the infield, but as Bellhorn threw to Ortiz, playing first, Suppan stopped partway down the line. Third-base coach Jose Oquendo yelled at him to run home, and he started up again, but then held up and decided to scamper back to third. Ortiz never could have expected Suppan's stutter-start dance, but alertly picked up what was happening, took a couple of steps across the infield toward third, and threw a bullet to Bill Mueller, who got Suppan with the tag. It was a rare 4-3-5 double play. Pedro got Albert Pujols to ground out. Walker hit his second home run of the Series off Keith Foulke in the bottom of the ninth, but there was no general uprising, and the game ended at 4–1.

So St. Louis was down 0–3. As we learned in the American League championship series, only one team in baseball history had ever come back from an

0–3 deficit and won—in a game which ended just one week earlier. Now the Red Sox were the ones up three games to none. There was a full lunar eclipse in progress, timed to begin just as Game Four got under way; the whole Red Sox run seemed both improbable and magical.

In Game Four, Derek Lowe started against Jason Marquis. There was some irony that Lowe started the game that could be the deciding game of the World Series. He'd pitched uncertainly all season long, and it was by no means certain that he would start any game in the postseason, but in the bottom of the first, he took the rubber in a game that offered the Red Sox the opportunity to win their first World Series since 1918. Lowe already had a slim lead; Johnny Damon had homered off Marquis to lead off the game. It was the 17th time a leadoff batter homered to start a World Series game, but it served notice on St. Louis that the Red Sox remained determined. The Red Sox scored first in every one of the four games, and they hadn't wasted any time doing it—they scored in the first inning each time.

Cardinals leadoff batter Tony Womack singled off Lowe, and St. Louis had their big guns up. Larry Walker, already hitting .417 in the Series, might have powered out his third homer of the Series to give the Cardinals the lead. Instead, he bunted to move Womack to second. Albert Pujols, second in the league in slugging, with 46 homers and 123 RBIs to his credit, grounded out to second base. Scott Rolen, second in the league in RBIs, but who had not yet had a hit in the Series, grounded out to the pitcher, unassisted.

The St. Louis slump continued in the second, when Jim Edmonds (just behind Pujols, third in the league in slugging) flew out to left. Lowe set the Cardinals down 1-2-3 in the second, third, and fourth innings. In the meantime, Trot Nixon had doubled home two more Red Sox runs in the top of the third. Boston led 3–0, and Derek Lowe's sinker was sinking St. Louis.

Lowe held St. Louis hitless until the fifth inning, when Edgar Renteria doubled. Lowe then threw a wild pitch and Renteria scampered to third. It looked like a crack in the armor, but Lowe bore down and struck out John Mabry and then induced an easy grounder to Cabrera at short.

Marquis kept the game from getting any worse, holding the Sox scoreless in the middle innings. He was lifted for a pinch hitter, Marlon Anderson, in the bottom of the sixth, but Anderson just grounded out to Lowe, who flipped to first. Lowe walked Walker with two out in the sixth, and allowed a single to Renteria in the seventh, but those were the only other base runners the Cardinals got off him.

Lowe was lifted for a pinch hitter in the eighth, but he'd held St. Louis scoreless through seven, with just three scattered hits and one base on balls.

Arroyo and Embree shared the eighth. Arroyo got the first out, but then walked Reggie Sanders. Boston manager Terry Francona summoned Embree to pitch to Womack, and St. Louis skipper Tony La Russa called on Hector Luna to pinch-hit for Sanders. Sanders stole second off Embree, but died there as Luna struck out and Walker popped up to Cabrera.

Everyone playing their roles, Keith Foulke was asked to close it out. Pujols singled off Foulke to lead the ninth; he finished the Series with a good .333 average, but Scott Rolen never had a hit in any of the four games; he flied out to Gabe Kapler, on defensively in right field. Jim Edmonds had 42 home runs in the regular season but batted just .067 in the World Series; he whiffed for the second out.

Here the Red Sox were, as they had been in 1986, one out away from a world championship. Edgar Renteria was the potential last out. He already had two of the four Cardinal hits, but he couldn't even tie the game with a home run, though he could have made it more interesting. Instead, he grounded weakly to Foulke, who fielded it cleanly and had time to run to first for the out, but took the safer route and flipped softly underhand to Doug Mientkiewicz at first base.

Over many long years, the Red Sox had seemingly specialized in turning victories into last-minute defeats. Haunted Red Sox fans worldwide were afraid to breathe, anticipating horror, half assuming that the ball would sail wildly and get

OCTOBER 27, 2004: BOSTON AT ST. LOUIS																	
Boston Red Sox	AB	R	H	RBI	BB	SO	PO	A	**St. Louis Cardinals**	AB	R	H	RBI	BB	SO	PO	A
Damon cf	5	1	2	1	0	0	3	0	Womack 2b	3	0	1	0	0	0	1	3
Cabrera ss	5	0	0	0	0	1	1	3	Luna ph,2b	1	0	0	0	0	1	0	0
Ramirez lf	4	0	1	0	1	1	1	0	Walker rf	2	0	0	0	1	0	2	0
Ortiz 1b	3	1	1	0	1	0	8	0	Pujols 1b	4	0	1	0	0	1	7	3
Mientkiewicz 1b	1	0	0	0	0	0	1	0	Rolen 3b	4	0	0	0	0	0	0	3
Varitek c	5	1	1	0	0	2	6	0	Edmonds cf	4	0	0	0	0	1	4	0
Mueller 3b	4	0	1	0	1	0	1	1	Renteria ss	4	0	2	0	0	0	1	0
Nixon rf	4	0	3	2	0	0	2	0	Mabry lf	3	0	0	0	0	2	2	0
Kapler pr,rf	0	0	0	0	0	0	1	0	Isringhausen p	0	0	0	0	0	0	0	0
Bellhorn 2b	1	0	0	0	3	1	1	1	Molina c	2	0	0	0	0	1	9	0
Reese pr,2b	0	0	0	0	0	0	1	0	Cedeno ph	1	0	0	0	0	0	0	0
Lowe p	2	0	0	0	0	1	1	2	Matheny c	0	0	0	0	0	0	0	0
Millar ph	1	0	0	0	0	1	0	0	Marquis p	1	0	0	0	0	0	0	1
Arroyo p	0	0	0	0	0	0	0	0	Anderson ph	1	0	0	0	0	0	0	0
Embree p	0	0	0	0	0	0	0	0	Haren p	0	0	0	0	0	0	1	0
Foulke p	0	0	0	0	0	0	0	1	Sanders lf	0	0	0	0	1	0	0	0
Totals	35	3	9	3	6	7	27	8	**Totals**	30	0	4	0	2	6	27	10

Boston Red Sox	IP	H	R	ER	BB	SO	HR	**St. Louis Cardinals**	IP	H	R	ER	BB	SO	HR
Lowe (W)	7	3	0	0	1	4	0	Marquis (L)	6	6	3	3	5	4	1
Arroyo	0.1	0	0	0	1	0	0	Haren	1	2	0	0	0	1	0
Embree	0.2	0	0	0	0	1	0	Isringhausen	2	1	0	0	1	2	0
Foulke (S)	1	1	0	0	0	1	0	**Totals**	9	9	3	3	6	7	1
Totals	9	4	0	0	2	6	0								

	1	2	3	4	5	6	7	8	9		R	H	E
BOS A	1	0	2	0	0	0	0	0	0		3	9	0
STL N	0	0	0	0	0	0	0	0	0		0	4	0

by Mientkiewicz, starting off a rally that would lead to a Cardinals win in Game Four, and turn the tide in the Series. No, the Yankees were safe: they could still retain the greatest-choke title. Mientkiewicz caught the million-dollar ball, and the Red Sox piled on each other in the traditional winner's ritual.

Derek Lowe got the win, and earned the unusual distinction of being the winning pitcher in the final games of the ALDS, the ALCS, and now the World Series.

The Red Sox swept the World Series from the team with the most 2004 wins of any major league ball club. The Sox had scored first in every game and were never behind in any game. The combined ERAs of the Game Two, Game Three, and Game Four starters was 0.00. After the drama of Game One, it became about as convincing a rout as there had ever been.

It was a long time coming. Would it be 86 years before the Red Sox won another? Time alone will tell.

Extra Innings

- The Cardinals had a formidable offense. The team had won 105 games in the regular season, more than any other team in the majors. The heart of the Cardinals' order was Pujols, Rolen, and Edmonds. Each one of them was a legitimate MVP candidate. Among them they had hit 122 home runs in the regular season and driven in an astronomical 358 runs. The Red Sox must have had some great advance scouts, and St. Louis succumbed to one of the greatest collective power droughts, as their trio of titans combined to manage just six hits in 45 at-bats (.133), without even one home run and just one run batted in. The lone RBI was Rolen's, late in Game Two, on a sacrifice fly; he never did get a hit. Pujols doubled twice; the other four hits were singles.

- Most accounts of the Series focus on the shortfall of St. Louis's offense. Another significant deficit was the loss of pitcher Chris Carpenter. The right-hander was sidelined late in the season with a September 18 arm injury described as nerve damage in the right biceps. The Cardinals hoped that he would be able to be activated by the time of the playoffs. It was a major loss; Carpenter had the best winning percentage (15–5), the best strikeouts-to-walks ratio (152 : 38), and the best ERA (3.46) of any starter on the team.

- After the Series was over, Boston hosted the biggest public event in the history of New England. An estimated 3 million or more thronged the streets of Boston to welcome their heroes for a victory parade. The city of Boston proper has a population of just under 600,000. Hence the crowd was five times as many people as even lived within the city limits.

The 50 Games Ranked 1 to 50

This list evolved through the input of both authors, our ongoing research and experiences, as well as the suggestions of friends, colleagues, and fans on the Internet. Eventually we whittled the list down to 49 games, then posted a poll of all the remaining suggestions onto various Web sites, allowing fans to choose the final game for inclusion. The game the fans chose, by almost twice as many votes as the second-place choice, was September 13, 1946, the game in which Ted Williams's sole inside-the-park home run was the difference in a 1–0 game that also happened to be the pennant clincher. The game first came to our attention because several of the players we interviewed agitated for its inclusion, and the fans agreed.

Some of the games that were left off the list were not excluded for a lack of inherent "greatness" but for other reasons. For example, we already have Pedro facing Roger Clemens in two games in the book, and between the two of them they appear as major figures in seven of the 50 games. To add another, like the memorable Sunday night duel they pitched on May 28, 2000, would have been too much. We also felt it was important to include at least one game from each decade, which was particularly challenging for the 1920s—but we found a worthy selection, a victory over the Yankees, no less.

Satisfied with the selection of 50, we then scored them based on the following criteria:

- How well remembered is this game?

- What was this game's historical significance, whether on or off the field?

- Did this game involve interesting characters in Red Sox history, or an intriguing back story?

- Was this game "momentous," as part of a pennant race, postseason, or World Series?

- Did this game involve bizarre twists of Fate of unbelievable luck, good or bad?

- Was the opponent the New York Yankees?

- Was the game exciting or suspenseful for the fans watching/listening?

- How often was the game nominated in our polls?

- Did the game involve an ignominious failure by the Red Sox?

The "ignominy" score, by the way, deducted points from the total score, not added. The two authors scored the games independently and then combined their scores. The highest possible score would have been 40.

The 50 Greatest Red Sox Games Ranked 1 to 50

#1. October 17 and 18, 2004: The curse reverses on New York

#2. October 12, 1986: Henderson's home run in Anaheim

#3. October 21, 1975: Fisk's body-English homer

#4. October 2, 1978: Bucky "Bleepin'" Dent

#5. October 16, 2003: Aaron goes Boone

#6. October 25, 1986: Bill Buckner

#7. April 29, 1986: The Rocket's 20Ks, first time

#8. October 10, 1904: Grabbing the pennant from New York

#9. June 23, 1917: Ernie Shore's "perfect game" in relief

#10. September 28, 1941: Ted Williams 6-for-8, hits .406

#11. October 15, 1946: Slaughter's mad dash

#12. September 28, 1960: Ted Williams's final at-bat

#13. May 5, 1904: Cy Young's perfect game

#14. October 1, 1967: The Impossible Dream final game

#15. October 1 and 2, 1949: The pennant race, lost

#16. September 10, 1999: Pedro's 17Ks in Yankee Stadium

#17. October 18, 1912: World Series, the Snodgrass Muff

#18. October 4, 1948: One-game playoff vs. Cleveland

#19. October 16, 1999: Pedro demolishes Clemens in ALCS

#20. October 27, 2004: After 86 years, World Series clincher!

#21. August 1, 1962: Monbouquette no-hitter

#22. July 29, 1911: Smoky Joe Wood no-hitter

#23. June 27, 2003: 10 runs before first out recorded

#24. October 12, 1967: World Series Game Seven

#25. October 6, 2003: Capping a wild, weird ALDS over the A's

#26. September 18, 1996: Roger Clemens's 20Ks, again

#27. October 18, 1986: World Series opener, beat Mets 1–0

#28. September 13, 1946: Ted inside-the-park HR clinches pennant

#29. September 5, 1918: World Series Game One, Ruth wins 1–0

#30. June 18, 1961: Ninth-inning comeback from 7 runs down

#31. October 9, 1967: World Series Game Five, Lonborg 3-hitter

#32. September 2, 1996: Mike Greenwell 9-RBI game

#33. July 23, 2002: Nomar hits 3 home runs on his birthday

#34. October 9, 1915: Rube Foster three-hitter in World Series

#35. October 15, 1975: World Series Game Four, Tiant triumphs

#36. October 9, 1916: World Series Game Two, Ruth 14-inning 1–0 win

#37. September 11, 1918: Carl Mays wins World Series clincher

#38. April 27, 2002: Derek Lowe no-hitter

#39. October 6, 1946: Return to the World Series, 3–2 win

#40. August 28, 1950: Comeback from 12–1 down, win 15–14!

#41. October 13, 1915: World Series clincher, Harry Hooper

#42. September 5, 1927: Fans crash the gates, Sox beat Lou/Babe

#43. August 17, 1947: Galehouse 11-inning complete-game shut out

#44. October 12, 1912: World Series Game Five, beat Mathewson

#45. October 2, 1903: First World Series, Dinneen 3-hitter

#46. October 13, 1903: Clinching first World Series title

#47. September 12, 1931: Durham 13-inning complete-game shut out

#48. April 12, 1992: Matt "Sigh" Young losing no-hitter

#49. June 24, 1949: Record offense: Boston 21, St. Louis 2

#50. May 18, 1955: Worst shut out in team history 19–0

The "Other" Greatest Games

And here are the contenders that did not make it into the book. Some of these were suggested by fans; others were on our original list before the 2004 post-season came along and bumped them off. Some are historic, some are painful, some are fun. Many are mentioned in the course of the chapters as lead-ins to games we did choose, but here is a recap of some of the other great games in Sox history.

May 8, 1901 The franchise plays their first home game, beating the Philadelphia Athletics 12–4 behind the pitching of Cy Young. The game was played at the Huntington Avenue Grounds.

August 17, 1904 Jesse Tannehill pitches the first Red Sox no-hitter, a 6–0 win over Chicago. His brother Lee plays for the White Sox and goes 0-for-3.

September 27, 1905 Bill Dinneen pitches a no-hitter, a 2–0 win. The White Sox are the victims again. Dinneen would become an umpire after his pitching career ended.

June 30, 1908 Cy Young, who threw a perfect game in 1904, pitches his third no-hitter. Boston clobbers New York 8–0, and only a single walk prevents this from being another perfect game.

April 9, 1912 The first game played at Fenway Park. The Red Sox defeat Harvard 2–0 in an exhibition game played in the snow.

September 6, 1912 Smoky Joe Wood faces off against Walter Johnson at Fenway. Wood was going for his 14th win in a row, while Johnson had set the record at 16 wins in a row earlier in the same season. It was a World Series atmosphere, with fans standing in the outfield and ticket sales cut off half an hour prior to game time.

June 21, 1916 George "Rube" Foster pitches the first no-hitter at Fenway Park. The Yankees are the victims and lose 2–0.

August 30, 1916 Hubert Benjamin "Dutch" Leonard pitches a no-hitter over the St. Louis Browns. He had taken the hill the day before and couldn't get out of the first inning, giving up two runs, two hits, a walk, hitting a batter, and throwing a wild pitch before being yanked.

June 13, 1918   After struggling with his control all season, Dutch Leonard notches another no-hitter, this one against Chicago, but he leaves the Sox a few weeks later with plans to enlist in the military.

September 7, 1923   Howard Ehmke pitches a no-hitter against the Philadelphia A's. Ehmke fans only one man, and actually gives up a double to the opposing pitcher, Slim Harriss. Harriss hits a drive to the wall in the seventh inning but is called out for failing to touch first base.

July 9, 1946   The All-Star Game at Fenway Park features eight Red Sox. Ted Williams belts a Rip Sewell "eephus" pitch for a homer, and with another homer, two singles, a walk, and four runs scored leads the American League to a 12–0 rout.

June 8, 1950   The Sox beat the St. Louis Browns by a record-setting score of 29–4. Pitcher Chuck Stobbs walks four times in four innings, and leadoff man Clyde Vollmer bats eight times in eight innings, the only time that has ever happened. The 58 total bases for the Sox is also a new record, and they score 17 runs in a single inning.

June 17 and 18, 1953   The Sox score big over the Tigers two days in a row, by scores of 17–1 and 23–3.

July 14, 1956   Lefty Mel Parnell throws the first no-hitter for the Red Sox in 33 years. Later in the season he is injured and retires as the winningest left hander in Red Sox history.

August 7, 1956   Willard Nixon pitches a tight 11-inning complete game, 1–0 shutout vs. the New York Yankees at Fenway Park.

June 26, 1962   Earl Wilson pitches a 2–0 no-hitter against the Angels, and hits a home run to boot. Wilson was the first black player signed by the Red Sox organization, but Pumpsie Green beat him to the majors thanks to Wilson's two years of military service.

September 16, 1965   Dave Morehead pitches a no-hitter to beat the Cleveland Indians 2–0, though the day is significantly remembered as the day GM Mike "Pinky" Higgins was fired by the Sox.

April 14, 1967   Twenty-one-year-old rookie Billy Rohr makes his major league debut facing Whitey Ford at Yankee Stadium. He comes within one strike of a no-hitter before giving up a hit to Elston Howard. Rohr nails down the 3–0 shutout but wins only two more games in the majors after that.

July 23, 1967   Tony Conigliaro becomes the youngest player in American League history to reach the 100-home-run milestone, at age 22.

April 8, 1969   Tony C returns to the lineup for the first time after his 1967 beaning, vision still blurry, yet hits a two-run homer in the 10th inning, and then after the Orioles tie it up again, walks to lead off the 12th and scores the winning run.

May 16, 1969   In the highest-scoring 11th inning ever, the Seattle Pilots score six runs, but then Boston charges back, scoring five, including a home run by Rico Petrocelli. Unfortunately, the comeback falls short. Jim Bouton gets the win with three shutout innings in relief.

May 28, 1971   Sonny Siebert and Vida Blue face off in a standing-room-packed Fenway on a beautiful summer night, for one of the most hyped matchups of the decade. (Many fans nominated this game, though some thought the pitchers were Lee Stange and Blue Moon Odom.)

October 11, 1975   Game One of the World Series; the great El Tiante stops the Big Red Machine cold.

October 22, 1975   Game Seven of the World Series. As in 1946, the Sox are valiant but fall short in the ultimate game of the year.

May 20, 1976   The Sox hammer the Yanks 8–2. A major brawl erupts at home plate, and Bill Lee is injured. A new generation of Red Sox fans is indoctrinated into a visceral hatred of Yankees with this one.

October 1, 1978   On the final day of the season, the Sox beat the Blue Jays, while the Cleveland Indians beat the New York Yankees. "Thank You, Rick Waits" appears on the Fenway Park scoreboard, in appreciation of Cleveland's winning pitcher.

August 21, 1986   The Sox trounce the Indians at Cleveland, 24–5. Oil Can Boyd beats Greg Swindell (his major league debut). Boyd is prompted to say, "That's what you get when you build a stadium by the ocean."

September 5, 1988   Marty Barrett pulls off the third hidden-ball trick of his Red Sox career, in Baltimore. (He also got Doug DeCinces of California on July 21 1985, just two weeks after getting Bobby Grich in California!)

June 4, 1989   In a game against Toronto, the Sox are leading 10–0 after six innings. They give up 11 runs, then tie the game at 11-all in ninth. Unfortunately, they lose in the 13th when Junior Felix hits a two-run shot.

June 23 and 24, 1990   Pitcher Jeff Gray earns his first win on the first day, and gets his first save on the next.

October 3, 1990   The Sox clinch the East Division title against the White Sox on Tom Brunansky's spectacular catch.

May 13, 1991   Popular utility man Steve Lyons pulls the hidden-ball trick on Ozzie Guillen in the fourth inning. As of press time, it was the last time a Red Sox player successfully used the trick.

July 8, 1994   John Valentin turns an unassisted triple play and the Sox beat the Mariners 4–3.

April 10, 1998   The Fenway home opener. Seattle's Randy Johnson pitches a two-hitter through eight, protecting a 7–2 lead. But the Sox score seven runs in the ninth inning, the final four on a walk-off grand slam by Mo Vaughn off Mike Timlin.

July 13, 1999   The All-Star Game at Fenway Park. Not only is there a stirring appearance by Ted Williams, in which major league stars flock around him, but also Pedro Martinez strikes out Barry Larkin, Larry Walker, Sammy Sosa, and Mark McGwire to start the game.

October 10, 1999   Game four of the American League division series against the Indians. The Sox deliver a 23–7 shellacking as John Valentin notches 7 RBIs.

October 11, 1999   Game five of the American League division series. The Indians are up 8–7 after three innings, when Pedro comes out of the bullpen, ignores his injuries, and pitches shutout ball the rest of the way. Boston wins 12–8 and moves on to face the Yankees for the pennant.

May 28, 2000   In their first meeting since a matchup in the ALCS the previous October, Pedro Martinez opposes Roger Clemens in a Sunday night hyped-up ESPN matchup. The duel lives up to the hype as both pitchers fire shutouts for the first eight innings before Trot Nixon takes Clemens deep.

August 29, 2000   Pedro faces the Devil Rays in Tampa and hits the first batter, but then retires the next 24 men in a row. Rays catcher John Flaherty breaks up the no-hitter with a single in the ninth, but the Red Sox win 8–0. Also, eight Devil Rays, including the manager and two coaches, are ejected during the game; Brian Daubach and Lou Merloni are injured in a brawl; and Carl Everett almost hits for the cycle, needing only a single to complete it.

April 4, 2001   Hideo Nomo becomes the first Red Sox pitcher to pitch a no-hitter in his debut for the team.

September 2, 2001   Mike Mussina almost pitches a perfect game for the Yankees at Fenway Park. Even Sox fans get into the game, as a gutty, washed-up David Cone pushes himself to the limit to match Mussina pitch for pitch. Carl Everett breaks up the perfect game with a clean single with two out and two strikes in the ninth.

April 13, 2002   Shea Hillenbrand hits a three-run dinger over the Green Monster off the Yankees' Mariano Rivera in the eighth inning, and Alfonso Soriano ends the game getting caught stealing second.

October 4, 2003   Down 0–2 in the ALDS and facing elimination, the Sox turn the corner, beating Oakland at Fenway on a two-run walk-off home run by Trot Nixon.

July 24, 2004   On a day when the Yankees' Alex Rodriguez brawled with Sox catcher Jason Varitek, Bill Mueller caps the action with a walk-off homer off Mariano Rivera.

October 23, 2004   Game One of the World Series turns into a slugfest at Fenway, setting a new record for total runs in a World Series game (20), plus 14 walks and five errors. The Sox win it 11–9 on a two-run home run by Mark Bellhorn in the eighth.

April 11, 2005   The home opener at Fenway Park and the raising of the World Series championship flag. The day was special even if the game didn't turn out that exciting.

Acknowledgments

Many people's input, support, and understanding went into making this book, and we'll try not to forget anyone.

First, thanks to Lori Perkins, whose talent as an agent is unmatched, and to Stephen Power, our editor at Wiley, who we hope had as much fun with the book as we did.

A number of SABR members provided research help, made suggestions for improvement, and checked facts, including Charlie Bevis, Clem Comly, Paul Hirsch, R. J. Lesch, John Lewis, Rod Nelson, Steve Steinberg, Bob Timmerman, Alain Usereau, and Fred Worth. Bill in particular would like to thank Roger Abrams, Peter M. Collery, Ted Fischer, Herm Krabbenhoft, Wayne McElreavy, Thomas Mueller, Chris Savage, and Neal Traven. Cecilia would also like to thank Leigh Grossman, David Laurila, and Eric Van.

David Smith at Retrosheet went beyond the call in helping us to find play-by-play records of hard-to-find games and track down discrepancies in newspaper accounts. Bill Burdick at the National Baseball Hall of Fame and Museum did a great job of unearthing photos of Red Sox players for us.

We also would like to thank the many Red Sox fans on the Internet who participated in our discussion forums, voted in our polls, and forwarded our calls for nominations to their friends, and in particular Kelly at the Triumphant Red Sox Fan Forum, redsoxjamie at Sons of Sam Horn, and Cambridge of the Royal Rooters at RedSoxNation.net.

Thanks also to the Boston Red Sox, and the players and former players who made time to speak with us about their experiences. You're all champions.

Notes on Sources and Technological Advances

To re-create the play-by-play action in the 50 greatest Red Sox games, the authors began with hundreds of newspaper accounts—far too many individual articles to conveniently list. We compared both home and away accounts of each game, relying mostly on the *Boston Herald*, the *Boston Globe*, the *Boston Post*, and the *Boston Journal* for the Hubcentric views, with occasional looks at the plethora of other New England papers that chronicle the Red Sox, from the *Lawrence Eagle-Tribune* to the *Providence Journal*. Both authors spent time in the microfilm departments of the Boston Public Library, the New York Public Library, Harvard University, and Tufts University to gather maximum coverage, but thanks to the march of technology, we have also been able to search collections that would otherwise not be available to us.

Through the Society for American Baseball Research (SABR, pronounced "saber") and the society's subscription to the Pro Quest Historical Newspapers database, we could search the microfilm archives of the *New York Times*, the *Washington Post*, and the *Los Angels Times* right from the convenience of our home computers. ProQuest has since added the *Christian Science Monitor*, the *Wall Street Journal*, and the *Atlanta Constitution*, and continues to expand. Another Web site, Paper of Record (www.paperofrecord.com), archives the complete run of *The Sporting News*, dating back to 1886. NewspaperArchive.com allowed us to sometimes find coverage in tiny, obscure local newspapers.

Where we could, we supplemented our initial newspaper research with radio calls, videotape, and, of course, interviews with players. Historical and biographical information came from numerous sources, including books, of course, but also Web sites and Web databases that have been built online by SABR and/or other dedicated baseball enthusiasts. These online resources are changing the nature of baseball research. Retrosheet, the Baseball Library, the Baseball Almanac, SABR's ever-growing BioProject, and the like have made it possible to conjure up factoids, anecdotes, biographical blurbs, and stats at the press of a button. For the most part we have double-checked what we found online with print sources, but the day is coming when the online sources will be the canonical ones. Already MLB.com, the official Web site of Major League Baseball, has replaced *The Sporting News* as the current source for team updates and box scores, and now with players starting their own Web sites and blogs, the availability of online multimedia archives, and the march of libraries toward total digitization, it won't be long before "bibliographies" go the way of flannel uniforms and the four-man rotation.

The Internet also aided our research in another way, in that it gives us near instantaneous access to the minds of our fellow researchers. Through the SABR-L email list, for example, we were able to solve two mysteries about the 1912 World Series within 24 hours. While fact-checking the book, we noticed that the Red Sox team ERA for the Series was recorded in some sources as 2.92, in some as 2.80, and in others as 2.55. The discrepancies hinged on an inning where the number of runs earned was in question. Newspapers, box scores, play-by-play records—none of the material we had could verify which was the correct assertion. Some box scores showed an error that did not appear in the play-by-play records. An error would have explained why some sources thought Joe Wood earned only nine of 11 runs he gave up, while other sources concluded that he earned all 11. We emailed our SABR cohort and by the next morning had an answer: a SABR member in Iowa found a definitive account in the 1913 *Reach Guide* that not only verified the error, it also described exactly how it was made and why it affected the scoring decision. It turns out that all our previous sources were then wrong about the Red Sox team ERA, which should have been 2.67. The other mysterious fact we had trouble verifying was why a certain ball hit into the stands counted as a double instead of a home run. Our microfilm sources gave only partial explanations and not a complete picture. SABR-L again extended our reach, and several quotes from newspapers we had not seen clarified the situation.

It is the dedication of the folks in SABR, who are by and large unpaid enthusiasts whose love of the game spurs them to delve into the historical record and attempt to set it straight, that has made it possible for original research on historical topics to be undertaken. Bill Nowlin, coauthor of this volume, researched the use of the nickname "Pilgrims" for the early Boston American League team and found that the nickname was unlikely to have been in prevalent use at the time of the 1903 World Series. Many history books refer to the Boston Pilgrims as if this were a commonly accepted and commonly used nickname for the team all along. But the nickname appears not to have taken root until 1907, when writers at the *Washington Post*, the *Boston Herald*, and the *Boston Journal* took a liking to it. The nickname was fairly short-lived, however; in December 1907 owner John I. Taylor decided that his players would wear red stockings and bear the name Red Sox.

Recent delvings on Bill's part have also revealed why it is that Big Bill Dinneen's name changed spelling between his playing days and his umpiring days. All through his career as a player he bore the name "Dineen," apparently in error, according to a December 1933 column in *The Sporting News*, which reads: "William Henry Dinneen . . . had quite a time getting scribes to place three *n*'s in his last name." As of this writing, we are hoping to obtain a copy of his signature that may settle once and for all how he spelled it himself.

References

Books

Abrams, Roger. *The First World Series and the Baseball Fanatics of 1903*. Boston: Northeastern University Press, 2003.

Adelman, Tom. *The Long Ball*. Boston: Little, Brown, 2003.

Baldassaro, Lawrence. *Ted Williams: Reflections on a Splendid Life*. Boston: Northeastern University Press, 2003.

Baseball Writers of the *New York Times* and the *Boston Globe*. *The Rivals*. New York: St. Martin's Press, 2004.

Berry, Henry. *Boston Red Sox*. New York: Collier, 1975.

Bevis, Charlie. *Sunday Baseball*. Jefferson, NC: McFarland, 2003.

Boston Globe. Believe It. Chicago: Triumph Books, 2004.

Boston Herald. Boston Red Sox, 2004 World Champions. Champaign, IL: Sports Publishing, 2004.

Boston Red Sox. *Boston Red Sox Media Guide*. Boston: Boston Red Sox, 2005.

Bradford, Rob. *Chasing Steinbrenner*. Dulles, VA: Brassey's, 2004.

Browning, Reed. *Cy Young: A Baseball Life*. Amherst: University of Massachusetts Press, 2000.

Bryant, Howard. *Shut Out*. New York: Routledge, 2002.

Buckley, James Jr. *Perfect*. Chicago: Triumph Books, 2002.

Buckley, Steve. *Red Sox: Where Have You Gone?* Champaign, IL: Sports Publishing, 2005.

Campbell, Peter A. *Old-Time Baseball and the First Modern World Series*. Brookfield, CT: Millbrook, 2002.

Castiglione, Joe, and Doug Lyons. *Broadcast Rites and Sites: I Saw It on the Radio with the Boston Red Sox*. Lanham, MD: Taylor, 2004.

Cataneo, David. *Tony C*. Nashville: Rutledge Hill Press, 1997.

Chadwick, Bruce, and David M. Spindel. *The Boston Red Sox*. New York: Abbeville, 1991.

Chapman, Con. *The Year of the Gerbil*. Danbury, CT: Rutledge Books, 1998.

Cinquanti, Michael. *A Year's Worth of Red Sox Birthdays*. Amsterdam, NY: Genium, 2005.

Clark, Ellery. *Boston Red Sox 75th Anniversary History*. Hicksville, NY: Exposition Press, 1975.

———. *Red Sox Fever*. Hicksville, NY: Exposition Press, 1979.

Clemens, Roger, and Peter Gammons. *Rocket Man*. Lexington, MA: Stephen Greene, 1987.

Cole, Milton, and Jim Kaplan. *The Boston Red Sox*. North Dighton, MA: JG Press, 2005.

Coleman, Ken, with Dan Valenti. *Diary of a Sportscaster.* Pittsfield, MA: Literations, 1982.

Coleman, Ken. *So You Want to Be a Sportscaster.* New York: Hawthorn, 1973.

———. *Talking on Air.* Champaign, IL: Sports Publishing, 2000.

Conigliaro, Tony, with Jack Zanger. *Seeing It Through.* New York: Macmillan, 1970.

Creamer, Robert. *Babe: The Legend Comes to Life.* New York: Simon & Schuster, 1974.

———. *Baseball in '41.* New York: Viking, 1991.

Crehan, Herb. *Red Sox Heroes of Yesteryear.* Cambridge, MA: Rounder Books, 2005.

Crehan, Herb, and James W. Ryan. *Lightning in a Bottle.* Boston: Branden, 1992.

Daniel, W. Harrison. *Jimmie Foxx.* Jefferson, NC: McFarland, 1996.

Dawidoff, Nicholas. *The Catcher Was a Spy.* New York: Vintage, 1994.

DiMaggio, Dom, with Bill Gilbert. *Real Grass, Real Heroes.* New York: Zebra, 1990.

Dolan, Edward F. Jr., and Richard B. Lyttle. *Fred Lynn: The Hero from Boston.* New York: Doubleday, 1978.

Enders, Eric. *100 Years of the World Series.* New York: Barnes & Noble, 2003.

Femia, Vin. *The Possible Dream.* Worcester, MA: Chandler House Press, 2004.

Ferroli, Steve. *Hit Your Potential.* Indianapolis: Masters Press, 1998.

Frommer, Harvey. *Baseball's Greatest Rivalry.* New York: Atheneum, 1982.

Frommer, Harvey, and Frederic J. Frommer. *Red Sox vs. Yankees: The Great Rivalry.* Champaign, IL: Sports Publishing, 2004.

Gammons, Peter. *Beyond the Sixth Game.* Lexington, MA: Stephen Greene, 1986.

Glebe, Iris Webb. *The Earl of Dublin.* Privately printed, 1988.

Golenbock, Peter. *Red Sox Nation.* Chicago: Triumph, 2005.

Gorman, Lou. *One Pitch from Glory.* Champaign, IL: Sports Publishing, 2005.

Gowdy, Curt. *Cowboy at the Mike.* Garden City, NY: Doubleday, 1966.

Grossman, Leigh. *The Red Sox Fan Handbook.* Cambridge, MA: Rounder Books, 2005.

Halberstam, David. *Summer of '49.* New York: William Morrow, 1989.

Halloran, Bob. *Destiny Derailed.* Salt Lake City: Millennial Mind Publishing, 2004.

Harrelson, Ken, with Al Hirshberg. *Hawk.* New York: Viking, 1969.

Hirshberg, Al. *The Red Sox, the Bean, and the Cod.* Boston: Waverly House, 1947.

———. *What's the Matter with the Red Sox?* New York: Dodd, Mead, 1973.

Holway, John. *The Last .400 Hitter.* Dubuque, IA: William C. Brown, 1992.

Honig, Donald. *The Boston Red Sox.* Englewood Cliffs, NJ: Prentice-Hall, 1990.

———. *The Boys of October.* Chicago: Contemporary Books, 2003.

James, Bill, and Rob Neyer. *The Neyer/James Guide to Pitchers.* New York: Simon & Schuster, 2004.

Johnson, Dick, and Glenn Stout. *Ted Williams: A Portrait in Words and Pictures.* New York: Walker, 1991.

Kaiser, David. *Epic Season: The 1948 American League Pennant Race.* Amherst: University of Massachusetts Press, 1998.

Kaplan, Jim. *Lefty Grove: American Original.* Cleveland: Society for American Baseball Research, 2000.

Keene, Kerry, Raymond Sinabaldi, and David Hickey. *The Babe in Red Stockings.* Champaign, IL: Sagamore, 1997.

Kettmann, Steve. *One Day at Fenway.* New York: Atria, 2004.

Krantz, Les, ed. *Not Till the Fat Lady Sings: The Most Dramatic Sports Finishes of All Time.* Chicago: Triumph Books, 2003.

Lally, Dick. *The Boston Red Sox.* New York: Bonanza, 1991.

Lautier, Jack. *Fenway Voices.* Camden, ME: Yankee Books, 1990.

Lee, Bill, with Dick Lally. *The Wrong Stuff.* New York: Viking Press, 1984.

Lee, Bill, with Jim Prime. *The Little Red (Sox) Book.* Chicago: Triumph Books, 2004.

Lieb, Frederick. *The Boston Red Sox.* 1974. Reprint, Carbondale: Southern Illinois University Press, 2001.

Linn, Ed. *The Great Rivalry.* New York: Ticknor and Fields, 1991.

———. *Hitter.* New York: Harcourt, Brace, 1993.

Lowry, Philip. *Green Cathedrals.* Reading, MA: Addison-Wesley, 1992.

Lyle, Sparky, with Peter Golenbock. *The Bronx Zoo.* New York: Outlet, 1979.

Lyons, Steve. *PSYCHOAnalysis.* Champaign, IL: Sagamore, 1995.

Marchildon, Phil, with Brian Kendall. *Ace.* Toronto: Penguin Books Canada, 1993.

Markusen, Bruce. *Ted Williams.* Westport, CT: Greenwood Press, 2004.

Martin, George I. *The Golden Boy.* Portsmouth, NH: Peter E. Randall, 2000.

Masur, Louis P. *Autumn Glory.* New York: Hill & Wang, 2003.

McDermott, Mickey, with Howard Eisenberg. *A Funny Thing Happened on the Way to Cooperstown.* Chicago: Triumph Books, 2003.

McGrath, Patrick J., and Terrence K. McGrath. *Bright Star in a Shadowy Sky.* Pittsburgh: Dorrance, 2002.

McSweeney, Bill. *The Impossible Dream.* New York: Coward-McCann, 1968.

Millikin, Mark. *Jimmie Foxx: The Pride of Sudlersville.* Lanham, MD: Scarecrow, 1998.

Montville, Leigh. *Ted Williams.* New York: Doubleday, 2004.

———. *Why Not Us?* New York: Public Affairs, 2004.

Neft, David S., and Richard M. Cohen. *The World Series.* New York: St. Martin's Press, 1990.

Neft, David S., Michael L. Neft, Bob Carroll, and Richard M. Cohen. *The Red Sox Fan Book.* New York: St. Martin's Press, Griffin, 2005.

Neyer, Rob. *Feeding the Green Monster.* New York: Warner Books, 2001.

Nowlin, Bill. *Fenway Lives.* Cambridge, MA: Rounder Books, 2004.

———. *Mr. Red Sox: The Johnny Pesky Story.* Cambridge, MA: Rounder Books, 2004.

————, ed. *The Kid: Ted Williams in San Diego.* Cambridge, MA: Rounder Books, 2005.

Nowlin, Bill, and Jim Prime. *Blood Feud: The Red Sox, The Yankees, and the Struggle of Good versus Evil.* Cambridge, MA: Rounder Books, 2005.

————. *Ted Williams: A Splendid Life.* Chicago: Triumph Books, 2002.

Nowlin, Bill, and Mike Ross with Jim Prime. *Fenway Saved.* Champaign, IL: Sports Publishing, 1999.

Nowlin, Bill, and Cecilia Tan, eds. *The Fenway Project.* Cambridge, MA: Rounder Books, 2004.

O'Nan, Stewart, and Stephen King. *Faithful.* New York: Scribner, 2004.

Piersall, Jim, and Al Hirshberg. *Fear Strikes Out.* Lincoln, NE: Bison Books, 1999.

Prime, Jim, and Ted Williams. *Ted Williams' Hit List.* Indianapolis: Masters Press, 1996.

Prime, Jim, and Bill Nowlin. *More Tales from the Red Sox Dugout: Yarns from the Sox.* Champaign, IL: Sports Publishing, 2002.

————. *Tales from the Red Sox Dugout.* Champaign, IL: Sports Publishing, 2000.

————. *Ted Williams: The Pursuit of Perfection.* Champaign, IL: Sports Publishing, 2002.

————. *Ted Williams: A Tribute.* Indianapolis: Masters Press, 1997.

Redmount, Robert. *The Red Sox Encyclopedia.* Champaign, IL: Sports Publishing, 1998.

Remy, Jerry, with Corey Sandler. *Watching Baseball.* Boston: Globe Pequot, 2004.

Reynolds, Bill. *Lost Summer: The '67 Red Sox and the Impossible Dream.* New York: Warner Books, 1992.

Richter, Francis, ed. *Reach Guide.* Philadelphia: Reach Sporting Goods, 1913.

Riley, Dan. ed. *The Red Sox Reader.* Boston: Houghton Mifflin, Mariner, 1999.

Ritter, Lawrence S. *The Glory of Their Times: The Story of the Early Days of Baseball Told by the Men Who Played It.* New York: William Morrow, 1984.

Rucker, Mark, and Bernard M. Corbett. *The Boston Red Sox: From Cy to the Kid.* Charleston, SC: Arcadia, 2002.

Ryan, Bob. *When Boston Won the World Series.* Philadelphia: Running Press, 2003.

Sammarco, Anthony Mitchell. *Boston's Fenway.* Charleston, SC: Arcadia, 2002.

Sampson, Arthur. *Ted Williams.* New York: A. S. Barnes, 1950.

Seidel, Michael. *Ted Williams: A Baseball Life.* Chicago: Contemporary Books, 1991.

Shaughnessy, Dan. *The Curse of the Bambino.* New York: Penguin, 1991.

————. *At Fenway.* New York: Three Rivers, 1996.

————. *One Strike Away.* New York: Beaufort, 1987.

————. *Reversing the Curse.* Boston: Houghton Mifflin, 2004.

Shaughnessy, Dan, and Stan Grossfeld. *Fenway: A Biography in Words and Pictures.* Boston: Houghton Mifflin, 1999.

Smith, Curt, *Our House.* Chicago: Masters Press, 1999.

The Sporting News. Curse Reversed. St. Louis: Sporting News Books, 2004.

Stout, Glenn, ed. *Impossible Dreams.* Boston: Houghton Mifflin, 2003.

Stout, Glenn, and Richard Johnson. *Red Sox Century.* Boston: Houghton Mifflin, 2004.

Sugar, Burt. *The Baseball Maniac's Almanac.* New York: McGraw-Hill, 2005.

Sullivan, George. *The Picture History of the Boston Red Sox.* Indianapolis: Bobbs-Merrill, 1979.

Tan, Cecilia. *The 50 Greatest Yankee Games.* New York: John Wiley & Sons, 2005.

Tebbetts, Birdie, with James Morrison. *Birdie.* Chicago: Triumph Books, 2002.

Thompson, Dick. *The Ferrell Brothers of Baseball.* Jefferson, NC: McFarland, 2005.

Thorn, John, Phil Birnbaum, and Bill Deane. *Total Baseball.* Toronto: Sport Classic, 2004.

Tiant, Luis, and Joe Fitzgerald. *El Tiante.* Garden City, NY: Doubleday, 1976.

Tsiotos, Nick, and Andy Dabilis. *Harry Agganis: The Golden Greek.* Brookline, MA: Hellenic College Press, 1995.

Valenti, Dan. *Clout!* New York: Stephen Greene Press, 1989.

———. *From Florida to Fenway.* Pittsfield, MA: Literations, 1982.

Walton, Ed. *This Date in Red Sox History.* New York: Scarborough, 1978.

———. *Red Sox Triumphs and Tragedies.* New York: Stein & Day, 1980.

Waterman, Ty, and Mel Springer. *The Year the Red Sox Won the Series.* Boston: Northeastern University Press, 1999.

Werber, Bill, and C. Paul Rogers III. *Memories of a Ballplayer.* Cleveland: Society for American Baseball Research, 2001.

Williams, Dick, and Bill Plaschke. *No More Mr. Nice Guy.* New York: Harcourt Brace Jovanovich, 1990.

Williams, Ted, and David Pietrusza. *Teddy Ball Game.* Toronto: Sport Classic Books, 2002.

Williams, Ted, with John Underwood. *My Turn at Bat.* New York: Simon & Schuster, Fireside Books, 1988.

Wood, Allan. *1918.* Lincoln, NE: Writers Club Press, 2000.

Yastrzemski, Carl, and Gerald Eskenazi. *Yaz: Baseball, the Wall, and Me.* New York: Doubleday, 1990.

Yastrzemski, Carl, and Al Hirshberg. *Yaz.* New York: Viking, 1968.

Zingg, Paul J. *Harry Hooper.* Urbana: University of Illinois Press, 1993.

Personal Interviews

Bell, Gary. Interview with Cecilia Tan. By phone. January 4, 2005.

Damon, Johnny. Interview with Cecilia Tan. City of Palms Park, Fort Myers, FL. March 22, 2005.

DiMaggio, Dom. Interview with Cecilia Tan. By phone. February 22, 2005.

Ferriss, Dave "Boo." Interview with Cecilia Tan. By phone. January 14, 2005.

Gile, Don. Interview with Cecilia Tan. By phone. January 3, 2005.

Gutteridge, Don. Interview with Cecilia Tan. By phone. January 10, 2005.

Macleod, Bill. Interview with Cecilia Tan. By phone. January 4, 2005.

Miller, Rick. Interview with Cecilia Tan. By phone. January 14, 2005.

Pesky, Johnny. Interview with Cecilia Tan. City of Palms Park, Fort Myers, FL. March 22, 2005.

Tiant, Luis. Interview with Cecilia Tan. City of Palms Park, Fort Myers, FL. March 22, 2005.

Varitek, Jason. Interview with Cecilia Tan. City of Palms Park, Fort Myers, FL. March 22, 2005.

Web Sites

ASAP Sports. 1996–2004. ASAP Sports, Long Island, NY.
   <www.asapsports.com>

The Baseball Almanac. 2000–2005. Baseball Almanac, Miami, FL.
   <www.baseballalmanac.com>

The Baseball Library. 2002–2005. The Idea Logical Company, New York, NY.
   <www.baseballlibrary.com>

The Baseball Page. 1995–2005. Kirk Robinson and Dan Holmes, Cooperstown, NY.
   <www.thebaseballpage.com>

Baseball Reference. 2000–2005. Sean L. Forman, Philadelphia, PA.
   <www.baseballreference.com>

CNN/SI. 1998–2005. CNN Sports Illustrated, New York, NY.
   <sportsillustrated.cnn.com>

The Diamond Angle. 2001–2005. James Floto, ed. Kihei, HI.
   <www.thediamondangle.com>

MLB.com. 2002–2005. Major League Baseball Advanced Media, New York, NY.
   <www.mlb.com>

National Baseball Hall of Fame. National Baseball Hall of Fame and Museum, Inc.
   Cooperstown, NY.
   <www.baseballhalloffame.org>

Retrosheet. 1996–2004. Retrosheet, Newark, DE.
   <www.retrosheet.org>

YES Network. 2002–2005. Yankees Entertainment and Sports, New York, NY.
   <www.yesnetwork.com>

Index